bell hooks (1952–2021) was the author of over thirty books, including the feminist classic *Ain't I a Woman*, the memoir *Bone Black*, and the *New York Times* bestselling *All About Love*.

Also by bell hooks

Teaching to Transgress:
Education as the Practice of Freedom

Outlaw Culture:
Resisting Representations

Sisters of the Yam:
Black Women and Self-Recovery

Black Looks:
Race and Representation

Breaking Bread:
Insurgent Black Intellectual Life
(with Cornel West)

Yearning:
Race, Gender, and Cultural Politics

Talking Back:
Thinking Feminist, Thinking Black

Feminist Theory:
From Margin to Center

Ain't I a Woman:
Black Women and Feminism

Art on My Mind

Visual Politics

bell hooks

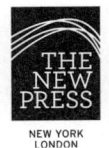

NEW YORK
LONDON

Requests for permission to reproduce selections from this book should
be made through our website: https://thenewpress.com/contact.

Originally published in the United States by
The New Press, New York, 1995
This edition published in the United States by
The New Press, New York, 2025
Distributed by Two Rivers Distribution

ISBN 978-1-62097-926-6 (pb)
ISBN 978-1-62097-929-7 (ebook)
CIP data is available

The New Press publishes books that promote and enrich public
discussion and understanding of the issues vital to our democracy
and to a more equitable world. These books are made possible by
the enthusiasm of our readers; the support of a committed group of
donors, large and small; the collaboration of our many partners in the
independent media and the not-for-profit sector; booksellers, who often
hand-sell New Press books; librarians; and above all by our authors.

www.thenewpress.com

Composition and book design by Brian Mulligan
This book was set in Bembo
Printed in the United States of America

2 4 6 8 10 9 7 5 3 1

until we meet again . . .
"the diasporic is an act of will and memory"

Art is a habit of the intellect, developed with practice over time, that empowers the artist to make the work right and protects him . . . from deviating from what is good for the work. It unites what he is with what his material is. It leads him to seek his own depths. Its purpose is not his self-enhancement, his having fun or feeling good about himself. These are byproducts. It aims solely towards bringing a new thing into existence in the truest manner possible. It is about truth and, as such, has to do with ultimates and, as such, posits self-sacrifice and consecration.

This passage by Nell Sonneman specifically addresses the work of the artist Martin Puryear, yet it names a philosophical approach to art making that shapes the way I think, dream, feel, and imagine art.
—b.h.

Contents

Foreword
Mickalene Thomas

In 2002, during my artist-in-residence at the Studio Museum in Harlem, I began reading bell hooks. This was at the same time I started of my first teaching job as a visiting artist faculty at Rhode Island School of Design. Sandra Jackson-Dumont, the director of education at the time, administered the teaching program and mentored me as I leaned into this new role. She reframed my perspective on education and showed me how to see it as a transformative social practice that could enhance an artist's engagement with their art: that education is not a substitute for creativity, but a catalyst to stay grounded, connected, and nurtured in our artistic journeys.

This was all new to me, juggling my studio practice with my responsibilities as a teacher-facilitator, especially since my only previous experience was as a teaching assistant for elementary school students. I knew I needed to learn more, and that I lacked the training for this new level of pedagogy. It was a friend and fellow artist, David Antonio Cruz, who introduced me to bell hooks's *Teaching to Transgress*, which offered valuable insights into the evolving relationship between teachers and students. With this, I now had the tools to embark on my journey as an educator. I also had a newfound thirst to delve deeper into hooks's oeuvre of brilliant wisdom, which led me to her other works: *Communion*, *The Will to Change*, *Ain't I a Woman*, *Belonging*, and most recently *All About Love*.

Now, more than twenty years later, it's an honor to have my reflections alongside such an incomparable genius who has gifted the world her voice, intelligence, philosophy, and advocacy. I hope that *Art on My Mind* resonates as deeply with others as it still does with me; bell hooks has had a profound influence on my artistic practice. In 2002 my residency at the Studio Museum concluded, and my artistic journey began. I committed to crafting a distinct aesthetic language, capturing the beauty and strength of Black women through vibrant, meaningful images. My work encompasses photography, film, installations, and multimedia paintings, often using rhinestones, acrylic, and enamel. The goal of my work is to command space while eloquently occupying it, exploring the complex intersections of Black and female identity. My 2024 exhibition "All About Love" demands for Black women to be seen and understood, and for viewers to become what hooks calls "practitioners of love." hooks's words have always inspired me to create deeply personal and culturally resonant art that refuses Western paradigms.

My most treasured section in *Art on My Mind* is bell hooks's dialogue with Carrie Mae Weems, who is the reason I'm a celebrated artist today. When I saw Weems's *Kitchen Table* series at the Portland Art Museum in 1995, it was a transformative moment for me. That marked my first encounter with the work of a Black female contemporary artist whose art touched me in a profound way. Knowing and feeling that art could have such power opened my eyes to the many possibilities of image making. I owe my artistry to that moment, taking in the power of Weems's photography. And as I continued to engage with her work, I began to understand what art can achieve: a blend of realism with fantasy that tells authentic and impactful stories. The images I saw were beautifully composed yet deeply rooted in familiarity. In a 1993 interview with the *Los Angeles Times* Weems said, "I got my first camera when I was 21—my boyfriend gave it to me for my birthday—but at that

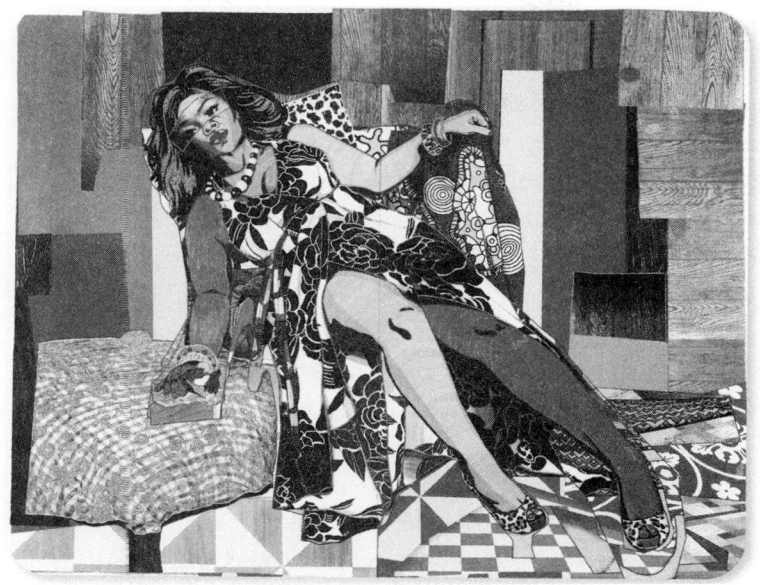

Mickalene Thomas, She Ain't a Child No More #2, *2015.*
Rhinestones, acrylic, oil, and enamel on wood panel. 96" x 120".
243.8 cm x 304.8 cm. MTPT15-003. © Mickalene Thomas.

point politics was my life, and I viewed the camera as a tool for
expressing my political beliefs rather than as an art medium."
Weems used art as a political frame in which to hang her vision
for the world. Knowing this, I began to view image making as
a way to convey a sense of truth regarding our lives—a portrait
of how we perceive ourselves and are perceived by others. We
control the narrative.

By centering artists like Carrie Mae Weems, bell hooks broke
open paradigm-shifting dialogues about representation and
identity that echo in my mind, as I believe they still do in the art
world writ large. hooks spoke plainly about the way Black art
is commodified and stripped of its cultural significance to fit a
Eurocentric mold. By naming this truth, she illuminated a path

for me to resist reductive white narratives and assert my unique voice as a Black queer woman and artist. Through hooks, I learned that it is essential for us to carve out our own spaces— it is non-negotiable. As hooks writes in the introduction, "The uses of time, the choices we make with respect to what to think and write about, are part of visual politics. . . . As we critically imagine new ways to think and write about visual art, as we make spaces for dialogue across boundaries, we engage a process of cultural transformation that will ultimately create a revolution in vision." As a Black artist, there is an onus I bear that white artists do not have. I must be discerning about what is nonnegotiable in my life to fine-tune my cultural barometer, define my values, establish my boundaries, and recognize what I will and will not accept—to know that I am more than merely a vessel through which people understand what it means to be Black.

If cultural transformation through visual politics is to be had, radical change in how art is made, valued, and exhibited is also necessary. In *Art on My Mind*, hooks urges us to challenge the institution of art itself. In this sense, I also contend with hooks's emphasis on communion by working to create liberatory spaces that reimagine what creative institutions can look like. This, along with her call for critical pedagogy and intersectionality, inspired me to co-found Pratt>FORWARD, Soula's House, and Sister Outsider. All three of these projects provide spaces, both digital and physical, for Black women to build creative networks that nurture their growth and dissolve the institutional barriers to success that we typically face. hooks said, "rarely, if ever, are any of us healed in isolation. Healing is an act of communion." In order to heal ourselves, and our world, we need to be surrounded by our community. To find strength from each other.

This is also why *Art on My Mind* is a critical text for helping us build new ways of art making. It offers a foundational framework for Black artists navigating a world full of obstacles and complexities. However, the world hooks wrote about thirty years ago has changed dramatically, particularly with the rise of technology and the internet, which have transformed how art is produced. exhibited, manipulated, and consumed. Yet, despite these changes, hooks's perspective is prescient. At the time of *Art on My Mind*'s publication in 1995, she was critiquing the politics of representation in mainstream media and art institutions that were predominantly controlled by white male gatekeepers, ordaining whose stories were told and how they were portrayed. I do see the transition within these spaces, but not all has been transformed.

The internet age has democratized art production and distribution, allowing marginalized people to bypass traditional gatekeepers and reach global audiences directly. This shift challenges the dominance of traditional art institutions, but the issues hooks raised are still pertinent. New iterations of white male gatekeepers now own the digital marketplace, and oppressive frameworks still undergird the infrastructure of the internet. Algorithms on social media can reinforce existing biases, often amplifying certain voices while marginalizing others. The very same social media networks that artists rely on to circumvent institutional exclusivity can also replicate institutional oppression. Social media can also breed forms of isolation, loneliness, and dystopia. Thus, hooks's critical engagement with notions of representation and interconnectedness is more important than ever, as artists and audiences navigate the complex interplay of visibility, power, and control in digital spaces.

Art on My Mind is also deeply critical of how capitalist structures commodify art by reducing complex social and political messages to marketable products. This commodification, hooks argued, strips art of its radical potential, turning it into a tool for maintaining the status quo rather than challenging it. In the internet age, this critique is even more relevant. hooks's insights encourage artists to resist market pressures and remain committed to creating art that defies dominant power structures. As an artist, it is important to become aware of, and take control of, new tools by researching best practices and understanding how technological changes in our craft can be used to uphold or push back against the status quo. Embracing new technologies allows us to adapt our art form and connect with the wider world. Newness in the digital age, like the widespread use of AI, can feel foreign or out of reach, but I see it as a new language for us to create and communicate.

The internet age has also made the boundary between artist and audience increasingly porous. Online spaces can be sites of intense scrutiny and harassment, particularly for artists from marginalized communities. The anonymity and reach of the internet can amplify negative reactions, making it challenging for artists to maintain their vision amid public pressure. hooks's call for critical consciousness among audiences is vital in this context. She asks viewers of art to consider their active role in interpreting it, to engage thoughtfully and consider its social and political implications.

Art shapes and reflects our identities, histories, struggles, and successes. It has the power to inspire radical change, a belief that bell hooks held fiercely. Today her wisdom continues to fuel my creative framework, not only for art, but also for life, moving me to create from a place of love, joy, and celebration. Throughout her career, which spans decades and epistemologies, bell hooks was relentlessly committed to the notion of freedom as a practice, in many forms. Education as a practice of freedom. Love as a practice of freedom. Art as a practice of freedom. Art matters because the practice of freedom matters. As such, *Art on My Mind* is a revolutionary spark—a rallying cry to reclaim our humanity and join the fight against oppressive power.

Thank you, bell hooks, for empowering me to create art that matters. Your legacy will continue to inspire generations to come.

Mickalene Thomas
December 2024

---

1. Kristine McKenna, "Photography: The Evolution of a Tough Cookie: Racism, Sexism and Classism Permeate Carrie Mae Weems' Photographic Palette," *Los Angeles Times*, June 1993.

Introduction
Art Matters

One of the first paintings I ever made is hidden in my basement. It was not put there for safekeeping. Damp dank spaces are no place for art work one treasures. All the other pictures I painted growing up have been destroyed, thrown away. They were not valued. This one survived because I took it with me when I left home at seventeen. The assignment we had been given in our art class was to choose a style of painting used by an artist whose work we admired. I loved the work of painters using abstract expressionism because it represented a break with rigid notions of abstract painting; it allowed one to be passionate, to use paint in an expressive way while celebrating the abstract. Studying the history of painting by African Americans, one sees that abstract expressionism influenced the development of many artists precisely because it was a critical intervention, an expansion of a closed turf. It was a site of possibility.

The artist whose work served as a catalyst for my painting was Willem de Kooning. As a young student in the segregated South, where we never talked race, it was not important to situate a painter historically, to contextualize a work. The "work" was everything. There are times when I hunger for those days: the days when I thought of art only as the expressive creativity of a soul struggling to self-actualize. Art has no race or gender. Art, and most especially painting, was for me a realm where every imposed boundary could be transgressed. It was the free world of color where all was possible. When I studied de Kooning's use of paint, those broad brush strokes, the thick layering of color, I was in paradise. To be able to work with paint and create textures, to try and make color convey through density an intensity of feeling—that was the lesson I wanted to learn.

My pleasure in abstract expressionism has not diminished over the years. It has not been changed by critical awareness of race, gender, and class. At times that pleasure is disrupted when I see that individual white men who entered the art world as rebels have been canonized in such a way that their standards and aesthetic visions are used instrumentally to devalue the works of new rebels in the art world, especially artists from marginal groups.

Most Black artists I know—myself included—have passionately engaged the work of individual white male artists deemed great by the mainstream art world. That engagement happens because the work of these artists has moved *us* in some way. In our lived experience we have not found it problematic to embrace such work wholeheartedly, and to simultaneously subject to rigorous critique the institutional framework through which work by this group is more valued than that of any other group of people in this society. Sadly, conservative white artists and critics who control the cultural production of writing about art seem to have the greatest difficulty accepting that one can be critically aware of visual politics—the way race, gender, and class shape art practices (who makes art, how it sells, who values it, who writes about it)—without abandoning a fierce commitment to aesthetics. Black artists and critics must continually confront an art world so rooted in a politics of white-supremacist capitalist patriarchal exclusion that our relationship to art and aesthetics can be submerged by the effort to challenge and change this existing structure. While there are now more working Black artists than ever before in the United States, the number of Black critics writing about art and aesthetics is only slowly increasing.

More than any other Black cultural critic or art historian, Michele Wallace has consistently endeavored to link the dilemmas Black artists face with the dearth of critical Black voices thinking and writing about art. Her writings on art continually inspire me. In her essay "'Why Are There No Great Black Artists?' The Problem of Visuality in African American Culture," Wallace insists that Black folks must engage the work of Black visual artists fully, and that includes understanding "how regimens of visuality enforce racism, how they literally hold it in place." The system of white-supremacist capitalist patriarchy is not maintained solely by white folks. It is also maintained by all the rest of us who internalize and enforce the values of this regime. This means that Black people must be held accountable when we do not make needed critical interventions that would create the "revolution in vision" Wallace calls for. Indeed, Wallace's essay, first given as the closing talk at a conference she organized on Black popular culture, challenged Black intellectuals to place visual arts on the critical agenda and to reconceptualize aesthetic criteria. Contemporary cultural criticism by African Americans has nicely highlighted the need to uncover subjugated knowledge in Black communities that relates to art and aesthetics—all too often it is simply assumed that visual arts are not important. Although individual progressive Black females (Sylvia Ardyn Boone, Judith Wilson, Kellie Jones, Coco Fusco, and myself, to name just a few) have been at the forefront of critical writing about art that seeks to address the issues Wallace raises, often our work does not receive attention from the conservative mainstream or from more progressive audiences who purport to be our allies in struggle. When it appears either that there is no audience for one's work or that one's work will be appropriated and not directly acknowledged, the will to do more of that work is diminished. Patriarchal politics in the realm of the visual frequently insure that works by powerful men, and that includes men of color, receive more attention and are given greater authority of voice than works by women. While feminist thinkers of all races have made rebellious critical interventions to challenge the art world and art practices, much of their groundbreaking work is used, but not cited, by males.

Concurrently, progressive white critics working from critical standpoints that include race and gender have been persistent in their efforts to produce a body of work focusing on visual politics. Yet this interest often leads such critics to appropriate the discussion in ways that deny the critical contribution of those rare individual Black critics who are writing on art. This is especially true with respect to the work of Black female critics. For example: Maurice Berger, a white male critic, recently edited an anthology titled *Modern Art and Society.* In the introduction he describes the book: "More than a primer on modernism's exclusions and biases, this anthology will hopefully be seen as a valuable methodological tool for art historians. Through various theoretical and critical processes, these essays, whether they discuss the work of one artist or many, offer new ways of thinking about the visual arts." Positioned as a critical intervention, Berger's anthology functions similarly to more conservative texts in the way in which it both appropriates and excludes the voices of Black females writing about art. Most of the essays Berger includes make no reference to art by Black women or to critical work about art by Black women, even though several of the essays build upon a critical foundation laid by Black female critics. The anthology opens with Cornel West's insightful essay "The New Cultural Politics of Difference," which draws on the themes of invisibility and erasure of Black voices on art and aesthetics, themes that have been so powerfully highlighted in the work of individual Black female critics. West even acknowledges that "the decisive push of postmodern Black intellectuals toward a new cultural politics of difference has been made by the powerful critiques and constructive explorations of Black diaspora women." The work of Black female critics informs this essay, yet our names go unmentioned.

In "Cotton and Iron," Trinh T. Minh-ha makes this useful point: "Liberation opens up new relationships of power, which have to be controlled by practices of liberty. Displacement involves the invention of new forms of subjectivities, of pleasures, of intensities, of relations, which also implies the continuous renewal of a critical work that looks carefully and intensively at the very system of values to which one refers in fabricating the tools of resistance." Progressive men who write about art and visual politics and who highlight difference, especially race and gender, must be vigilant in their critical efforts so that they do not subsume the voices and ideas of women within a critical rubric that reinforces male supremacy. The same may be said about curatorial practices. In both arenas, work by male artists and critical writing by male thinkers tend to receive more serious attention than similar work by female peers. Race does not mediate patriarchal politics in the realm of visual arts.

Art on My Mind: Visual Politics emerged as a response to the dearth of progressive critical writing by African Americans on art and aesthetics. The book represents my critical response to the ongoing dialogues about art, visual politics, and aesthetics, and it shares many of the ideas that have emerged from discussions I've had with Black folks and our allies in the struggle relating to the visual arts. Significantly, conversations with the art historian Sylvia Ardyn Boone and the cultural critic Michele Wallace were a major catalyst compelling me to explore more fully discussions I had begun about art and aesthetics in earlier work, particularly around the issue of subjugated knowledge—the attitudes and ways of thinking about art that Black folks from different class positionalities hold and that are rarely talked about.

Even though visual arts fascinated me long before feminist thinking informed my critical consciousness, it was not until I fully engaged the politics of feminism in conjunction with liberatory Black struggle that emphasized decolonization of our minds and imagination that I began to recognize the importance of taking the time to write a body of work addressing art and aesthetics. One obvious reason there are so few Black folks writing about art is that there are so few rewards to be had for such writing. And the reality is that, as Black female critics entering this domain, we risk having our ideas appropriated or go unacknowledged by those who enjoy more power, greater authority of voice, within the existing structure. This can lead us to choose silence. Audre Lorde spent a lifetime warning us of the danger in such a choice, reminding us that our silence will not save us. When I first began to search for and read art criticism on the work of artists from marginal groups, particularly the work of African American artists, I was appalled by the dearth of material, by the lack of serious critical engagement. I felt both a tremendous sadness and an intense rage. Constructively grappling with these feelings by writing about the work of African American artists, about art in Black life, I began this collection. Some of the work is brand new; other essays have been published before but in specific contexts where they could easily go unnoticed or read only by a privileged few.

When I began these essays and conversations with individual artists, I did not plan to focus the majority of my attention on the work of Black women artists. The book evolved in this direction only as I began to critically examine spaces of lack. I found that even those Black women artists whose work is widely acclaimed and receives attention on a number of fronts, both within the mainstream art world and outside, rarely receive serious consideration by art critics. Often critiques of their work are descriptive rather than critically interpretative. Every artist whose work I have chosen to write about makes art that I value. I have had the good fortune to live with pieces by every artist in this book. In some cases their work has sustained me during hard times. Recently, at the end of a lecture on art and aesthetics at the Institute of American Indian Arts in Santa Fe, I was asked whether I thought art mattered, if it really made a difference in our lives. From my own experience, I could testify to the transformative power of art. I asked my audience to consider why in so many instances of global imperialist conquest by the West, art has been either appropriated or destroyed. I shared my amazement at all the African art I first saw years ago in the museums and galleries of Paris. It occurred to me then that if one could make a people lose touch with their capacity to create, lose sight of their will and their power to make art, then the work of subjugation, of colonization, is complete. Such work can be undone only by acts of concrete reclamation.

The works of art I write about here have all had a transformative impact on my life. I first encountered Margo Humphrey's work when I was a graduate student. Lacking the money to buy the real thing, I bought a poster of her print *The Getaway*. During the many years that I remained in a relationship that was heartbreaking, I found hope and renewal for my spirits in this image of union between lovers, of joyous escape. This print was placed so that I would look at it every day when I awakened. It worked magic in my soul. Andres Serrano's photograph *Circle of Blood* was similarly healing to my spirit. In a period of long illness when I was in danger of bleeding my life away, I developed a hatred of blood so intense that it disrupted my capacity to function effectively. Serrano's image restored my appreciation for blood as a life-giving force. These are just two examples of the ways in which beautiful works of art have concretely and constructively influenced my thoughts, my habits of being.

Most art critics write about work that engages them deeply. The arbitrary nature of our choices struck me as I chose works to write about for this collection. Two of my favorite works of art are by white male artists, Leon Golub and John Baldessari. I chose not to write about these pieces at this time because the work of these two artists has received so much critical attention. That does not mean that writing about this work from my perspective would not add to the body of critical work that already exists; it just means that the uses of time, the choices we make with respect to what to think and write about, are part of visual politics. It is my hope that the essays included here will, in conjunction with the work of other progressive critics, stand as acts of critical resistance that actively introduce change within existing visual politics. As we critically imagine new ways to think and write about visual art, as we make spaces for dialogue across boundaries, we engage a process of cultural transformation that will ultimately create a revolution in vision.

As *Art on My Mind* progressed, I felt the need to take my first painting out of the shadows of the basement where it had been hidden, to stand it in the light and look at it anew. The outline of two houses, shacks, is visible. It is autumn. The yellow light of early fall emerges in the midst of earthy brown and red shades. There is chaos and turbulence in the image. It is a time of change and transition. Yet nothing can disturb the inner sanctuary—the place where the soul lives. These are the dwelling places of the spirit. Returning to them, I come again to the memory of a free world of color where ultimately only our engagement with the work suffices—makes art matter.

Art on My Mind

In high school I painted pictures that won prizes. My art teacher, a white man whom we called Mr. Harold, always promoted and encouraged my work. I can still remember him praising me in front of my parents. To them art was play. It was not something real—not a way to make a living. To them I was not a talented artist because I could not draw the kind of pictures that I would now call documentary portraits. The images I painted never looked like our familiar world and therefore I could not be an artist. And even though Mr. Harold told me I was an artist, I really could not believe him. I had been taught to believe that no white person in this newly desegregated high school knew anything about what Black people's real lives were all about. After all, they did not even want to teach us. How, then, could we trust what they taught? It did not matter that Mr. Harold was different. It did not matter to grown folks that in his art classes he treated Black students like we had a right to be there, deserved his attention and his affirmation. It did not matter to them, but it began to matter to *us*: We ran to his classes. We escaped there. We entered the world of color, the free world of art. And in that world we were, momentarily, whatever we wanted to be. That was my initiation. I longed to be an artist, but whenever I hinted that I might be an artist, grown folks looked at me with contempt. They told me I had to be out of my mind thinking that Black folks could be artists—why, you could not eat art. Nothing folks said changed my longing to enter the world of art and be free.

Life taught me that being an artist was dangerous. The one grown Black person I met who made art lived in a Chicago basement. A distant relative of my father's, cousin Schuyler was talked about as someone who had wasted his life dreaming about art. He was lonely, sad, and broke. At least that was how folks saw him. I do not know how he saw himself, only that he loved art. He loved to talk about it. And there in the dark shadows of his basement world he initiated me into critical thinking about art and culture. Cousin Schuyler talked to me about art in a grown-up way. He said he knew I had "the feeling" for art. And he chose me to be his witness: to be the one who would always remember the images. He painted pictures of naked Black women, with full breasts, red lips, and big hips. Long before Paul Gauguin's images of big-boned naked brown women found a place in my visual universe, I had been taught to hold such images close, to look at art and think about it, to keep art on my mind.

Now when I think about the politics of seeing—how we perceive the visual, how we write and talk about it—I understand that the perspective from which we approach art is overdetermined by location. I tell my sister G., who is married to a man who works in an auto factory in Flint, Michigan, and has three children, that I am thinking about art. I want to know whether she thinks about art, and, more importantly, if she thinks most Black folks are thinking about art. She tells me that art is just too far away from our lives, that "art is something—in order to enjoy and know it, it takes work." And I say, "But art is on my mind. It has always been on my mind." She says, "Girl, you are different, you always were into this stuff. It's like you just learned it somehow. And if you are not taught how to know art, it's something you learn on your own."

We finish our late-night conversation and it's hours later when, staring into the dark, art on my mind, I remember Mr.

Harold. I close my eyes and see him looking over my work, smell him, see the flakes of dandruff resting on his black shirt. In the dark, I conjure an image of him: always in black, always smiling, willing to touch our Black hands while the other white folks hate and fear contact with our bodies. In the dark of memory, I also remember cousin Schuyler, the hours of listening and talking about art in his basement, the paintings of naked brown women. And I think Sister G. is wrong. I did not just learn to think about art on my own—there were always teachers who saw me looking, searching the visual for answers, and who guided my search. The mystery is only why I wanted to look while others around me closed their eyes—that I cannot yet explain.

When I think of the place of the visual in Black life, I think most Black folks are more influenced by television and movie images than by visual arts like painting, sculpture, and so on. My sister G. told me: "We can identify with movies and we don't feel we know how to identify with art." Black folks may not identify with art due to an absence of representation. Many of us do not know that Black folks create diverse art, and we may not see them doing it, especially if we live in working-class or underclass households. Or art (both the product and the process of creation) may be so devalued—not just in underclass communities, but in diverse Black contexts, and, to some extent, in our society as a whole—that we may deem art irrelevant even if it is abundantly in our midst. That possibility aside, the point is that most Black folks do not believe that the presence of art in our lives is essential to our collective well-being. Indeed, with respect to Black political life, in Black liberation struggles—whether early protests against white supremacy and racism during slavery and Reconstruction, during the civil rights movement, or during the more recent Black power movements—the production of art and the creation of a politics of the visual that would not only affirm artists but also see the development of an aesthetics of viewing as central to claiming subjectivity have been consistently devalued. Taking our cues from mainstream white culture, Black folks have tended to see art as completely unimportant in the struggle for survival. Art as propaganda was and is acceptable, but not art that was concerned with any old subject, content, or form. And Black folks who thought there could be some art for art's sake for Black people, well, they were seen as being out of the loop, apolitical. Hence, Black leaders have rarely included in their visions of Black liberation the necessity to affirm in a sustained manner creative expression and freedom in the visual arts. Much of our political focus on the visual has been related to the issue of good and bad images. Indeed, many folks think the problem of Black identification with art is simply the problem of underrepresentation, not enough images, not enough visible Black artists, not enough prestigious galleries showing their work.

Representation is a crucial location of struggle for any exploited and oppressed people asserting subjectivity and decolonization of the mind. Without a doubt, if all Black children were daily growing up in environments where they learned the importance of art and saw artists that were Black, our collective Black experience of art would be transformed. However, we know that, in the segregated world of recent African American history, for years Black folks created and displayed their art in segregated Black communities, and this effort was not enough to make an intervention that revolutionized our collective experience of art. Remembering this fact helps us to understand that the question of identifying with art goes beyond the issue of representation.

We must look, therefore, at other factors that render art meaningless in the everyday lives of most Black folks. Identification with art is a process, one that involves a number of different factors. Two central factors that help us to understand Black folks' collective response to art in the United States are, first, recognition of the familiar—that is, we see in art something that resembles what we know—and, second, that we look with the received understanding that art is necessarily a terrain of defamiliarization: it may take what we see/know and make us look at it in a new way.

In the past, particularly in segregated school settings, the attitude toward art was that it had a primary value only when it documented the world as is. Hence the heavy-handed emphasis on portraiture in Black life that continues to the present day, especially evident if we look at the type of art that trickles down to the masses of Black folks. Rooted in the African American historical relation to the visual is a resistance to the idea of art as a space of defamiliarization. Coming to art in search only of exact renderings of reality, many Black folks have left art dissatisfied. However, as a process, defamiliarization takes us away from the real only to bring us back to it in a new way. It enables the viewer to experience what the critic Michael Benedikt calls in his manifesto *For an Architecture of Reality* "direct esthetic experiences of the real." For more Black folks to identify with art, we must shift conventional ways of thinking about the function of art. There must be a revolution in the way we see, the way we look.

Such a revolution would necessarily begin with diverse programs of critical education that would stimulate collective awareness that the creation and public sharing of art is essential to any practice of freedom. If Black folks are collectively to affirm our subjectivity in resistance, as we struggle against forces of domination and move toward the invention of the decolonized self, we must set our imaginations free. Acknowledging that we have been and are colonized both in our minds and in our imaginations, we begin to understand the need for promoting and celebrating creative expression.

The painter Charles White, commenting on his philosophy of art, acknowledged: "The substance of man is such that he has to satisfy the needs of life with all his senses. His very being cries out for these senses to appropriate the true riches of life: the beauty of human relationships and dignity, of nature and art, realized in striding towards a bright tomorrow . . . . Without culture, without creative art, inspiring to these senses, mankind stumbles in a chasm of despair and pessimism." While employing sexist language, White was voicing his artistic understanding that aesthetics nurture the spirit and provide ways of rethinking and healing psychic wounds inflicted by assault from the forces of imperialist, racist, and sexist domination.

As Black artists have broken free from imperialist white-supremacist notions of the way art should look and function in society, they have approached representation as a location for contestation. In looking back at the lives of Lois Mailou Jones and Romare Bearden, it is significant to note that they both began their painting careers working with standard European notions of content and form. Their attempt to assimilate the prevailing artistic norms of their day was part of the struggle to gain acceptance and recognition. Yet it was when they began to grapple within their work with notions of what is worthy of representation—when they no longer focused exclusively on European traditions and drew upon the cultural legacy of the African American diasporic experience—that they fully discovered their artistic identity.

Lois Mailou Jones has said that it was an encounter with the critic Alain Locke that motivated her to do work that directly reflected Black experience. Locke insisted that Black artists had to do more with the Black experience and, especially, with their heritage. Although Romare Bearden was critical of Locke and felt that it was a mistake for Black folks to think that all Black art had to be protest art, Bearden was obsessed with his ancestral legacy, with the personal politics of African American identity and relationships. This subject matter was the groundwork that fueled all his art. He drew on memories of Black life—the images, the culture.

For many Black folks, seeing Romare Bearden's work redeems images from our lives that many of us have previously responded to only with feelings of shame and embarrassment. When Bearden painted images reflecting aspects of Black life that emerged from underclass experience, some Black viewers were disturbed. After his work appeared in a 1940s exhibition titled "Contemporary Negro Art," Bearden wrote a letter to a friend complaining about the lack of a sophisticated critical approach to art created by Black folks. "To many of my own people, I learn, my work was very disgusting and morbid—and portrayed a type of Negro that they were trying to get away from." These Black audiences were wanting art to be solely a vehicle for displaying the race at its best. It is this notion of the function of art, coupled with the idea that all Black art must be protest art, that has served to stifle and repress Black artistic expression. Both notions of the function of art rely on the idea that there should be no nonrepresentational Black art. Bearden's work challenged the idea that abstraction had no place in the world of Black art. He did not accept that there was any tension between the use of Black content and the exploration of diverse forms. In 1959 Bearden wrote, "I am, naturally, very interested in form and structure—in a personal way of expression which can perhaps be called new. I have nothing, of course, against representational images, but the demands, the direction of the sign factors in my painting now completely obliterate any representational image."

Although Bearden was a celebrated artist when he died in 1988, his work has reached many more Black folks since his death. Those Black audiences who have learned to recognize the value of Black artistic expression revere Bearden for his having dared to make use of every image of Black life available to his creative imagination. As so much traditional Black folk experience is lost and forgotten, as we lose sight of the rich experience of working-class Black people in our transnational corporate society, many of us are looking to art to recover and claim a relationship to an African American past in images.

The Black playwright August Wilson, extolling the liberatory powers of art in his foreword to the book *Romare Bearden: His Life and Art*, described his first encounter with Bearden's work:

> What I saw was black life presented in its own terms, on a grand and epic scale, with all its richness and fullness, in a language that was vibrant and which, made attendant to everyday life, ennobled it, affirmed its value, and exalted its presence. It was the art of a large and generous spirit that defined not only the character of black American life, but also its conscience. I don't recall what I said as I looked at it. My response was visceral. I was looking at myself in ways I hadn't thought of before and have never ceased to think of since.

Wilson's testimony to the power of art, images, the visual as an experience that can convert and serve as a catalyst for transformation is the kind of witnessing that is necessary if we are to change the way masses of Black folks think about art. Collectively, Black folks must be able to believe fully in the transformative power of art if we are to put art on our mind in a new way.

The writer Ntozake Shange offers testimony similar to Wilson's in *Ridin' the Moon in Texas*. In a "note to the reader" at the beginning of the book, she shares the place of art in her life. Talking first about growing up with a father who painted, who had a darkroom, she continues: "As I grew I surrounded myself with images, abstractions that drew warmth from me or wrapped me in loveliness. . . . Paintings and poems are moments, capturing or seducing us, when we are so vulnerable. These images are metaphors. This is my life, how I see and, therefore, am able to speak. Praise the spirits and the stars that there are others among us who allow us visions that we may converse with one another."

Revealing to the reader her privileged background in this note, Ntozake evokes a domestic Black world in which art had a powerful presence, one that empowered her to expand her consciousness and create. While writing this piece, I have spoken with many Black folks from materially privileged backgrounds who learned in their home life to think about art and sometimes to appreciate it. Other Black folks I have talked with who have access to money mention seeing Black art on the walls while watching *The Cosby Show* and developing an interest. They speak about wanting to own Black art as an investment, but they do not speak of an encounter with the visual that transforms. Though they may appreciate Black art as a commodity, they may be as unable to identify with art aesthetically as are those who have no relation at all to art.

I began this essay sharing bits and pieces of a conversation that did not emerge from a bourgeois standpoint. My sister G. considered the role of art in Black life by looking critically at the experiences of Black working-class, underclass, and lower-middle-class folks in the world she has known most intimately. Looking at Black life from that angle, from those class locations that reflect the positionality of most Black folks, she made relevant observations. We both agreed that art does not have much of a place in Black life, especially the work of Black artists.

Years ago most Black people grew up in houses where art, if it was present at all, took the form of cheap reproductions of work created by white artists featuring white images; some of it was so-called great art. Often these images incorporated religious iconography and symbols. I first saw cheap reproductions of art by Michelangelo and Leonardo da Vinci in Southern Black religious households. We identified with these images. They appealed to us because they conveyed aspects of religious experience that were familiar. The fact of whiteness was subsumed by the spiritual expression in the work.

Contemporary critiques of Black engagement with white images that see this engagement solely as an expression of internalized racism have led many folks to remove such images from their walls. Rarely, however, have they been replaced by the work of Black artists. Without a radical counterhegemonic politics of the visual that works to validate Black folks' ability to appreciate art by white folks or any other group without reproducing racist colonization, Black folks are further deprived of access to art, and our experience of the visual in art is deeply diminished. In contemporary times, television and cinema may be fast destroying any faint desire that Black folks might have, particularly those of us who are not materially privileged, to identify with art, to nurture and sustain our engagement with it as creators and consumers.

Our capacity to value art is severely corrupted and perverted by a politics of the visual that suggests we must limit our responses to the narrow confines of a debate over good versus bad images. How can we truly see, experience, and appreciate all that may be present in any work of art if our only concern is whether it shows us a positive or negative image? In the valuable essay "Negative/Positive," which introduces Michele Wallace's collection *Invisibility Blues*, Wallace cautions us to remember that the binary opposition of negative versus positive images too often sets the limits of African American cultural criticism. I would add that it often sets the limits of African American creative practice, particularly in the visual arts. Wallace emphasizes that this opposition ties "Afro-American cultural production to racist ideology in a way that makes the failure to alter it inevitable." Clearly, it is only as we move away from the tendency to define ourselves in reaction to white racism that we are able to move toward that practice of freedom which requires us first to decolonize our minds. We can liberate ourselves and others only by forging in resistance identities that transcend narrowly defined limits.

Art constitutes one of the rare locations where acts of transcendence can take place and have a wide-ranging transformative impact. Indeed, mainstream white art circles are acted upon in radical ways by the work of Black artists. It is part of the contemporary tragedy of racism and white supremacy that white folks often have greater access to the work of Black artists and to the critical apparatus that allows for understanding and appreciation of the work. Current commodification of Blackness may mean that the white folks who walk through the exhibits of work by such artists as Bettye and Alison Saar are able to be more in touch with this work than most Black folks. These circumstances will change only as African Americans and our allies renew the progressive Black liberation struggle—reenvisioning Black revolution in such a way that we create collective awareness of the radical place that art occupies within the freedom struggle and of the way in which experiencing art can enhance our understanding of what it means to live as free subjects in an unfree world.

The Poetics of Soul:
Art for Everyone

Black people comprise half the population of the small midwestern town that I have lived in for the past six years, even though the neighborhood where my house is remains predominately white. Cooking in my kitchen one recent afternoon, I was captivated by the lovely vernacular sounds of Black schoolchildren walking by. When I went to the window to watch them, I saw no Black children, only white children. They were not children from a materially privileged background. They attend a public school in which Black children constitute a majority. The mannerisms, the style, even the voices of these white children had come to resemble their Black peers—not through any chic acts of cultural appropriation, not through any willed desire to "eat the other." They were just there in the same space sharing life—becoming together, forming themselves in relation to one another, to what seemed most real. This is just one of the many everyday encounters with cultural difference, with racial identity, that remind me of how constructed this all can be, that there is really nothing inherent or "essential" that allows us to claim in an absolute way any heritage.

Sadly, at a time when so much sophisticated cultural criticism by hip intellectuals from diverse locations extols a vision of cultural hybridity, border crossing, subjectivity constructed out of plurality, the vast majority of folks in this society still believe in a notion of identity that is rooted in a sense of essential traits and characteristics that are fixed and static. Many contemporary African Americans, especially those from nonmaterially

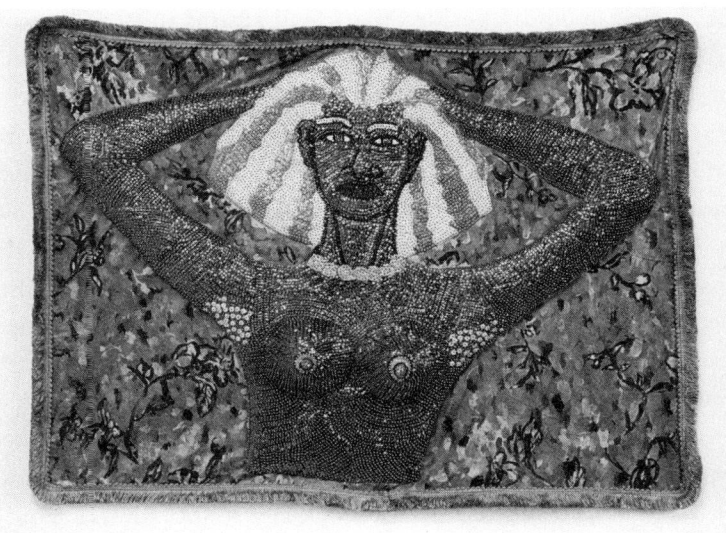

Alison Saar, Sapphire, 1986. Beads and sequins. 25" × 34".
© Alison Saar. Courtesy of L.A. Louver, Venice, CA.

privileged backgrounds, are seductively engaging a narrow nationalist identity politics that leads them to invest in notions of ethnic purity, that makes them both fearful and dismissive of those individuals who do not share the same set of assumptions. Among the Black poor and destitute, whose lives are ravaged by exploitative and oppressive institutionalized structures of domination, narrow nationalism takes hold because it intrudes on the concrete realities of postmodern malaise. When the ground is shaking under one's feet, fundamentalist identity politics can offer a sense of stability. The tragedy is that it deflects attention from those forms of struggle that might have a more constructive, transformative impact on Black life.

Black folks who are interrogating essentialist assumptions about Black identity are engaged in an act of decolonization that empowers and liberates. In the essay "Minimal Selves," the

Black British cultural critic Stuart Hall affirms this: "It may be true that the self is always, in a sense, a fiction, just as the kind of 'closures' which are required to create communities of identification—nation, ethnic group, families, sexualities, etc.—are arbitrary closures; and the forms of political action, whether movements, or parties, those too are temporary, partial, arbitrary. It is an immensely important gain when one recognizes that all identity is constructed across difference." Given this reality, acts of appropriation are part of the process by which we make ourselves. Appropriating—taking something for one's own use—need not be synonymous with exploitation. This is especially true of cultural appropriation. The "use" one makes of what is appropriated is the crucial factor.

These days it is often assumed that any act of cultural appropriation wherein one ethnic group draws on the experiences of a group to which they do not belong is suspect. Issues of authenticity are raised to devalue work that emerges from cultural borrowings. For a more expansive understanding of cultural appropriation to emerge in this society, critical thinkers would need to construct both a revised ontology and radically different theories of knowledge. This would mean taking seriously ways of knowing that may not be deemed rational. Right now, direct experience is privileged in many of the debates surrounding identity politics as the most relevant way to apprehend reality. Experience is clearly one way to know, yet there are many other ways as well.

The appeal to experience is central for all claims of authenticity. This has been the case especially with respect to Black vernacular culture and its appropriation by individuals who are not Black, or by Black folks who are from materially privileged backgrounds, or who were raised in predominately white environments, or with mixed ethnic or racial parentage. Countering claims to Black authenticity in the essay "Black Art and the

Burden of Representation," Kobena Mercer contends: "When the trope of 'authenticity' is used to define the question of aesthetic and political value, it often reduces to an argument about who does, and does not, 'belong' in the Black communities." Oftentimes the issue of authenticity is raised when individual Black artists produce work that is well received by the white mainstream. Within the realm of cultural production, as more white producers and consumers traffic in the commodification of Blackness, showing both interest in and fascination with subject matter related to Black experience, particularly to Black vernacular culture, issues of cultural appropriation, ownership, and authenticity come to the fore. Individual African American artists are more likely to be interrogated about issues of identity than ever before.

When Alison Saar recently exhibited her work at the Hirshhorn Museum in Washington, D.C., African American critics and artists were among those who judged her work from the standpoint of narrow identity politics. Accused by critics of self-consciously appropriating Black folk art in an attempt to mask her privileged upbringing, Saar found that her identity and not her aesthetic became the central issue. Hank Burchard's review of the exhibit in the *Washington Post* was particularly scathing. In a mean-spirited, ridiculing tone, Burchard asserted: "She seems not so much a talented African American in search of her artistic identity as an accomplished artist in search of an African American identity. The immediate, powerful impact of her sculptures fades rather than builds because one cannot help seeing that Saar 'dumbs down' her first-class craft skills in imitation of the rude execution of folk art." This comment is highly ironic since it is precisely the self-conscious display of artistic skill and craft evident in Saar's work that is meant to startle audiences, making them aware that they are looking not at folk art but, indeed, at art that is informed by the aesthetic principles and ideals of that gentle art. Saar's work fuses traditional academic study of art, both history and craft, and Saar's own aesthetic experience of folk art traditions. That fusion necessarily carries with it mimetic traces that proudly assert themselves in the work, even as Saar reveals her unique artistic vision. Unfortunately, reviews of the Hirshhorn exhibit that focused narrowly on questions of personal background deflected attention from Saar's artistic vision. It was as though the exhibit was the *To Tell the Truth* game show and the only question that needed to be asked was "Will the real Black person please stand up?"

Robyn Johnson-Ross's short polemical piece "Ersatz Africa: Alison Saar at the Hirshhorn" was even more aggressive in its insistence that the value of the work could be assessed without direct consideration of anything except the artist's identity and personal history. Asserting that the artist is, "after all, neither black nor white, but something in between," Ross negates all understanding of identity as locally constructed, formed by both choice and context. In the first half of the piece she addresses Saar's failure to render an "authentic" version of the biblical narrative of Salome—as though this were the function of art, to document already existing narratives. Throughout her review Johnson-Ross demonstrates no interest in Saar's aesthetic vision and is content to dismiss her work as inauthentic, as "willed rather than lived." Ultimately, this dismissal is directed at a white museum structure that Johnson-Ross perceives to be showing too great an interest in validating art that clearly in no way interests her. "You could say that African American themes have, at present, a great hold on the contemporary gallery and museum agenda, so even the New Directions, which has a reputation for 'difficult' art, will have a place for Alison Saar's narrative folk sculpture." Indeed, if this contention were true, we would be witnessing major needed transformations in the art world. Unfortunately, it is the type of uninformed hyperbolic assertion that misleads, even as it deflects attention from the extent to which structures of domination based on race, sex, and class remain unchanged and intact in galleries and museums, functioning to exclude marginal groups or dismiss their work through the use of the binary paradigms Johnson-Ross relies on.

Trained in traditional institutions to think about art in the usual Eurocentric ways, Alison Saar chose to break with that thinking and reeducate herself. That process of nurturing critical consciousness enabled her to form an oppositional perspective that could embrace her holding in high esteem vernacular aesthetic practices, especially folk art, even as she continued to be interested in canonical works within white Western classical traditions. Freed of the academic biases common in old-school art departments, which devalue folk art and vernacular culture, Saar looked to those traditions as resources, allowing them to shape her aesthetic.

Studying African and African American art with the Black female artist Samella Lewis as a teacher, Saar found her new directions affirmed. She embarked on research to uncover subjugated knowledge about African American artists and became passionately engaged with folk artists, in particular those who believe their work to be visionary, metaphysically guided by powers greater than humankind. These artists offered an aesthetic pedagogy that ran counter to the notion of "great art" produced primarily for elite audiences. Saar was impressed by the depths of their commitment to making art, not for fame or money but for the elevation of the human spirit. To these artists, making art was tantamount to religious service, and to Saar's amazement they were devout in their aspiration "to make art for anyone who would take the time to look at it." Drawing on these patterns of devotion, commitment, and a vision of both the artist and the individual work as functioning to serve and sustain life, Saar began to realize her own artistic destiny.

Like her predecessors, she searched in the world around her for material to use in making art. Working with salvaged "found" objects, as well as with specifically selected and sought-after materials, Saar began to create a body of work celebrating fusion, cultural borrowing, and intermixing that bears witness to a poetics of soul.

Against a backdrop of postmodern nothingness, fragmentation, and loss, Saar's work invites us to engage the mysteries of the soul. Yet as an early piece like *Enchante* suggests, the soul is complicated. That which lures us to pleasure also takes us close to danger. The soul evoked in Saar's work is not a simplistic metaphysical construction. It is, as Thomas Moore suggests in *Care of the Soul*, "closely connected to fate, and the turns of fate almost always go counter to the expectations and often to the desires of the ego." The figures that inhabit the world of Saar's work know this. They know the unpredictability of life and circumstance, how quickly the good can change to evil, the darkness to light. It is this paradoxical mystery Saar calls us to embrace in a modern world that privileges order and control, that denies the power of destiny and fate.

Sexual longing and desire remain one of the spaces of human need where mystery is encountered, where the will to surrender overwhelms rational concerns. Many of Saar's images, including *Ju Ju Eugene, Invisible Man*, and *La Pierna Blanca*, depict dangerous desire: Men who seek to possess and lure, who leave their lovers lost and wondering. Women who lust with a vengeance, whose will to possess and consume the desired object is as intense and potentially violent as that of any man. An odd mixture of torment and delight surfaces in Saar's pieces. *Wallflower* is one of the few sculptures displaying an entire body that is light-colored. The blank downcast look on this

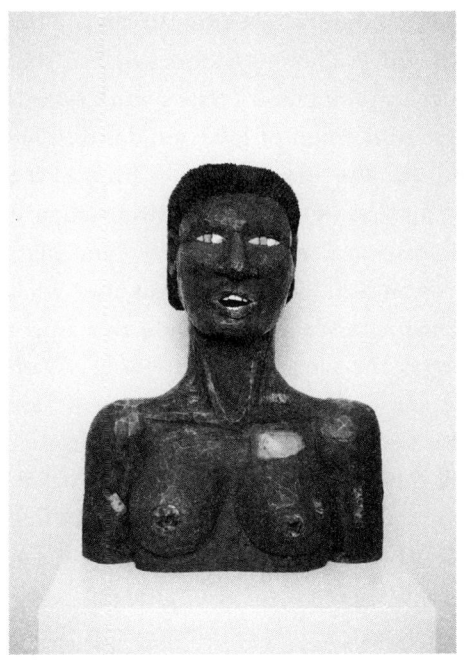

Alison Saar,
Diva, *1988.*
Wood, tin, paint.
25" × 17" × 9"
(63.5 × 43.2 × 22.9 cm).
Collections of the Jordan
Schnitzer Family
Foundation.
© *Alison Saar.*
Courtesy of L.A. Louver,
Venice, CA.

blond-haired light body bespeaks the existence of a world beyond the white-supremacist aesthetics that overvalue these very traits. In this lopsided world, such traits are not markers that incite interest and desire. In Saar's sculpture *Sapphire*, she shows an image of conflicted longings, the Black female who sees herself as most desirable when she has a look of whiteness. Although she appears strong and capable, when her heart and soul are bared she reveals that she has fragments, bits and pieces, where her heart would be. In the dark blue *Diva*, the Black female figure with songbird magic in her chest is incomplete, uncertain, has a look of hesitation. Her longing is so intense she appears otherworldly, as though what she sees from her bright green eyes is a world so astounding it cannot be expressed in mere speech. Installations such as *Love Potion #9* evoke the desperate yearning for love that leads folks to lose their minds to, as we used to say in the South, "a shoot-and-cut kinda love," the "if I can't have you nobody will." Thomas Moore suggests that "soul is to be found in the vicinity of taboo." Saar's work reveals a fascination with the tragic dimension of love and desire. Figures like *Sweet Thang* and *Heathen Tea at Trump's* hint at the power of desire to disrupt and challenge norms. Even when it comes to structures of domination, racism, sexism, and class boundaries, love and desire can lead folks astray, can alter what appeared to be a fixed dynamic, a set location. It is this aspect of desire that Saar captures in the piece *Fear and Passion*. With intense longing comes the fear and possibility of betrayal. Saar highlights the Black female body precisely because within sexist and racist iconography it is often depicted as a site of betrayal. Just as the white female in racist sexist iconography most often symbolizes innocence and virtue, the absence of sexual passion, the black female body is usually marked as the opposite.

Many of the naked Black female bodies pictured in Saar's work assume seductive poses, their bodies open for entry. As "sweet thangs," Black females must use sexuality as a means to survive. Saar suggests that there is integrity in this choice. For example, Saar's sculpture *Cleo* posits that female longing can be positioned as worthy even as the female remains sexual, driven by passion. Clearly, Saar depicts Salome as a woman driven by unrequited longing to destroy the object of her affection and desire. In Saar's sculpture, Salome tenderly cradles the head of John the Baptist. Her mouth is open as though she hopes to breathe life, to nurture and restore all that mad desire has driven her to destroy. That the death of the longed-for mate does not release Salome from torment is the most tragic and sorrowful culmination of this taboo desire. It has driven her to the edge but not afforded her peace. These are love's fatalities—envy and jealously are emotions that can strip away reason, creating unresolvable inner tension and conflict. Yet it is this surrender to an all-consuming yearning that exposes Salome's soul, the vulnerability she would use power, status, and position to mask.

Paradox and contradiction are the mysteries of the soul. The weird, the uncanny are sources of knowledge. To know the self, Saar's work suggests, one must open the heart wide and search every part. This requires facing the unacceptable, the perverse, the strange, even the sick. Without this critical embrace of metaphysical complexity the soul cannot be understood. Moore contends: "Sometimes deviation from the usual is a special revelation of truth. In alchemy this was referred to as the *opus contra naturam*, an effect contrary to nature. We might see the same kind of artful unnatural expression within our own lives. When normality explodes or breaks out into craziness or shadow, we might look closely, before running for cover and before attempting to restore familiar order, at the potential meaningfulness of the event. If we are going to be curious about the soul, we may need to explore its deviations, its perverse tendency to contradict expectations." Unlike the visionary folk artists who inspire her, Saar does not see the soul as in need of spiritual purification. For her the soul is a site for excavation—holding archeological stores of emotional meaning to be examined without judgment. Refusal to embrace a negative, darker side of being is tantamount to denial. Truth, particularly about the self, cannot be known if any aspect of the soul is repudiated. The true seeker who longs for self-realization journeys wherever the soul leads.

It is this relentless searching that is ever-present in Saar's work: the constant yearning for clarity of vision and insight that may or may not come. Value is found in the nature of searching. That yearning is expressed politically, in grieving for sorrows in the past that were not acknowledged. To see Saar's *Dying Slave* in a white-supremacist culture that would have everyone suppress both the horror and pain of that historical moment is to engage in an act of ritual remembering. *Star Song* blindly evokes that pain. Saar will not allow the hurt inflicted upon the body to be forgotten. It is the intensity of suffering that creates the passion of remembrance.

With the installation *Fertile Ground*, Saar constructs visual monuments that bear witness to the holocaust of slavery and its aftermath. Her intent is to remind us, to work against the silence and erasures of the past. This work bears witness even as it demands recognition of the reality that Black people were and are more than merely our pain. This "more" can be understood only in a context where the soul is recognized—where the experiences of the body are not seen as the only markers of personal integrity. The state of being that surpasses the body and encompasses the soul is the ontological understanding that has always provided exploited and oppressed folks both the hope for and the concrete experience of transcendence. Enslaved Black bodies could care for the soul by forging intimate connections and communities with the land. The ground is precisely the space where the dehumanized aspect of the self can be laid to rest and an integrity of being that transcends the physical plane can be claimed and affirmed. This understanding of the power of the earth, present in the religious beliefs held by the Native American dwellers and the first Africans who journeyed here, not as slaves but as seekers, is a legacy of spiritual resistance that continues into the present day. Offering testimony, Saar shares her experience of standing on this ground as a non-Southerner, feeling "the spiritual presence in the landscape." The installation is commemorative. It does not take the place of the experience. Saar declares: "To actually *be* there, to see that, to have that feeling, to stand on that ground, to be in *that* place is important." Without being heavyhanded, Saar's *Fertile Ground* attests to the historical relation Black folks have had to land, to the agrarian South. Both *The Cotton Demon* and *The Tobacco Demon* are haunting figures. The spirit of aggressive emptiness and desolation conveyed by "the cotton demon" deconstructs the image of whiteness as pure and innocent. Here the whiteness of the soul, the interior self, as a sign of deprivation and lack, will be precisely the state of being imposed on those humans enslaved for profit, who must plant, pick, and harvest the product. Ultimately, it is a barrenness of spirit that drives this demon, an absence of soul.

In her recent work Saar continues to explore the way in which soullessness damages the human spirit even as she also creates images that celebrate soulfulness. The Black female depicted in the lithograph *Black Snake Blues* has no difficulty claiming a space where she can dream and desire, where she can engage in the soul's reverie. Although she longs for pleasure that is mingled with danger—the healing poison of the snake that would release her spirit, set it free—she can reach fulfillment alone. Her soul can be satisfied as she lies alone, engaged in passionate erotic reverie. Lying on red sheets, holding her breasts, she boldly claims her passion without fear or shame. Neglected by others, by lovers who do not appear, she cares for her soul and her body. Waiting, for her, is the space for contemplation and reverie.

More than among any other group of people in the United States, in African American vernacular there has always been a concern with the soul. Unfortunately, Thomas Moore's preoccupation with Eurocentric understandings of the soul leads him to ignore this focus on the soul that Black people have consistently highlighted and shared with mainstream white culture. The aesthetic vision of "soul music" was precisely one in which a need to care for the soul was foregrounded. As in Saar's work, that vernacular emphasis on cultivating the soul, searching for depth and meaning in life, was continually connected to experiences of pleasure and delight. While Saar constructs a poetics of soul in her work that compels recognition of its dangerous mysteries and power, she also revels in the pleasure of soulfulness. That spirit of play and revelry is present in much of her work. It is quintessentially expressed in the installation *Soul Service Station*. A superficial look at this installation might lead one to see only quaint folk art–like figures that seem merely flat and naive; artfully constructed, but lacking, perhaps, in depth. Yet anyone who looks at these images with an eye for spiritual complexity sees a barren landscape with a life force coming from a sign that, like the sun, promises to nurture. That sign says that the soul will be given care here—at a mock gasoline station. These images linking man and nature suggest that the ability to imagine technology that can invent the automobile, that can plunder the earth for resources to make gasoline to fuel cars, does not rid us of the need to care for the inner life, the world of the soul. Technology is presented here not as an evil but, rather, as a parallel universe. Just as the car must be given gas to go forward, to take us where we want to go, the soul must be acknowledged—cultivated and cared for—if we are to become self-realized human beings.

Saar's poetics of soul is situated within the context of everyday life, for it is there that our spirits dwell and stand in need of comfort and shelter. Rather than depicting the metaphysical plane as existing in some evolved higher state beyond the ordinary, Saar's work seeks to reveal the presence of holy spirit in our daily life. Saar endeavors to create art that awakens awareness of the metaphysical, showing that it may be, as A. David Napier suggests in *Foreign Bodies*, "embodied in the physical, even in what we recognize as the inanimate." It is this oppositional insight that inspires vernacular visionary artists. It allows Saar to testify: "I worked once with a tree. I thought about the African and American Indian belief that tree spirits had to be at peace before anything could be carved from them. I also think about the spirit of iron and the nature of iron." Napier contends: "At issue here is not simply what used to be called 'animism,' but an ontology, a system of connectedness by which an individual's awareness of self is predicated on a system of reciprocal exchanges in the visible world. In a universe of relations governed by Mauss's archaic notion of the gift—in which individuals 'know' themselves by actually exchanging with others those objects by which they are 'identified'—knowledge can exist in the absence of intellectualism, since much of what is worth knowing is quite literally self-evident. The self, in other words, becomes evident through a visible demonstration of its connectedness." It is this state of being, so often unfamiliar to those of us in contemporary culture, that Saar extols in her work. And for that reason the work is often critically misunderstood by both those individuals who celebrate it and those who see it as superficial. Years ago, when Saar first made the choice to commit herself to an art practice that would engage the ordinary, call out the beauty in the everyday, and celebrate the metaphysical, she did not contemplate the reality that no critical framework existed to theoretically validate and illuminate the significance of this shift, its political subversiveness. Now she has lived with the implications of her choice and understands more intimately what we sacrifice when we choose to dissent. The spirit of sacrifice is reflected with elegance and grace in her new piece *Heart and Sole*. The sole of the shoe is worn presumably by a rough journey, by the traversing of terrains that test and try the spirit. That the path walked is a journey to the spirit is evident by the heart that surrounds the hole in the sole. All that is sacrificed is made meaningful when the complexity of the soul is exposed, revealed, its beauty and integrity as ever-present witness.

Talking Art with Alison Saar

bell hooks: Alison, talking about your work, you have said, "I love the idea that materials have memory, the idea of working with materials that have experienced more than I have." There is in each of us and in the objects that surround us a place of primal memory. I believe that we have memories that extend beyond what we have consciously experienced. That we carry within us ancestral memory. When I look at your art, I am not troubled by the fact that you draw upon realities you have not directly experienced.

Alison Saar: We don't just remember things that we've experienced. There are the memories that come to us in visions—as dreams. It's similar to when you're growing up and there's this playing and pretending—an inventing of worlds. That's actually also where I started getting these materials from, and so those sorts of games are things I continue to do, to put myself in those places. Before I do a piece I spend time in that imaginative space. For example, the piece I did about South Africa came to me after I finished reading in the paper about the life of a boy there. I felt a psychic connection with his story and began from there to invent.

bh: Imagining as a way to be empathic, to move into worlds we have not experienced yet have come to understand, is a way of knowing reality that is no longer valued in our culture. I found that critics and reviewers commenting on your work don't discuss imagination. They are much more fascinated by your family history than by the way your imagination works. And they often assume that your aesthetic vision is shaped more by family tradition in art making than by your autonomous engagement with that imaginative realm you just talked about. You identify with something and create worlds around it. It is often assumed that if we have an experience to draw on, we do not need to rely on imagination, that it just sort of comes naturally to us in some way. When I look at your art work, I see it as coming out of a powerful imagination. I don't assume that your experiences as a Black person and your use of Black subject matter mean that you do not vigorously work to create. Everyone assumes that Picasso was inspired by African art that he imaged differently. Yet your engagement with African, Native American, and other cultures conveys an active, intellectual seeking for inspiring subject matter that can go unnoticed or be devalued. Your work is so dreamlike.

AS: Someone asked me if I dream any of my pictures. I don't. Actually, I dream all of my anxieties about making art.

bh: That dreaming, though, is part of the creative process.

AS: When I'm working with specific ideas, information from cultures outside of my own, I seek to understand them through my own personal experience in relation to everything I feel: my pain, my understanding of love or anger, what I hope for and dream about.

bh: The influence of dreams, whether those that happen when we are asleep or daydreaming, is evident in your work in pieces such as *Sanctified*, where you see this secret preacher doing his thing and, like a riff in a song, you take it and fly with it, take it somewhere else. On one hand, you're walking around like a normal person and you see an image in everyday life, but all of a sudden you begin to have a vision about that image, a kind of waking dream. It has a mystical dimension, as though you take that concrete image and you have these X-ray eyes or something, where that image begins to visually deconstruct and then is reinvented in this imaginative space as something similar to what it was yet different. That process is happening throughout your work.

AS: I make art about everyday experience and often the concrete process is very ordinary and mundane. I take the ordinary and go with it into the surreal.

bh: Talking with you about your work is different from other interviews I've done, because you are one of my girlfriends as well as a powerful artist whose work I knew, loved, and was moved really deeply by before I met you. Our speaking together is a more intimate thing. When I was writing my questions, I found myself preparing them differently, like I'd write, "Don't you just love it when Bessie Harvey says, 'When I first found him, he was a big limb, but I knew he was a beautiful man: I knew that when I pulled him out. I said to him, "Ain't you pretty?" He said, "Granny, I ain't nobody," but I saw him and I just couldn't wait to get him home.' " I love this statement— there is just something so basic yet deep in it. And it's just the earthiness, the matter-of-fact tone of this statement made by a Black woman folk artist that leads the complexity of vision behind that statement to be ignored, go unseen. When I think about Bessie Harvey's work, I am reminded of the Buddhist tea ceremony: the way she takes something that appears ordinary and exposes its elegance and grace. But she does so by bringing it to a space of simplicity. A similar energy is at work in your stuff. Both you and I love folk art; it enchants us. I am enchanted by your work because of this quality, the way that so much of it appears simple, but in actuality emerges from a very convoluted, complex visionary process.

AS: What's most amazing is that the piece was complete in Bessie Harvey's mind, and when she saw that thing, that piece was made.

bh: I know, that is so deep.

AS: And that's how she makes it, that way is mysterious. Other people can't see it. That's true of visionaries. They're just not bogged down with technical bullshit in terms of how the piece has to be realized. They just see this thing, tie it together with wire, or glue it together with spit, or whatnot. The fact that their mind does not consciously register the process doesn't mean that it hasn't happened. Most artists can't work that way.

bh: All visionary artists risk making work that will not be seen in its complexity because they maybe lack the skills to adequately articulate the process. We can see this in the way Horace Pippin's work was written about for the catalog accompanying the retrospective. Critics called attention to biographical details or the social context without speaking directly about the images. It's difficult to describe exactly what happens in visionary moments. I put a lot of sophisticated ideas into my head that come to me from books, from schooling, and from other people. However, when I sit down to write, often it's as though I'm transported to a magical space. I don't always remember what happens. I have a magical encounter with words where all of a sudden something appears on my page that is totally not in line with anything that I consciously thought. Artists like yourself, and other folks who've gone to school and been trained, also have those moments where all that training falls away and you're at that visionary moment where you see it and can make it happen. Intellectual elitism, certain academic ways of thinking about creating art, leads to the insistence that the process of a folk artist or a native artist is so radically different from that of an artist who's been trained. Because you have had academic training, the folk elements in your work that enable you to fuse the ordinary with the surrealistic can be, and sometimes are, perceived by people as "contrived."

AS: It's peculiar, because, again, you know, the separation of artists into these two camps happens in art magazines like *Artforum*, where these people are considered great artists because they're crazy, or because they're totally out there, and the reality is that it's a genuine clear vision that guides their work. Many artists, taught or untaught, still experience this magical process, but they are forced to demonstrate technical finesse to fit the work into this rigid, linear format. It has to go on this rigid track that art dons have dictated art has to go along. It has to go through all these machinations where one thing precedes another in a linear fashion that can be documented. There's this assumption that it's all cause and effect, that things happen one after another, but they don't always. At times things happen simultaneously. My art comes to me from directions that don't always follow a rational, linear process.

bh: The critic Susan Crane writes that "Art is not simply the discreet, delectable, beautiful object, but the transcendental power of creativity, the alchemical potential of materials." The primacy of material is always highlighted in your work, the way the material works on you. Unlike Bessie Harvey, you don't always have the image in mind; sometimes the material makes this demand on you. It's as though there is this kind of spirit power. Daddy Gus, my grandfather, used to say that there was a spirit force calling out to us in every object. Sometimes I look at a piece of yours and it's as though the material itself said, "Alison Saar, this is what you're going to do." And it's not—as people seem to think when they're writing about your work—that Alison Saar says, "Well, OK, I'm going to take my little journey to Mexico now, and I will appropriate such and such." It's not a conscious, premeditated process. Even moments of premeditation are disrupted by the unexpected. I was struck by a critic saying that they get the feeling that you don't just "use found objects," you use "sought-after" objects, and I thought, well, but one can go seeking and find something that one was not looking for. One can find something and see in it something that one has been seeking. The desire to flatten everything out into this binary model again and again is something that really blocks our understanding of the creative process. It is important, when we look at the work of any group of people who've been marginalized, whether we're talking about white immigrants or any of us, that there be a willingness to acknowledge complexity—profundity—multilayered possibility. There is so much cultural criticism that extols the virtues of cultural hybridity, traveling, the notion of bricolage, of moving between different environments, border crossing, all these terms—yet I am fascinated when critics don't bring these theoretical standpoints into the discussion of your work. They continually quote a phrase you once used where you said you often feel as though you are "floating between two worlds"—usually to refer to your having both African American and Euro-American ancestry. Since you talk about this mixed background, critics often ignore the significance of the "border crossings" you choose that are not "givens." Much of the passion in your work is expressed as you celebrate those border crossings that take place in the imagination, in the mind as well as in real life, and those journeys are not talked about enough.

AS: Actually, when I first used that phrase, "floating between two worlds," I was talking about the two worlds of reality and magic. Yet when critics applied the statement to my background, that made sense as well. Meanings change. Pieces that I made ten years ago have very different meanings for me now. When people ask me to help them understand this work, I have to state again and again that for me the work means different things at different times, depending on my experience and as I accumulate knowledge.

bh: Also, historical context changes. Much of your early work was very prophetic in that you were creating art that articulated ideas about border crossing way before there was all this fancy theory, before Benetton ads, before all of these things. Yet critics now act as though you do the "ethnic" thing because it's in style. And some of them demonize you by suggesting that the work appropriates the folk or Black underclass and poor experience in an opportunistic manner. Yet so much of your work predates that kind of hedonistic consumerist approach to the "other" that says, "Oh, yes, now I have all these ethnic shops where I can buy cool artifacts from Africa, Mexico, Tibet." I had this experience yesterday. I was hanging out with a friend who was looking for an apartment. He went into a building where we knew an apartment was for rent, a building I had once seen a South Asian woman exiting. So we went into the apartment for rent. There were all these South Asian artifacts and little Buddhist things. I was expecting to meet the South Asian woman I had seen before. We opened the door to the bedroom, and the tenant was sitting in there. Suddenly I thought about the assumptions I had made, that there would be this linear correlation between the interior vision all those objects in space were giving and the person who put them together. I think it's that kind of longing for linear order that people have in a xenophobic and crazy society. So many folks want to be able to identify, codify, contain everything. And we're constantly challenged when these fixed notions of identity are disrupted. I think there are some people who would have been offended by the fact that there were no artifacts in this space that came from white culture. To me, that gap is interesting. I don't want to place a sort of value judgment on a person, saying, "Oh, she's appropriating; that's bad." To me it is much more interesting to know what are the energies and longings that move her to those objects! And I feel like that same interest emerges when I see your work, the artifacts you borrow from diverse cultures.

AS: Sometimes because of the fact that I was doing my work long before there was any interest in multiculturalism, etc., people have come up to me and said, "Oh, the Whitney Biennial really just pissed me off, because here are all these artists of color being shown, and it was a barrage, and a multicultural bandwagon sort of thing." And I've pointed out to them that many of the artists in this show had been making art for twenty years. Yet it takes being in this show to legitimate the art—to make it more visible.

bh: The moment white people decide it's cool to "eat the other," the response to all our work changes. And suddenly issues of authenticity, of "Will the real Black person please stand up?" come into play.

AS: Right. It's clear that people are very suspicious.

bh: Alison, we were always involved with Frida Kahlo's work.

I've loved Frida Kahlo's work since I was a little girl, but then when it became this kind of hip sign of cool, I began to feel somehow like my claim to a relationship to that work is validated not through my experience as a Southern Black girl involved in spiritual mysticism or interested in Mexico or what have you, but filtered through the validation Kahlo now receives from white folks; validated by Madonna, saying in some magazine that she's interested in this. It becomes this wacky thing, because there's a part of us that wants then to pull back and let our fascination with that artist go, because you don't want folks to see it as coming out of this culture of consumerism—where everyone wants to "eat the other." Let's face it, the culture of consumerism that eats the other has indeed made Frida Kahlo a household word in places where she might never have been heard of, and there's a vulgarization of work and process there. However, to subvert this, all of us who have loved her work and who think critically about it have to lay claim to contextualize those moments in our lives when that work first came to us. The same is true of your work. A lot of your work calls for a recognition of the importance of subjugated knowledge. Your work and your being were actualized at a historical moment when there was this real demand on the part of African American people in resistance against racism for the recovery of subjugated knowledge. That process of recovery wasn't then related to class positionality or regional status—whether you are a Southern Black person or a Northern Black person, whether you grew up in a rich or poor neighborhood. It was related to the collective yearning to know more about ourselves as Black people in the diaspora. It's as though we were saying, "There's this knowledge that we don't have," and none of us have it. So much about Black life—Black history—has only recently been documented. Nobody had all the information. It's not as if poor people were sitting on it, and rich people went and took it from them or what have you; that just was not the case. Can you talk about your experience searching for subjugated knowledge? What did you want that knowledge to do in your life? I know when I went to Stanford University, I began to see the rural South that I came from in a new way. I went back to those artifacts that I had often taken for granted in my life and saw them in a new way. I hear that same shift when you talk about going to roots, both real and imaginary, that you might not have thought about in Laurel Canyon.

AS: Yeah, for example, I did this piece about the South, and I've never lived in the South. I can say that my mother's people came from there; but it was never a concrete part of my experience. Yet when I went there, I saw this place as a part of my heritage that I did not know anything about. To me, the South was Hollywood versions of it, *Gone with the Wind* and so on. I was shocked to find that when I went there I felt a deep kinship, a connection to these surroundings, that was transformative.

bh: And the reasons you felt that intense spiritual connection cannot be explained—they are part of life's mystery. You know, I've been in love with this man who lives in another country, and I was writing him a letter in which I said, "You return me to the South, even though you've never been there." That his presence does this is pure mystery. The danger of identity politics, and of too much narrow essentialist value being placed on direct experience, is that it denies the realm of magic, of mysticism.

AS: Everyone out there is just highly suspicious of any bond between cultures and folks that can't be documented and explained by hard facts, by direct experience. Most folks don't want to feel the magic happen. When individuals see my work and feel alienated, usually it's because they want my connection to the places to be explained in a way that makes sense. The work doesn't exactly work that way.

bh: No matter how much folks in the academy validate new espistemologies—ways of knowing that transcend reason—most folks want everything explained in a linear, rational way. For example, maybe reincarnation informs our sense of connection to places, people, objects we know nothing about. This is a realm of experience that many people in our society might say they don't believe in. Jung's notion of the collective unconscious is so tied to African diasporic notions of ancestral knowledge and to a belief in ancestral memory that lives within people. While many Afrocentric thinkers are eager to acknowledge that there are real artifacts that document African cultural retentions in the so-called New World, specifically from the culture of West Africa, these same individuals refuse to acknowledge psychic connections that bind people, that transcend time and space.

AS: That is why the work of an untraditional scholar such as Robert Farris Thompson has meant a lot to some of us. He's willing to look beyond the rational explanation. The first time I saw him, I must have been seventeen years old. After struggling with art history, seeing it through the eyes of Germans, of the English, seeing the limited way these great, powerful, wonderful art objects were talked about—so coldly and without passion or tenderness—I was delighted to see a professor who was willing to take his tie off and put it around his waist to show what a different posture in another culture looked like. When he talked about diasporic connections—a link between African music and the blues—folks did not want to hear it mixed up, really. They questioned how these connections could be documented.

bh: And connections that can't be scientifically documented are not recognized as meaningful by the academy. Yet when we do enter those subcultural worlds in the United States at Santeria, or in Yoruba, we enter into a world where people are totally comfortable with notions of a border crossing that's not concrete, that emerges from spirit possession. In those worlds, the idea that you can be entered by a force and speak a language you don't know, all of these things, is accepted. Many of the white folks who talk endlessly about multiculturalism would be uncomfortable with truly accepting ways of knowing that challenge the privileged place that reason occupies in the West. We lack ways of talking about that sense of a connection with an artifact from another culture that feels primal, like my obsession with altars. As a little child, I was drawn to altars. One of my favorite church songs was one that asked, "Is your all on the altar of sacrifice laid?" And it was sung with this kind of spirit of anguish and longing that intrigued me. I wanted to see altars—to know what they meant in our lives cross-culturally. I let that passion lead me to where altars can be found. That passion for altars that surfaced in a Southern Black church, in a little town, led me to France, to Montserrat, where I saw the shrine of the Black Madonna, where I saw all these white hands stroking that shrine. Rather than seeing no connection between the altar of that Southern Black church and the shrine of the Black Madonna, I see it as a palimpsest, where there's a thread that's woven through our lives that pulls us toward things. And you are lucky, Alison, because you were given some of these threads early in life.

When you talk about your dad being interested in pre-Columbian art and African art and Leonardo, he was offering a world where you could make certain connections.

AS: That's true.

bh: And what's exciting about your work is the way you make border crossing a sacred yet playful ritual. That spirit of playfulness that I see in you as a person, the way you like to mix the delightful with the deadly serious, is there in your work. The spirit of play in folk art or primitive art is so rarely talked about as ritualistic, as evoking a vision of life, an ontology, that we can use to apprehend reality. I see that ritual play in specific figures you have created, like *The Tobacco Demon* or *The Cotton Demon*, where, on the one hand, there is playfulness, yet these figures are constructed to embody evil, everything we might dread.

AS: I think I have to do that, mix the sacred and the profane in my work; it's a process of exorcism. If I didn't do it in the work, I'd just jump off a cliff. These are constructive ways of facing tragic, painful experiences. And that's how the slaves survived all that pain—through creating, by making music, dance, poetry. That's how, you know, we survive in Haiti, in Mexico. You just somehow turn it around; you're up against death, then you make death this buffoon, this trickster, and that's how you deal with what you face, and that's how you survive it, because otherwise you'd just lay down and die.

bh: I remember when I first learned in high school about carnival in other cultures. We did not learn its deeper meaning, about "eating of the flesh," those layered metaphysical dimensions, the issues of life and death that are a part of the carnival. Instead, we were taught to think of carnival as primitive play. For too long in this culture we have had to witness African art and African American art talked about in ways that deny there is something happening in the work that is deep—not obvious—that what you see on the surface may be a smiling face, but the smiling face may be tilted in a manner that speaks to suffering, that changes the meaning of that smile. That willingness to critically

engage art by Black folks in all its profundity is still very difficult in a culture of domination where people do not learn to look
beneath the surface. For example, many folks look at your piece
The Snake Charmer and see it as Grace Jones.

AS: It's curious, he becomes Grace Jones, in people's eyes,
because of his hairdo. But as I produced the piece, in my imagination, it was a snake charmer, a man who had these powers,
who could hold the snake suspended in his mouth. Whether he
was a shaman or a gypsy, he could go between people and stir
things up.

bh: You're articulating that there's this rupture between artistic intentionality and what is culturally received. Maybe somewhere in your unconscious you created this piece, which you
envision as male, in a likeness similar to a woman. And audiences associate that piece with Grace Jones. I even began to
think of it as her, or of her as a mysterious figure like a snake
charmer. I didn't have problems seeing this image in multiple
ways. Again, it goes back to breaking out of the culture-of-
domination's insistence on binaries: it has to be either/or, it has
to be what you intend, there has to be this control. And I think
what we've been addressing today is that art is interactive in the
sense that the pieces aren't just your intentionality. They aren't
just even your life experience—they are all of these diverse elements coming together.

AS: The people who see that piece as Grace Jones are addressing
issues in their own lives. And I think it's really great that these
images are so powerful that people are immediately drawn to
them and that somehow their lives are being addressed by these
images.

bh: On one hand, folks project onto your work much that you did not intend; on the other hand, they don't always pay attention to what is there. I am fascinated by the proactive sexual images in your work. Pieces such as *Fear and Passion, Love Potion #9,* and *Queen of Sheba* evoke pleasure and danger, and desire. Romance and desire not as the boy-meets-girl stuff, but as fatal attractions of erotic passion that drives folks wild. You make a link in the work between obsessive longing and suffering.

AS: My experience with passion is that it can easily turn into something really self-destructive. It's very scary and, at the same time, it's alluring, seductive. I made this piece *Dance with Danger,* and it's this woman doing a really hot dance, and there's this male figure that at one angle becomes a skeleton, and it's desire depicted as life-and-death struggle, as all-consuming. I've always been struggling with how far I can go out there to the edge without really endangering myself, without falling off. The danger isn't just physical; it's mental, psychic danger. We can let go or become so obsessed with a thing that it can really kill us and just drown out every rational thought in our heads. My work explores the tension between the wildness within, the primitive, and the rational animal. There is that dual quality within all of us. And both are really important aspects of who we are.

bh: There is this teasing, seductive quality in your work when you come face to face with danger. You present an image that is ordinary or archetypal, like the heart—using it to symbolize romance and desire. Then you expose the darker side, the vision of being driven mad by desire. When I think of fictional work that is akin to your art, works like Marguerite Duras's *The Ravishing of Lol Stein* and Clarisse Lispector's writings come to mind. Like these writers, you create a world where people's longings are so intense they threaten to consume the self.

AS: These pieces emerge from personal struggle. It was initially very difficult for me to make those pieces, because it felt like I was walking around naked.

bh: I participated in Shu Lea Cheang's installation *Those Fluttering Objects of Desire*, which was at the Whitney. The museum was not prepared for the responses it engendered. In the installation, you could put a quarter into these red phones and talk. I read a very intense, passionate love letter that I wrote to a man in my life, and I was really stunned by the number of people who listened to it over and over and over. There was even some tension in the museum about the fact that they were acquiring so many quarters. And people were raising the question Is this art? or Is it too much like the real thing? I mean, you're dialing 1-900-DESIRE. But I think what people heard on those phones that we don't often hear is anguish, an aspect of loving that we don't often talk about. African American expressive culture, particularly music, has always given voice to tragic dimensions of love. We rarely see an equivalent in art. We do in your work. Your sculpture *Sapphire* is an erotic, sexualized image. It articulates Black female notions of female desirability, the sense that the biracial woman, or white-looking Black woman, is truly sexual, truly exotic, but always tortured. In your work you expose the inner contradictions that may not be manifest on the outside. There's the outer surface and then there's this inner world that is full of interweavings and complexities. We can all draw that heart shape, yet you open up these figures and there's so much going on. In your *Black Snake Blues*, who is that mysterious lady on the bed?

AS: The idea for this piece came to me from the song "Black Snake Blues." It's about a Black snake crawling on this lady's bed—and it's a way to talk about infidelity, transgression. The woman's longing for some Black snake to come into her bed is exposed. She needs and desires more. People aren't really ready to deal with fierce female passion.

bh: The politics of passion and desire that is articulated throughout your work needs to be discussed more by critics. We need to do more to describe the naked Black figure. We need to talk about the vulnerability in these images—the passion of remembrance. These longings that we know to be universal in people, the longing to connect, to experience community, to embrace the mysterious. Your work calls us again and again to that realm of mystery.

Altars of Sacrifice: Re-membering Basquiat

Is your all on the altar of sacrifice laid?
—Black church song

At the opening of the exhibition of Jean-Michel Basquiat's work at the Whitney Museum in the fall of 1992, I wandered through the crowd talking to folks about the art. I had just one question. It was about emotional responses to the work. I asked, What do you feel looking at Basquiat's paintings? No one I talked with answered the question. People went off on tangents, said what they liked about Basquiat, recalled meetings, talked generally about the show, but something seemed to stand in the way, preventing them from spontaneously articulating the feelings the work evoked. If art moves us—touches our spirit—it is not easily forgotten. Images will reappear in our heads against our will. I often think that many of the works that are canonically labeled "great" are simply those that lingered longest in individual memory. And that they lingered because, while looking at them, someone was moved, touched, taken to another place, momentarily born again.

Those folks who are not moved by Basquiat's work are usually unable to think of it as "great" or even "good" art. Certainly this response seems to characterize much of what mainstream art critics think about Basquiat. Unmoved, they are unable to speak meaningfully about the work. Often with no subtlety or tact, they "diss" the work by obsessively focusing on Basquiat's life or the development of his career, all the while insisting that they are in the best possible position to judge the work's value

*Jean-Michel
Basquiat,*
Irony of a Negro
Policeman, *1981.
Acrylic and oil
paintstick on wood.
72" × 48".*
© *Estate of
Jean-Michel
Basquiat. Licensed
by Artestar,
New York.*

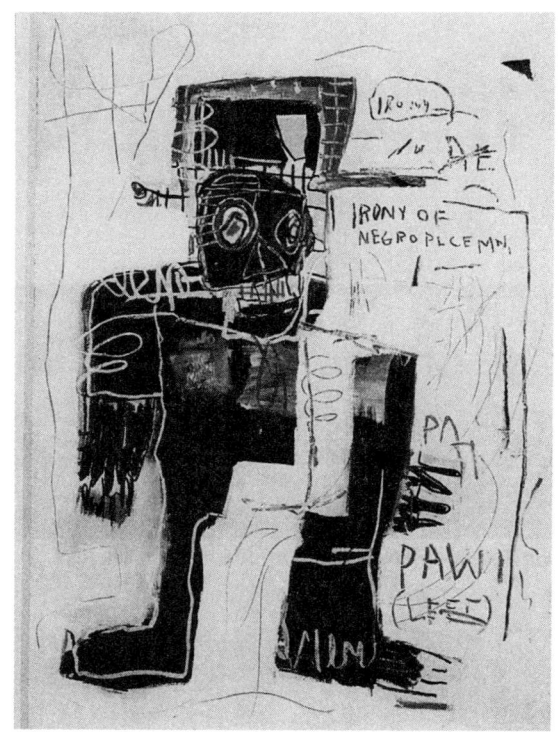

and significance. A stellar example of this tendency is Adam Gopnik's piece in the *New Yorker*.[1] Undoubtedly it is a difficult task to determine the worth and value of a painter's life and work if one cannot get close enough to feel anything, if indeed one can only stand at a distance.

Ironically, though Basquiat spent much of his short adult life trying to get close to significant white folks in the established art world, he consciously produced art that was a *vattier*, a wall between him and that world. Like a secret chamber that can be opened and entered only by those who can decipher hidden codes, Basquiat's painting challenges folks who think that by merely looking they can "see." Calling attention to this aspect of Basquiat's style, Robert Storr has written, "Everything about his work is knowing, and much is *about* knowing."[2] Yet the work resists "knowing," offers none of the loose and generous hospitality Basquiat was willing to freely give as a person.

Designed to be a closed door, Basquiat's work holds no warm welcome for those who approach it with a narrow Eurocentric gaze. That gaze which can recognize Basquiat only if he is in the company of Warhol or some other highly visible white figure. That gaze which can value Basquiat only if he can be seen as part of a continuum of contemporary American art with a genealogy traced through white males: Pollock, de Kooning, Rauschenberg, Twombly, and on to Andy. Rarely does anyone connect Basquiat's work to traditions of African American art history. While it is obvious that Basquiat was influenced and inspired by the work of established white male artists, the content of his work does not neatly converge with theirs. Even when Basquiat can be placed stylistically in the exclusive white-male art club that denies entry to most Black artists, his subject matter—his content—always separates him once again, and defamiliarizes him.

It is the content of Basquiat's work that serves as a barrier, challenging the Eurocentric gaze that commodifies, appropriates, and celebrates. In keeping with the codes of that street culture he loved so much, Basquiat's work is in-your-face. It confronts different eyes in different ways. Looking at the work from a Eurocentric perspective, one sees and values only those aspects that mimic familiar white Western artistic traditions. Looking at the work from a more inclusive standpoint, we are all better able to see the dynamism springing from the convergence, contact, and conflict of varied traditions. Many artistic Black folks I know, including myself, celebrate this inclusive dimension of Basquiat, a dimension emphasized in an insightful discussion of his life and work by his close friend, the attist and rapper Fred Braithwaite (a.k.a. Fab 5 Freddy). Braithwaite acknowledges the sweetness of their artistic bonding, and says that it had to do with their shared openness to any influence, the pleasure they took in talking to one another "about other painters as well as about the guys painting on the trains."[3]

Basquiat was in no way secretive about the fact that he was influenced and inspired by the work of white artists. It is the multiple other sources of inspiration and influence that are submerged, lost, when critics are obsessed with seeing him as connected solely to a white Western artistic continuum. These other elements are lost precisely because they are often not seen, or, if seen, not understood. When the art critic Thomas McEvilley suggests that "this black artist was doing exactly what classical-Modernist white artists such as Picasso and Georges Braque had done: deliberately echoing a primitive style," he erases all of Basquiat's distinct connections to a cultural and ancestral memory that linked him directly to "primitive" traditions.[4] This then allows McEvilley to make the absurd suggestion that Basquiat was "behaving like white men who think they are behaving like black men," rather than understand that Basquiat was grappling with both the pull of a genealogy that is fundamentally "Black" (rooted in African diasporic "primitive" and "high art" traditions) and a fascination with white Western traditions. Articulating the distance separating traditional Eurocentric art from his own history and destiny and from the collective fate of diasporic Black artists and Black people, Basquiat's paintings testify.

To bear witness in his work, Basquiat struggled to utter the unspeakable. Prophetically called, he engaged in an extended artistic elaboration of a politics of dehumanization. In his work, colonization of the Black body and mind is marked by the anguish of abandonment, estrangement, dismemberment, and death. Red paint drips like blood on his untitled painting of a Black female, identified by a sign that reads "Detail of Maid from 'Olympia.' " A dual critique is occurring here. First, the critique of Western imperialism, and, then, the critique of the way in which imperialism makes itself heard, the way it is reproduced in culture and art. This image is ugly and grotesque. That is exactly how it should be. For what Basquiat unmasks is the ugliness of those traditions. He takes the Eurocentric valuation of the great and beautiful and demands that we acknowledge the brutal reality it masks.

The "ugliness" conveyed in Basquiat's paintings is not solely the horror of colonizing whiteness; it is the tragedy of Black complicity and betrayal. Works such as *Irony of a Negro Policeman* (1931) and *Quality Meats for the Public* (1982) document this stance. The images are nakedly violent. They speak of dread, of terror, of being torn apart, ravished. Commodified, appropriated, made to "serve" the interests of white masters, the Black body as Basquiat shows it is incomplete, not fulfilled, never a full image. And even when he is "calling out" the work of Black stars—sports figures, entertainers—there is still the portrayal of incompleteness, and the message that complicity negates. These works suggest that assimilation and participation in a bourgeois white paradigm can lead to a process of self-objectification that is just as dehumanizing as any racist assault by white culture. Content to be only what the oppressors want, this Black image can never be fully self-actualized. It must always be represented as fragmented. Expressing a firsthand knowledge of the way assimilation and objectification lead to isolation, Basquiat's Black male figures stand alone and apart. They are not whole people.

It is much too simplistic a reading to see works such as *Jack Johnson* (1982), *Untitled (Sugar Ray Robinson)* (1982), and the like, as solely celebrating Black culture. Appearing always in these paintings as half-formed or somehow mutilated, the Black male body becomes, iconographically, a sign of lack and absence. This image of incompleteness mirrors those in works that more explicitly critique white imperialism. The painting *Native Carrying Some Guns, Bibles, Amorites on Safari* (1982) graphically evokes images of incomplete Blackness. With wicked wit, Basquiat states in the lower right-hand corner of the work, "I won't even mention gold, (oro)," as though he needed to remind onlookers of a conscious interrogating strategy behind the skeletal, cartoonlike images.

In Basquiat's work, flesh on the Black body is almost always falling away. Like skeletal figures in the Australian aboriginal bark painting described by Robert Edward (X-ray paintings, in which the artist depicts external features as well as the internal organs of animals, humans, and spirits, in order to emphasize "that there is more to a living thing than external appearances"[5]), these figures have been worked down to the bone. To do justice to this work, then, our gaze must do more than register surface appearances. Daring us to probe the heart of darkness, to move our eyes beyond the colonizing gaze, the paintings ask that we hold in our memory the bones of the dead while we consider the world of the Black immediate, the familiar.

To see and understand these paintings, one must be willing to accept the tragic dimensions of Black life. In *The Fire Next Time*, James Baldwin declared that "for the horrors" of Black life "there has been almost no language." He insisted that it was the privacy of Black experience that needed "to be recognized in language." Basquiat's work gives that private anguish artistic expression.

Stripping away surfaces, Basquiat confronts us with the naked Black image. There is no "fleshy" Black body to exploit in his work, for that body is diminished, vanishing. Those who long to be seduced by that Black body must look elsewhere. It is fitting that the skeletal figures displayed again and again in Basquiat's work resemble the shoe depicted in Gillies Turle's book *The Art of the Maasai*.[6] For both Maasai art and

Basquiat's work delineate the violent erasure of a people, their culture and traditions. This erasure is rendered all the more problematic when artifacts of that "vanishing culture" are commodified to enhance the esthetics of those perpetrating the erasure.

The world of Maasai art is a world of bones. Choosing not to work with pigments when making paintings or decorative art, the Maasai use bones from hunting animals in their art to give expression to their relationship with nature and with their ancestors. Maasai artists believe that bones speak—tell all the necessary cultural information, take the place of history books. Bones become the repository of personal and political history. Maasai art survives as a living memory of the distinctiveness of a Black culture that flourished most vigorously when it was undiscovered by the white man. It is this privacy that white imperialism violates and destroys. Turle emphasizes that while the bones are "intense focus points to prime minds into a deeper receptive state," this communicative power is lost on those who are unable to hear bones speak.

Even though socially Basquiat did not "diss" those white folks who could not move beyond surface appearances (stereotypes of entertaining darkies, pet Negroes, and the like), in his work he serves notice on that liberal white public. Calling out their inability to let the notion of racial superiority go, even though it limits and restricts their vision, he mockingly deconstructs their investment in traditions and canons, exposing a collective gaze that is wedded to an aesthetic of white supremacy. The painting *Obnoxious Liberals* (1982) shows us a ruptured history by depicting a mutilated Black Samson in chains and then a more contemporary Black figure no longer naked but fully clothed in formal attire, who wears on his body a sign that boldly states "Not For Sale." That sign is worn to ward off the overture of the large, almost overbearing white figure in the

painting. Despite the incredible energy Basquiat displayed playing the how-to-be-a-famous-artist-in-the-shortest-amount-of-
time game—courting the right crowd, making connections,
networking his way into high "white" art places—he chose to
make his work a space where that process of commodification is
critiqued, particularly as it pertains to the Black body and soul.
Unimpressed by white exoticization of the "Negro," he mocks
this process in works that announce an "undiscovered genius of
the Mississippi delta," forcing us to question who makes such
discoveries and for what reason.

Throughout his work, Basquiat links imperialism to patriarchy, to a phallocentric view of the universe where male egos
become attached to a myth of heroism. The image of the crown,
a recurring symbol in his work, calls to and mocks the Western obsession with being on top, the ruler. The art historian
Robert Farris Thompson suggests that the icon of the crown
reflects Basquiat's ongoing fascination with the subject matter
of "royalty, heroism, and the streets."[7] McEvilley interprets the
crown similarly, seeing it as representative of a "sense of double identity, a royal selfhood somehow lost but dimly remembered."[8] He explains that "in Basquiat's oeuvre, the theme of
divine or royal exile was brought down to earth or historicized
by the concrete reality of the African diaspora. The king that he
once was in another world (and that he would be again when he
returned there) could be imagined concretely as a Watusi warrior or Egyptian pharaoh."[9]

There is no doubt that Basquiat was personally obsessed with
the idea of glory and fame, but this obsession is also the subject of intense self-interrogation in his paintings. Both Thompson and McEvilley fail to recognize Basquiat's mocking, bitter
critique of his own longing for fame. In Basquiat's work the
crown is not an unambiguous image. While it may positively
speak of the longing for glory and power, it connects that desire

to dehumanization, to the general willingness on the part of males globally to commit an unjust act that will lead them to the top. In the painting *Crowns (Peso Neto)* (1981), Black figures wear crowns but are sharply contrasted with the lone white figure wearing a crown, for it is that figure that looms large, overseeing a shadowy world, as well as the world of Black glory.

In much of Basquiat's work the struggle for cultural hegemony in the West is depicted as a struggle between men. Racialized, it is a struggle between Black men and white men over who will dominate. In *Charles the First* (1982), we are told, "Most Young Kings Get Thier [sic] Head Cut Off." Evoking a political and sexual metaphor that fuses the fear of castration with the longing to assert dominance, Basquiat makes it clear that Black masculinity is irrevocably linked to white masculinity by virtue of a shared obsession with conquest, both sexual and political.

Historically, competition between Black and white males has been highlighted in the sports arena. Basquiat extends that field of competition into the realm of the cultural (the poster of him and Andy Warhol duking it out in boxing attire is not as innocent and playful as it appears to be), and the territory is music—in particular, jazz. Basquiat's work calls attention to the innovative power of Black male jazz musicians, whom he reveres as creative father figures. Their presence and work embody for him a spirit of triumph. He sees their creativity exceeding that of their white counterparts. They enable him not only to give birth to himself as Black genius but also to accept the wisdom of an inclusive standpoint.

Braithwaite affirms that Basquiat felt there was a cultural fusion and synthesis in the work of Black male jazz musicians that mirrored his own aspirations. This connection is misunderstood and belittled by Gopnik in his essay "Madison Avenue Primitive" (note the derision the title conveys) when he arrogantly voices his indignation at Basquiat's work being linked with that of great Black jazz musicians. With the graciousness and high-handed-ness of an old-world paternalistic colonizer, Gopnik declares that he can accept that the curator of the Basquiat show attempted to place the artist in a high-art tradition: "No harm, perhaps, is done by this, or by the endless comparisons in the catalogue of Basquiat to Goya, Picasso, and other big names." But, Gopnik fumes, "What *is* unforgivable is the endless comparisons in the catalogue essays of Basquiat to the masters of American jazz."

Gopnik speaks about Basquiat's own attempts to play jazz and then proceeds to tell us what a lousy musician Basquiat "really" was. He misses the point. Basquiat never assumed that his musical talent was the same as that of jazz greats. His attempt to link his work to Black jazz musicians was not an assertion of his own musical or artistic ability. It was a declara-tion of respect for the creative genius of jazz. He was awed by all the avant-garde dimensions of the music that affirm fusion, mixing, improvisation. And he felt a strong affinity with jazz artists in the shared will to push against the boundaries of conventional (white) artistic tastes. Celebrating that sense of connection in his work, Basquiat creates a Black artistic com-munity that can include him. In reality, he did not live long enough to search out such a community and claim a space of belonging. The only space he could claim was that of shared fame.

Fame, symbolized by the crown, is offered as the only pos-sible path to subjectivity for the Black male artist. To be unfa-mous is to be rendered invisible. Therefore, one is without choice. You either enter the phallocentric battlefield of repre-sentation and play the game or you are doomed to exist outside history. Basquiat wanted a place in history, and he played the game. In trying to make a place for himself—for Blackness—in the established art world, he assumed the role of employer/

colonizer. Wanting to make an intervention with his life and work, he inverted the image of the white colonizer.

Basquiat journeyed into the heart of whiteness. White territory he named as a savage and brutal place. The journey is embarked upon with no certainty of return. Nor is there any way to know what you will find or who you will be at journey's end. Braithwaite declares: "The unfortunate thing was, once one did figure out how to get into the art world, it was like, Well, shit, where am I? You've pulled off this amazing feat, you've waltzed your way right into the thick of it, and probably faster than anybody in history, but once you got in you were standing around wondering where you were. And then, Who's here with me?"[11] Recognizing art-world fame to be a male game, one that he could play, working the stereotypical darky image, playing the trickster, Basquiat understood that he was risking his life—that his journey was all about sacrifice.

What must be sacrificed in relation to oneself is that which has no place in whiteness. To be seen by the white art world, to be known, Basquiat had to remake himself, to create from the perspective of the white imagination. He had to become both native and nonnative at the same time—to assume the Blackness defined by the white imagination and the Blackness that is not unlike whiteness. As the anthropologist A. David Napier explains, "Strangers within our midst are indeed the strangest of all—not because they are so alien, but because they are so close to us. And so many legends of 'wildmen,' wandering Jews, and feral children remind us, strangers must be like us but different. They cannot be completely exotic, for, were they so, we could not recognize them."[12]

For the white art world to recognize Basquiat, he had to sacrifice those parts of himself they would not be interested in or fascinated by. Black but assimilated, Basquiat claimed the space of the exotic as though it were a new frontier, waiting only to be colonized. He made of that cultural space within whiteness (the land of the exotic) a location where he would be remembered in history even as he simultaneously created art that unsparingly interrogates such mutilation and self-distortion. As the cultural critic Greg Tate asserts in "Nobody Loves a Genius Child," for Basquiat "making it . . . meant going down in history, ranked beside the Great White Fathers of Western painting in the eyes of the major critics, museum curators and art historians who ultimately determine such things."[13]

Willingly making the sacrifice in no way freed Basquiat from the pain of that sacrifice. The pain erupts in the private space of his work. It is amazing that so few critics discuss configurations of pain in Basquiat's work, emphasizing instead its playfulness, its celebratory qualities. This reduces his painting to spectacle, making the work a mere extension of the minstrel show that Basquiat frequently turned his life into. Private pain could be explored in art because he knew that a certain world "caught" looking would not see it, would not even expect to find it there. Francesco Pellizzi begins to speak about this pain in his essay "Black and White All Over: Poetry and Desolation Painting," when he identifies Basquiat's offerings as "self-immolations, Sacrifices of the Self" that do not emerge "from desire, but from the desert of hope."[14] Rituals of sacrifice stem from the inner workings of spirit that inform the outer manifestation.

Basquiat's paintings bear witness, mirror this almost spiritual understanding. They expose and speak of the anguish of sacrifice. A text of absence and loss, they echo the sorrow of what has been given over and given up. McEvilley's insight that "in its spiritual aspect, [Basquiat's] subject matter is orphic—that is, it relates to the ancient myth of the soul as a deity lost, wandering from its true home, and temporarily imprisoned in a degradingly limited body," appropriately characterizes that anguish.[15] What limits the body in Basquiat's work is the construction of maleness as lack. To be male, caught up in the endless cycle of conquest, is to lose out in the realm of fulfillment.

Significantly, there are few references in Basquiat's work that connect him with a world of Blackness that is female or to a world of influences and inspirations that are female. That Basquiat, for the most part, disavows a connection to the female in his work is a profound and revealing gap that illuminates and expands our vision of him and his work. Simplistic pseudo-psychoanalytic readings of his life and work lead critics to suggest that Basquiat was a perpetual boy always in search of the father. In an essay included in the Whitney catalog, the critic Rene Ricard insists: "Andy represented to Jean the 'Good White Father' Jean had been searching for since his teenage years. Jean's mother has always been a mystery to me. I never met her. She lives in a hospital, emerging infrequently, to my knowledge. Andy did her portrait. She and Andy were the most important people in Jean's life."[16]

Since Basquiat was attached to his natural father, Gerard, as well as surrounded by other male mentor figures, it seems unlikely that the significant "lack" in his life was an absent father. Perhaps it was the presence of too many fathers—paternalistic cannibals who overshadowed and demanded repression of attention for and memory of the mother or any feminine/female principle—that led Basquiat to be seduced by the metaphoric ritual sacrifice of his fathers, a sort of phallic murder that led to a death of the soul.

The loss of his mother, a shadowy figure trapped in a world of madness that caused her to be shut away, symbolically abandoned and abandoning, may have been the psychic trauma that shaped Basquiat's work. Andy Warhol's portrait of Matilde Basquiat shows us the smiling image of a Black Puerto Rican woman. It was this individual, playfully identified by her son as "bruja" (witch), who first saw in Jean-Michel the workings of artistic genius and possibility. His father remembers, "His mother got imperialism started and she pushed him. She was actually a very good artist."[17] Jean-Michel also gave testimony: "I'd say my mother gave me all the primary things. The art came from her."[18] Yet this individual who gave him the lived texts of ancestral knowledge as well as that of the white West is an absent figure in the personal scrapbook of Basquiat as successful artist. It is as if his inability to reconcile the force and power of femaleness with phallocentrism led to the erasure of female presence in his work.

Conflicted in his own sexuality, Basquiat is nevertheless represented in the Whitney catalog and elsewhere as the stereotypical Black stud randomly fucking white women. No importance is attached by critics to the sexual ambiguity that was so central to the Basquiat diva persona. Even while struggling to come to grips with himself as a subject rather than an object, he consistently relied on old patriarchal notions of male identity despite the fact that he critically associated maleness with imperialism, conquest, greed, endless appetite, and, ultimately, death.

To be in touch with senses and emotions beyond conquest is to enter the realm of the mysterious. This is the oppositional location Basquiat longed for yet could not reach. This is the feared location, associated not with meaningful resistance but with madness, loss, and invisibility. Basquiat's paintings evoke a sense of dread. But the terror there is not for the world as it is, the decentered, disintegrating West, that familiar terrain of death. No, the dread is for that unimagined space, that location where one can live without the "same old shit."

Confined within a process of naming, of documenting violence against the Black male self, Basquiat was not able to chart the journey of escape. Napier asserts that "in naming, we relieve ourselves of the burden of actually considering the implication of how a different way of thinking can completely transform the conditions that make for meaningful social relations."[19] A master deconstructivist, Basquiat was not then able to imagine a concrete world of collective solidarities that could alter in any way the status quo. McEvilley sees Basquiat's work as an "iconographic celebration of the idea of the end of the world, or of a certain paradigm of it."[20] While the work clearly calls out this disintegration, the mood of celebration is never sustained. Although Basquiat graphically portrays the disintegration of the West, he mourns the impact of this collapse when it signals doom in Black life. Carnivalesque, humorous, playful representations of death and decay merely mask the magic, cover it with a thin veneer of celebration. Clinging to this veneer, folks deny that a reality exists beyond and beneath the mask.

The Black gay filmmaker Marlon Riggs recently suggested that many Black folks "have striven to maintain secret enclosed spaces within our histories, within our lives, within our psyches about those things which disrupt our sense of self."[21] Despite an addiction to masking/masquerading in his personal life, Basquiat used painting to disintegrate the public image of himself that he created and helped sustain. It is no wonder, then, that his work is subjected to an ongoing critique that questions its "authenticity and value." Failing to accurately represent Basquiat to that white art world that remains confident it "knew" him, critics claim and colonize the work within a theoretical apparatus of appropriation that can diffuse its power by making it always and only spectacle. That sense of "horrific" spectacle is advertised by the paintings chosen to don the covers of every publication on his work, including the Whitney catalog.

In the conclusion to *The Art of the Maasai*, Turle asserts: "When a continent has had its people enslaved, its resources removed, and its land colonized, the perpetrators of these actions can never agree with contemporary criticism or they would have to condemn themselves."[22] Refusal to confront the necessity of potential self-condemnation makes those who are least moved by Basquiat's work insist that they know it best. Understanding this, Braithwaite articulates the hope that Basquiat's work will be critically reconsidered, that the exhibition at the Whitney will finally compel people to "look at what he did."

But before this can happen, Braithwaite cautions, the established white art world (and, I would add, the Eurocentric, multiethnic viewing public) must first "look at themselves." With insight, Braithwaite insists: "They have to try to erase, if possible, all the racism from their hearts and minds. And then when they look at the paintings they can see the art."[23] Calling for a process of decolonization that is certainly not happening (judging from the growing number of negative responses to the show), Braithwaite articulates the only possible cultural shift in perspective that could lay the groundwork for a comprehensive critical appreciation of Basquiat's work.

The work by Basquiat that haunts my imagination, that lingers in my memory, is *Riding with Death* (1988). Evoking images of possession, of riding and being ridden in the Haitian *voudoun* sense—as a process of exorcism, one that makes revelation, renewal, and transformation possible—this work subverts the sense of dread provoked by so much of Basquiat's work. In place of dread is the possibility that the Black-and-brown figure riding the skeletal white bones is indeed "possessed." Napier invites us to consider possession as "truly an avant-garde activity, in that those in trance are empowered to go to the periphery of what is and can be known, to explore the boundaries, and to return unharmed."[24] No such spirit of possession guarded Jean-Michel Basquiat in his life. Napier reports that "people in trance do not—as performance artists in the West sometimes do—leave wounded bodies in the human world."[25] Basquiat must go down in history as one of the wounded. Yet his art will stand as the testimony that declares with a vengeance: We are more than our pain. That is why I am most moved by the one Basquiat painting that juxtaposes the paradigm of ritual sacrifice with that of ritual recovery and return.

1. Adam Gopnik, "Madison Avenue Primitive," *New Yorker*, Nov. 9, 1992, pp. 137–139.

2. Robert Storr, "Two Hundred Beats per Minute," in John Cheim, ed., *Basquiat Drawings*, New York, Robert Miller Gallery, 1990.

3. Fred Braithwaite, "Jean-Michel Basquiat," *Interview*, Oct. 1992, p. 119.

4. Thomas McEvilley, "Royal Slumming: Jean-Michel Basquiat Here Below," *Artforum*, Nov. 1992, p. 95.

5. Robert Edward, *Aboriginal Bark Painting*, Adelaide, Rigby Limited, 1959.

6. Gillies Turle, *The Art of the Maasai*, New York, Knopf, 1992.

7. Robert Farris Thompson, "Royalty, Heroism, and the Streets: The Art of Jean-Michel Basquiat," in Richard Marshall, ed., *Jean-Michel Basquiat*, New York, Whitney Museum of American Art, 1992.

8. Thomas McEvilley, "Royal Slumming," p. 96.

9. Ibid.

10. Gopnik, "Madison Avenue Primitive," p. 139.

11. Braithwaite, "Jean-Michel Basquiat," p. 123.

12. A. David Napier, "Culture as Self: The Stranger Within," in *Foreign Bodies: Performance, Art, and Symbolic Anthropology*, Berkeley, University of California Press, 1992, p. 147.

13. Greg Tate, "Nobody Loves a Genius Child," *Village Voice*, Nov. 14, 1989, p. 33.

14. Francesco Pellizzi, "Black and White All Over: Poetry and Desolation Painting," *Jean-Michel Basquiat*, New York, Vrej Baghoomian Gallery, 1989.

15. McEvilley, "Royal Slumming," p. 96.

16. Rene Ricard, "World Crown ©: Bodhisattva with Clenched Mudra," in Marshall, ed., *Jean-Michel Basquiat*, p. 49.

17. Gerard Basquiat, quoted in Marshall, ed., *Jean-Michel Basquiat*, p. 233.

18. Jean-Michel Basquiat, quoted in *Jean-Michel Basquiat*, p. 233.

19. Napier, *Foreign Bodies*, p. 51.

20. McEvilley, "Royal Slumming," p. 97.

21. Kalamu ya Salaam, "Interview with Marlon Riggs," *Black Film Review* 7, no. 3 (fall 1992), p. 8.

22. Turle, *The Art of the Maasai*.

23. Braithwaite, "Jean-Michel Basquiat," p. 140.

24. Napier, *Foreign Bodies*, p. 69.

25. Ibid.

Subversive Beauty:
New Modes of Contestation

When Keats wrote the lines "a thing of beauty is a joy forever, its loveliness increases, it will never pass into nothingness," he attributed to beauty the subversive function of sustaining life in the face of deprivation, unrelenting pain, and suffering. In the work of Felix Gonzalez-Torres beauty is also a life force, affirming the presence of intense intimacy, closeness, our capacity to know love, face death, and live with ongoing yet reconciled grief. Unlike Keats, Gonzalez-Torres insists in his work that beauty is not best expressed or contained in the enduring art object but, rather, in the moment of experience, of human interaction, the passion of remembrance that serves as a catalyst urging on the will to create. The art object is merely a mirror, giving a glimpse that is also a shadow of what was once real, present, concrete. It is this invitation to enter a world of shadows that Gonzalez-Torres's work extends.

Shadows become the location of our destiny, outlining the shape of past, present, and future possibility. There is always in Gonzalez-Torres's work—whether expressed in the enfolding Blackness that serves as a background for signs of decontextualized history (seemingly random but connected events); in the photographic image of a once inhabited but now vacant bed; or in a pattern of birds' flight among gray clouds—the insistence that elegance and ecstacy are to be found in daily life, in our habits of being, in the ways we regard one another and the world around us. It is sacrilege to reserve this beauty solely for art.

Taking the familiar, the everyday, the mundane, and removing them from the veiled and hidden realm of domesticity, Gonzalez-Torres's work disrupts boundaries, challenges us to see and acknowledge in public space all that we have been encouraged to reveal only in private. Bringing us face to face with our emotional vulnerability, our lack of control over our bodies, our intense longing for nurturance (for example, the bits of candy in an installation we are allowed to take and suck remind us of our engagement with the world of the senses), this art restores the primacy of our bond with flesh. It is about exposure and revelation. It indicts the audience. We are witnesses unable to escape the truth of what we have seen.

Jet-black backgrounds provide the perfect blank screens for the projection of our individual understanding of realities named yet undefined by the printed text. When we see photographs of a billboard that reads *"People With AIDS Coalition 1985 Police Harassment 1969 Oscar Wilde 1895 Supreme/Court 1986 Harvey Milk 1977 March on Washington 1987 Stonewall Rebellion 1969,"* we are not innocent onlookers asked to escape into a world of the artistic imaginary. Here, in this moment of testimony, art returns the gaze of the onlooker, demanding an interrogation of our individual subjectivity—our locations. Who were we, where were we, how did we experience these events?

All the pieces by Gonzalez-Torres that make use of "datelines" resist consumption as mere artifact by the inherent demand that audiences participate, that we make "sense" of the world mirrored here. As counterhegemonic art, Gonzalez-Torres's work requires not that we identify with the artist as iconic figure or with the beautiful art object but, rather, that we identify ourselves as subjects in history through our interaction with the work. This is not art that subliminally subjugates, coercively enthralls or enraptures. It welcomes our presence, our participation.

That presence is made more manifest by the spaces left vacant in the work that leave room for us. This was most evident in the photograph of the unmade bed, rumpled, marked by the imprint of missing bodies, that loomed large on billboards throughout New York City. This image taunted us with remembered connection. Where the body of love could be, where the intimacy of lying close could be seen, there was only absence. Each individual looking into that vacant space must come to terms with what is not there. Once again Gonzalez-Torres gives us art that is not meant to usurp, stand in for, or replace experience.

This art returns us to experience, to memory. What we feel and know with our senses determines what this absence means. There are many ways to "read" the image of the empty bed. Those who come to it with autobiographical details from Felix Gonzalez-Torres's life can see projected here the loss of his lover, the impact of AIDS, the power and pleasure of homosexual/homoerotic love and loss, the anguish of grief. Yet for the masses of viewers who saw this work without knowing the intimate details, this black and white image of an empty bed is a shadowy place to be entered not simply through empathy with the artist but by way of our own relationship to loss, to absence, to leave-taking, to remembered grief.

Inviting audiences to remember moments of closeness and separation, this image is a passage linking the particular losses we experience with a culture of collective grief. All our diverse losses, unnamed sorrows, undocumented deaths can find expression as we gaze upon this bed where living bodies might lie together, leave their mark. We confront an absence that is also a trace leading back so that we can we bear witness to the intimacy that was present. Although the bodies are gone, memories sustain the experience, allow the feelings these bodies generated—the warmth and passion—to be revealed, recalled, recorded.

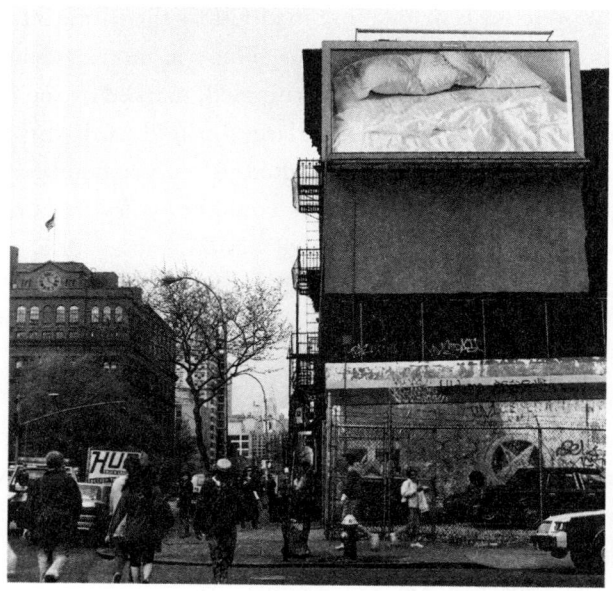

Felix Gonzales-Torres, Untitled, *1991.*
Billboard dimensions vary with installation © Estate Felix Gonzalez-
Torres. Courtesy Felix Gonzalez-Torres Foundation.
Photographer: Peter Muscato.

In the stillness of this image can be heard the sounds of lives content, fulfilled. It is that aura of satisfaction which this image embraces, resurrects, bringing to life a vision of hope and possibility. The absence in this image is not meaningless death. What we see is a pedagogy of mourning that teaches us to understand that life well-lived shapes the nature of our journey, our passage from the moment we are born to the day we die. There are intimations of immortality in this and in Gonzalez-Torres's newer work, a sense of eternity that extends from this image into the artist's recent images of dark clouds where solitary birds fly. Gonzalez-Torres gives us a "passport." This passport has no places for "irrelevant" details: where we were born, in what

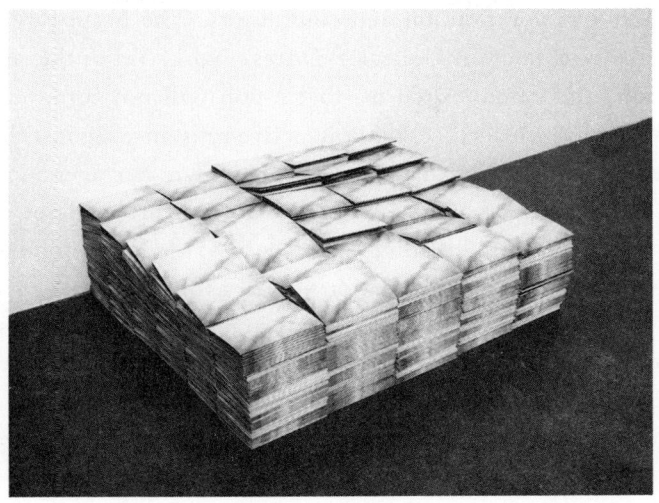

Felix Gonzalez-Torres, Untitled (Passport #II), *1993.*
Print on paper, endless copies. 20.3 cm at ideal height
× 76.2 × 61 cm (original size)
[8" at ideal height × 31 ½" × 29 ½" (original size)].
Each bound booklet, 12 pages: 15.2 × 10.2 cm each (original size)
[6" × 4" each (original size)].
© Estate Felix Gonzalez-Torres
Courtesy Felix Gonzalez-Torres Foundation.
Photographer: Marc Domage.

country, dates or numbers. A passport of dark clouds, of birds in flight, moves us to a space beyond history, a space of mystery where there is no record, no documentation, nothing to recall. What is captured here is a moment of utter oneness where the experience of union, of perfect love transcends the realm of the senses. No boundaries exist. There are no limits.

In the work of Felix Gonzalez-Torres this call for reunion is a political moment, an act of resistance. Once we embrace his vision of the collapse of public and private, the convergence of the individual and the collective, we open ourselves to the possibility of communion and community. The beauty of that union is celebrated in Gonzalez-Torres's work. Yet as the signs, symbols, and datelines tell us, that union will not come without struggle and sacrifice, without active resistance against those forces of domination that seek to shut down our agency, our will to be self-actualized. Gonzalez-Torres's art declares that to be political is to be alive—that beauty resides in moments of revolution and transformation—even as his work articulates "new modes of contestation." In his grappling with subversive beauty, with an aesthetics of loss, Gonzalez-Torres insists that our lives be that space where beauty is made manifest, where the power of human connection and interaction creates that loveliness that "will never pass into nothingness."

In Our Glory: Photography and Black Life

Always a daddy's girl. I was not surprised that my sister V. became a lesbian, or that her lovers were always white women. Her worship of Daddy and her passion for whiteness appeared to affirm a movement away from Black womanhood and, of course, away from that image of the woman we did not want to become—our mother. The only family photograph V. displays in her house is a picture of our dad, looking young with a mustache. His dark skin mingling with the shadows in the photograph. All of which is highlighted by the white T-shirt he wears.

In this snapshot he is standing by a pool table. The look on his face is confident, seductive, cool—a look we rarely saw growing up. I have no idea who took the picture, only that it pleases me to imagine that he cared for the person—deeply. There is such boldness, such fierce openness in the way he faces the camera. This snapshot was taken before marriage, before us, his seven children, before our presence in his life forced him to leave behind the carefree masculine identity this pose conveys.

The fact that my sister V. possesses this image of our dad, one that I had never seen before, merely affirms their romance, the bond between the two of them. They had the dreamed-about closeness between father and daughter, or so it seemed. Her possession of the snapshot confirms this, is an acknowledgment that she is allowed to know—yes, even to possess—that private life he always kept to himself. When we were children, he refused to answer our questions about who he was, how he acted, what he did and felt before us. It was as though he did not want to remember or share that part of himself, as though remembering hurt. Standing before this snapshot, I come closer to the cold, distant, dark man who is my father, closer than I can ever come in real life. Not always able to love him there, I am sure I can love this version of him, the snapshot. I gave it a title: "in his glory."

Before leaving my sister's place, I plead with her to make a copy of this picture for my birthday. She says she will, but it never comes. For Christmas, then. It's on the way. I surmise that my passion for it surprises her, makes her hesitate. My rival in childhood—she always winning, the possessor of Dad's affection—she wonders whether to give that up, whether she is ready to share. She hesitates to give me the man in the snapshot. After all, had he wanted me to see him this way, "in his glory," he would have given me the picture.

My younger sister G. calls. For Christmas, V. has sent her a "horrible photograph" of Dad. There is outrage in her voice as she says, "It's disgusting. He's not even wearing a shirt, just an old white undershirt." G. keeps repeating, "I don't know why she has sent this picture to me." She has no difficulty promising to give me her copy if mine does not arrive. Her lack of interest in the photograph saddens me. When she was the age our dad is in the picture, she looked just like him. She had his beauty then, the same shine of glory and pride. Is this the face of herself that she has forgotten, does not want to be reminded of, because time has taken such glory away? Unable to fathom how she cannot be drawn to this picture, I ponder what this image suggests to her that she cannot tolerate: a grown Black man having a good time, playing a game, having a drink maybe, enjoying himself without the company of women.

Although my sisters and I look at this snapshot and see the same man, we do not see him in the same way. Our "read-

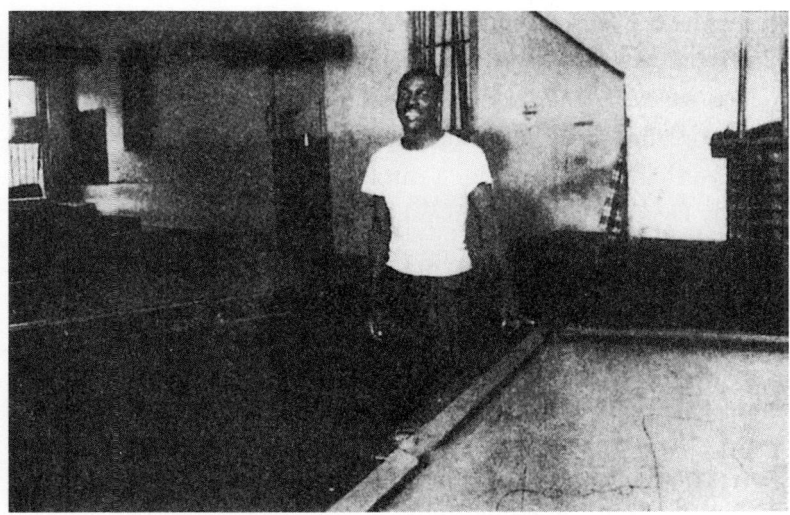

Snapshot of Veodis Watkins, 1949.
Courtesy of bell hooks. Photographer unknown.

ing" and experience of this image is shaped by our relationship with him, with the world of childhood and the images that make our lives what they are now. I want to rescue and preserve this image of our father, not let it be forgotten. It allows me to understand him, provides a way for me to know him that makes it possible to love him again, despite all the other images, the ones that stand in the way of love.

Such is the power of the photograph, of the image, that it can give back and take away, that it can bind. This snapshot of Veodis Watkins, our father, sometimes called Ned or Leakey in his younger days, gives me a space for intimacy between the image and myself, between me and Dad. I am captivated, seduced by it, the way other images have caught and held me, embraced me like arms that would not let go.

Struggling in childhood with the image of myself as unworthy of love, I could not see myself beyond all the received images, which simply reinforced my sense of unworthiness. Those ways of seeing myself came from voices of authority. The place where I could see myself, beyond imposed images, was in the realm of the snapshot. I am most real to myself in snapshots—there I see an image I can love.

My favorite childhood snapshot, then and now, showed me in costume, masquerading. Long after it had disappeared, I continued to long for it, and to grieve. I loved this snapshot of myself because it was the only image available to me that gave me a sense of presence, of girlhood beauty and capacity for pleasure. It was an image of myself I could genuinely like. At that stage of my life I was crazy about Westerns, about cowboys and Indians. The camera captured me in my cowgirl outfit, white ruffled blouse, vest, fringed skirt, my one gun and my boots. In this image I became all that I wanted to be in my imagination.

For a moment, suspended in this image: I am a cowgirl. There is a look of heavenly joy on my face. I grew up needing this image, cherishing it—my one reminder that there was a precious little girl inside me able to know and express joy. I took this photograph with me on a visit to the house of my father's cousin Schuyler.

His was a home where art and the image mattered. No wonder, then, that I wanted to share my "best" image. Making my first real journey away from home, from a small town to my first big city, I needed the security of this image. I packed it carefully. I wanted Lovie, cousin Schuyler's wife, to see me "in my glory." I remember giving her the snapshot for safekeeping: only, when it was time for me to return home, it could not be found. This was for me a terrible loss, an irreconcilable grief. Gone was the image of myself I could love. Losing that snapshot, I lost the proof of my worthiness—that I had ever been a bright-eyed child capable of wonder—the proof that there was a "me of me."

The image in this snapshot has lingered in my mind's eye for years. It has lingered there to remind me of the power of snapshots, of the image. As I slowly complete a book of essays titled *Art on My Mind*, I think about the place of art in Black life, connections between the social construction of Black identity, the impact of race and class, and the presence in Black life of an inarticulate but ever-present visual aesthetic governing our relationship to images, to the process of image making. I return to the snapshot as a starting point to consider the place of the visual in Black life—the importance of photography.

Cameras gave to Black folks, irrespective of class, a means by which we could participate fully in the production of images. Hence it is essential that any theoretical discussion of the relationship of Black life to the visual, to art making, make photography central. Access and mass appeal have historically made photography a powerful location for the construction of an oppositional Black aesthetic. Before racial integration there was a constant struggle on the part of Black folks to create a counterhegemonic world of images that would stand as visual resistance, challenging racist images. All colonized and subjugated people who, by way of resistance, create an oppositional subculture within the framework of domination recognize that the field of representation (how we see ourselves, how others see us) is a site of ongoing struggle.

The history of Black liberation movements in the United States could be characterized as a struggle over images as much as it has also been a struggle for rights, for equal access. To many reformist Black civil rights activists, who believed that desegregation would offer the humanizing context that would challenge and change white supremacy, the issue of representation—control over images—was never as important as equal access. As time has progressed and the face of white supremacy has not changed, reformist and radical Blacks would likely agree

that the field of representation remains a crucial realm of struggle, as important as the question of equal access, if not more
important. Roger Wilkins emphasizes this point in his recent
essay "White Out."

> In those innocent days, before desegregation had
> really been tried, before the New Frontier and the
> Great Society, many of us Blacks had lovely, naive
> hopes for integration . . . In our naiveté, we believed
> that the power to segregate was the greatest power
> that had been wielded against us. It turned out that
> our expectations were wrong. The greatest power
> turned out to be what it had always been: the power
> to define reality where Blacks are concerned and to
> manage perceptions and therefore arrange politics
> and culture to reinforce those definitions.

Though our politics differ, Wilkins's observations echo my
insistence, in the opening essay of *Black Looks: Race and Representation*, that Black people have made few, if any, revolutionary
interventions in the arena of representation.

In part, racial desegregation—equal access—offered a vision
of racial progress that, however limited, led many Black people to be less vigilant about the question of representation.
Concurrently, contemporary commodification of Blackness
creates a market context wherein conventional, even stereotypical, modes of representing Blackness may receive the greatest
reward. This leads to a cultural context in which images that
would subvert the status quo are harder to produce. There is
no "perceived market" for them. Nor should it surprise us that
the erosion of oppositional Black subcultures (many of which
have been destroyed in the desegregation process) has deprived
us of those sites of radical resistance where we have had primary

control over representation. Significantly, nationalist Black freedom movements were often concerned only with questions of "good" and "bad" imagery and did not promote a more expansive cultural understanding of the *politics* of representation. Instead they promoted notions of essence and identity that ultimately restricted and confined Black image production.

No wonder, then, that racial integration has created a crisis in Black life, signaled by the utter loss of critical vigilance in the arena of image making—by our being stuck in endless debate over good and bad imagery. The aftermath of this crisis has been devastating in that it has led to a relinquishment of collective Black interest in the production of images. Photography began to have less significance in Black life as a means—private or public—by which an oppositional standpoint could be asserted, a mode of seeing different from that of the dominant culture. Everyday Black folks began to see themselves as not having a major role to play in the production of images.

To reverse this trend we must begin to talk about the significance of Black image production in daily life prior to racial integration. When we concentrate on photography, then, we make it possible to see the walls of photographs in Black homes as a critical intervention, a disruption of white control over Black images.

Most Southern Black folks grew up in a context where snapshots and the more stylized photographs taken by professional photographers were the easiest images to produce. Displaying these images in everyday life was as central as making them. The walls of images in Southern Black homes were sites of resistance. They constituted private, Black-owned and -operated gallery space where images could be displayed, shown to friends and strangers. These walls were a space where, in the midst of segregation, the hardship of apartheid, dehumanization could be countered. Images could be critically considered, subjects positioned according to individual desire.

Growing up inside these walls, many of us did not, at the time, regard them as important or valuable. Increasingly, as Black folks live in a world so technologically advanced that it is possible for images to be produced and reproduced instantly, it is even harder for some of us to emotionally contextualize the significance of the camera in Black life during the years of racial apartheid. The sites of contestation were not *out there*, in the world of white power, they were *within* segregated Black life. Since no "white" galleries displayed images of Black people created by Black folks, spaces had to be made within diverse Black communities. Across class boundaries Black folks struggled with the issue of representation. This issue was linked with the issue of documentation; hence the importance of photography. The camera was the central instrument by which Blacks could disprove representations of us created by white folks. The degrading images of Blackness that emerged from racist white imagination and that were circulated widely in the dominant culture (on salt shakers, cookie jars, pancake boxes) could be countered by "true-to-life" images. When the psychohistory of a people is marked by ongoing loss, when entire histories are denied, hidden, erased, documentation can become an obsession. The camera must have seemed a magical instrument to many of the displaced and marginalized groups trying to carve out new destinies for themselves in the Americas. More than any other image-making tool, the camera offered African Americans, disempowered in white culture, a way to empower ourselves through representation. For Black folks, the camera provided a means to document a reality that could, if necessary, be packed, stored, moved from place to place. It was documentation that could be shared, passed around. And, ultimately, these images, the world they recorded, could be hidden, to be discovered at another time. Had the camera been there when slavery ended, it could have provided images that would have helped folks searching for lost kin and loved ones. It would have been a powerful tool of cultural recovery. Half a century later, the generations of Black folks emerging from a history of loss became passionately obsessed with the camera. Elderly Black people developed a cultural passion for the camera, for the images it produced, because it offered a way to contain memories, to overcome loss, to keep history.

Though rarely articulated as such, the camera became in Black life a political instrument, a way to resist misrepresentation as well as a means by which alternative images could be produced. Photography was more fascinating to masses of Black folks than other forms of image making because it offered the possibility of immediate intervention, useful in the production of counterhegemonic representations even as it was also an instrument of pleasure. The camera allowed Black folks to combine image making, resistance struggle, and pleasure. Taking pictures was fun!

Growing up in the 1950s, I was somewhat awed and at times frightened by our extended family's emphasis on picture taking. From the images of the dead as they lay serene, beautiful, and still in open caskets to the endless portraits of newborns, every wall and corner of my grandparents' (and most everybody else's) home was lined with photographs. When I was young I never linked this obsession with self-representation to our history as a domestically colonized and subjugated people.

My perspective on picture taking was also informed by the way the process was tied to patriarchy in our household. Our father was definitely the "picture-takin' man." For a long time cameras remained mysterious and off limits to the rest of us. As the only one in the family who had access to the equipment, who could learn how to make the process work, my father exerted control over our images. In charge of capturing our family history with the camera, he called and took the shots.

We were constantly being lined up for picture taking, and it was years before our household could experience this as an enjoyable activity, before any of the rest of us could be behind the camera. Until then, picture taking was serious business. I hated it. I hated posing. I hated cameras. I hated the images that cameras produced. When I stopped living at home, I refused to be captured by anyone's camera. I did not wish to document my life, the changes, the presence of different places, people, and so on. I wanted to leave no trace. I wanted there to be no walls in my life that would, like gigantic maps, chart my journey. I wanted to stand outside history.

That was twenty years ago. Now that I am passionately involved with thinking critically about Black people and representation, I can confess that those walls of photographs empowered me, and that I feel their absence in my life. Right now I long for those walls, those curatorial spaces in the home that express our will to make and display images.

Sarah Oldham, my mother's mother, was a keeper of walls. Throughout my childhood, visits to her house were like trips to a gallery or museum—experiences we did not have because of racial segregation. We would stand before the walls of images and learn the importance of the arrangement, why a certain photograph was placed here and not there. The walls were fundamentally different from photo albums. Rather than shutting images away, where they could be seen only upon request, the walls were a public announcement of the primacy of the image, the joy of image making. To enter Black homes in my childhood was to enter a world that valued the visual, that asserted our collective will to participate in a noninstitutionalized curatorial process.

For Black folks constructing our identities within the culture of apartheid, these walls were essential to the process of decolonization. In opposition to colonizing socialization, interna_ized racism, these walls announced our visual complexity. We saw ourselves represented in these images not as caricatures, cartoonlike figures; we were there in full diversity of body, being, and expression, multidimensional. Reflecting the way Black folks looked at themselves in those private spaces, where those ways of looking were not being overseen by a white colonizing eye, a white-supremacist gaze, these images created ruptures in our experience of the visual. They challenged both white perceptions of Blackness and that realm of Black-produced image making that reflected internalized racism. Many of these images demanded that we look at ourselves with new eyes, that we create oppositional standards of evaluation. As we looked at Black skin in snapshots, the techniques for lightening skin that professional photographers often used when shooting Black images were suddenly exposed as a colonizing aesthetic. Photographs taken in everyday life, snapshots in particular, rebelled against all those photographic practices that reinscribed colonial ways of looking and capturing the images of the Black "other." Shot spontaneously, without any notion of remaking Black bodies in the image of whiteness, snapshots posed a challenge to Black viewers. Unlike photographs constructed so that Black images would appear as the embodiment of colonizing fantasies, snapshots gave us a way to see ourselves, a sense of how we looked when we were not "wearing the mask," when we were not attempting to perfect the image for a white-supremacist gaze.

Although most Black folks did not articulate their desire to look at images of themselves that did not resemble or please white folks' ideas about us, or that did not frame us within an image of racial hierarchies, that desire was expressed through our passionate engagement with informal photographic practices. Creating pictorial genealogies was the means by which one could ensure against the losses of the past. Such genealogies were a way to sustain ties. As children, we learned who our ancestors were by listening to endless narratives as we stood in front of these pictures.

In many Black homes, photographs—especially snapshots—were also central to the creation of "altars." These commemorative places paid homage to absent loved ones. Snapshots or professional portraits were placed in specific settings so that a relationship with the dead could be continued. Poignantly describing this use of the image in her novel *Jazz*, Toni Morrison writes:

> . . . a dead girl's face has become a necessary thing for their nights. They each take turns to throw off the bedcovers, rise up from the sagging mattress and tiptoe over cold linoleum into the parlor to gaze at what seems like the only living presence in the house: the photograph of a bold, unsmiling girl staring from the mantelpiece. If the tiptoer is Joe Trace, driven by loneliness from his wife's side, then the face stares at him without hope or regret and it is the absence of accusation that wakes him from his sleep hungry for her company. No finger points. Her lips don't turn down in judgment. Her face is calm, generous and sweet. But if the tiptoer is Violet, the photograph is not that at all. The girl's face looks greedy, haughty and very lazy. The cream-at-the-top-of-the-milkpail face of someone who will never work for anything, someone who picks up things lying on other people's dressers and is not embarrased when found out. It is the face of a sneak who glides over to your sink to rinse the fork you have laid by your place. An inward face—whatever it sees is its own self. You are there, it says, because I am looking at you.

I quote this passage at length because it attests to a kind of connection to photographic images that has not been acknowledged in critical discussions of Black folks' relationship to the visual. When I first read these sentences, I was reminded of the passionate way we related to photographs when I was a child. Fictively dramatizing the extent to which a photograph can have a "living presence," Morrison describes the way that many Black folks rooted in Southern tradition once used, and still use, pictures. They were and remain a mediation between the living and the dead.

To create a palimpsest of Black folks' relation to the visual in segregated Black life, we need to follow each trace, not fall into the trap of thinking that if something was not openly discussed, or only talked about and not recorded, it lacks significance and meaning. Those pictorial genealogies that Sarah Oldham, my mother's mother, constructed on her walls were essential to our sense of self and identity as a family. They provided a necessary narrative, a way for us to enter history without words. When words entered, they did so in order to make the images live. Many older Black folks who cherished pictures were not literate. The images were crucial documentation, there to sustain and affirm memory. This was true for my grandmother, who did not read or write. I focus especially on her walls because I know that, as an artist (she was an excellent quiltmaker), she positioned the photos with the same care that she laid our her quilts.

The walls of pictures were indeed maps guiding us through diverse journeys. Seeking to recover strands of oppositional worldviews that were a part of Black folks' historical relationship to the visual, to the process of image making, many Black folks are once again looking to photography to make the connection. The contemporary African American artist Emma Amos maps our journeys when she mixes photographs with painting, making connections between past and present. Amos uses snapshots inherited from an uncle who once took pictures for a living. In one piece, Amos paints a map of the United States and identifies diaspotic African presences, as well as particular Native American communities with Black kin, marking each spot with a family image.

Drawing from the past, from those walls of images I grew up with, I gather snapshots and lay them out to see what narratives the images tell, what they say without words. I search these images to see if there are imprints waiting to be seen, recognized, and read. Together, a Black male friend and I lay out the snapshots of his boyhood to see when he began to lose a certain openness, to discern at what age he began to shut down, to close himself away. Through these images, my friend hopes to find a way back to the self he once was. We are awed by what our snapshots reveal, what they enable us to remember.

The word *remember* (*re-member*) evokes the coming together of severed parts, fragments becoming a whole. Photography has been, and is, central to that aspect of decolonization that calls us back to the past and offers a way to reclaim and renew life-affirming bonds. Using images, we connect ourselves to a recuperative, redemptive memory that enables us to construct radical identities, images of ourselves that transcend the limits of the colonizing eye.

Diasporic Landscapes
of Longing

*We take home and language for granted; they become
nature and their underlying assumptions recede into dogma
and orthodoxy.*

*The exile knows that in a secular and contingent world,
homes are always provisional. Borders and barriers, which
enclose us within the safety of familiar territory, can also
become prisons, and are often defended beyond reason or
necessity. Exiles cross borders, break barriers of thought and
experience.*

—Edward Said, "Reflections on Exile"

When I was a little girl in the rural South, we would
sometimes go to country churches. Traveling down narrow,
dusty, unpaved roads, past fields and fields of crops and chew-
ing tobacco, we would ride into a wilderness of nature, arrive
late, and yet be welcomed into a hot, crowded sanctuary full
of holiness and grace. To awaken a spirit of ecstatic reverie, the
choir would sing this song with a line that just made folks shout
and cry out with joy, "I wouldn't take nothing for my journey
now." This line affirmed a vision of life in which all experience,
good and bad, everything that happened, could retrospectively
be seen as a manifestation of divine destiny. It called on believers to lay claim to an inclusive spirit of unconditional acceptance
that would enable all of us to see every path we had taken in life,
whether chosen or not, as a necessary one—preparing us for that
return to a home we could only dream about. The multilayered

vision of life's journey celebrated in this old-time Black church song, where every bit of history and experience is seen as essential to the unfolding of one's destiny, is rearticulated in the artistic practices of Carrie Mae Weems.

Traditionally trained in mainstream art schools where there was little or no awareness of the way in which the politics of white supremacy shaped and informed academic pedagogies of photographic practice, Weems made a conscious decision to work with Black subjects. This choice preceded contemporary academic focus on decentering Western civilization, which necessarily requires that attention shift from a central concern with white subjects. Ironically, for the most part, cultural criticism that calls for acts of intervention that would decenter the West tend to reprivilege whiteness by investing in a politics of representation that merely substitutes the central image of colonizing oppressive whiteness with that of a *newly* reclaimed radical whiteness portrayed as liberatory. Whiteness then remains the starting point for all progressive cultural journeying—that movement across borders which invites the world to take note, to pay attention, to give critical affirmation. The much talked-about discourse of postcoloniality is a critical location that, ironically, often maintains white cultural hegemony. The less well-recognized discursive practices of anticolonialism, on the other hand, decenter, interrogate, and displace whiteness. This discourse disrupts accepted epistemologies to make room for an inclusive understanding of radical subjectivity that allows recognition and appreciation of the myriad ways individuals from oppressed or marginalized groups create oppositional cultural strategies that can be meaningfully deployed by everyone. This constructive cultural appropriation happens only as shifts in standpoint take place, when there is ongoing transformation of ways of seeing that sustain oppositional spheres of representation.

The work of Carrie Mae Weems visually engages a politics of anticolonialism. Concretely decentering the white subject, she challenges viewers to shift their paradigms. Although her work encourages us not to see the Black subject through the totalizing lens of race, it is often discussed as though the sign of racial difference is the only relevant visual experience her images evoke. This way of seeing actively reappropriates the work and reinscribes it within the dominant cultural hegemony of Western imperialism and colonialism. By choosing to concentrate attention on Black subjects, Weems risks this oversimplification of her artistic practice. In her work, however, she consistently invites us to engage the Black subject in ways that call attention to the specificity of race even as we engage an emotional landscape that challenges us to look beyond race and recognize the multiple concerns represented. Unfortunately, the failure to move beyond a conventional practice of art criticism that consistently confines Black artists within a discourse that is always and only about racial otherness characterizes much critical writing about Weems's work. Transforming ways of seeing means that we learn to see race—thereby no longer acting in complicity with a white-supremacist aesthetic that would have us believe issues of color and race have no place in artistic practices—without privileging it as the only relevant category of analysis. Carrie Mae Weems's photoworks create a cartography of experience wherein race, gender, and class identity converge, fuse, and mix so as to disrupt and deconstruct simple notions of subjectivity.

While Weems's decision to concentrate on Black subjects was a challenge to white cultural hegemony, it signaled, more importantly, the emergence of a lifelong commitment to recover and bring to the foreground subjugated knowledge relating to African American experience. Although Weems was initially captivated by mainstream documentary photography, learning from the work of photographers from Henri Cartier-

Bresson to Roy DeCarava, she critically engages a process of image making that fuses diverse traditions and engages mixed media. Early in her artistic development, she was particularly inspired by DeCarava's visual representations of Black subjects that invert the dominant culture's aesthetics, in which, informed by racist thinking, Blackness was iconographically seen as a marker of ugliness. DeCarava endeavored to reframe the Black image within a subversive politics of representation that challenged the logic of racist colonization and dehumanization. Moving among and within the public and private worlds of poor and working-class Black experience, which mainstream white culture perceived only as a location of deprivation and spiritual and emotional "ugliness," DeCarava created images of Black folks embodying a spirit of abundance and plenty; he claimed Blackness as the aesthetic space of ethereal beauty, of persistent, unsuppressed elegance and grace.

Such work fits most neatly into the category that the critic Saidiya Hartman identified as artistic practice aimed at "rescuing and recovering the Black subject" via a "critical labor of the positive. It is a resolutely counterhegemonic labor that has at its aim the establishment of other standards of aesthetic value and visual possibility. The intention of the work is corrective representation." Weems extended DeCarava's legacy beyond the investment in creating positive images. Her images problematizing Black subjectivity expand the visual discursive field. Weem's journey, beginning with this "critical labor of the positive," is fundamentally altered and refigured as her relation to the Black image is transformed by a politics of dislocation. In her early work, Weems's perception of Black subjectivity departed from a concern with the positive and refigured itself within a field of contestation, wherein identity is always fluid, always changing.

Weems is engaged in a process of border crossing, of living within a social context of cultural hybridity. Her understanding of Black subjectivity is informed by what Paul Gilroy identified as "the powerful effects of even temporary experiences of exile, relocation, and displacement." Indeed, it is the effort to recover subjugated knowledge within the realm of visual representation that brings Weems face to face with the limitations of essentialist constructions of Black identity.

Contrary to critical discussion that sees Weems as laying claim to an "authentic" Black experience, her explorative journeys of recovery and return merely expose how reality is distorted when a unitary representation of Black subjectivity is reinscribed rather than consistently challenged. When Weems made the decision to focus on Black subjects—as she put it, to "dig in my own backyard"—she was motivated by a longing to restore knowledge, not by a desire to uphold an essentialist politics of representation. (A distinction must be made here between the critical project that seeks to promote a notion of authentic Blackness and efforts to reclaim the past that are a gesture of critical resistance and remembrance.) While Weems drew on her family history in the series *Family Pictures and Stories*, her narrative deflects any one-dimensional construction of these works as "positive" images deployed to challenge racist stereotypes. She not only named her location as that of the outsider who has journeyed away from family and community of origin to return with new perspectives, she juxtaposed and contrasted her memories of people with the present reality. Balancing image making that commemorates the past with the act of highlighting the ways in which the meaning of this past is changed by interrogations in the present, Weems celebrated what Roger Simon called "processes of collective remembrance." He explained: "Central to these processes is a procedure within which images and stories of a shared past are woven together with a person (or group's) feelings and comprehension of their embodied presence in time and space. These processes of remembrance are organized and

Carrie Mae Weems,
What are the three
things you can't give a
Black person?,
1987–1988.
14 ½" x 14 ½".
Gelatin silver print.
© Carrie Mae Weems.
Courtesy of the artist and
Gladstone Gallery,
New York, Fraenkel
Gallery, San Francisco,
and Galerie Barbara
Thumm, Berlin.

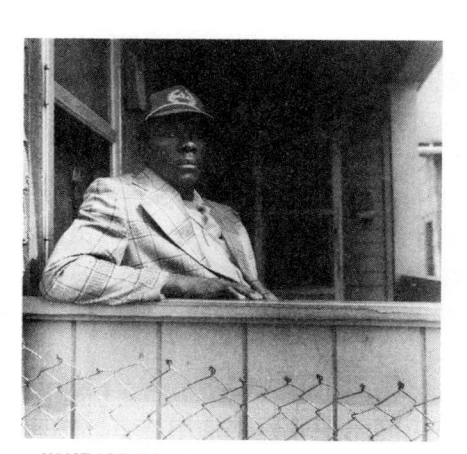

WHAT ARE THE THREE THINGS YOU CAN'T
GIVE A BLACK PERSON?

produced within practices of commemoration which initiate and structure the relation between a representation of past events and that constellation of affect and information which define a standpoint from which various people engage such representations."

Commemoration is central to Weems's artistic practice. From early work that focused on constructing images and narratives of families, she moved into an exploration of the journey from Africa to the so-called New World. There she looked at African American ideas of home, community, and nation, particularly as expressed in vernacular, working-class culture. Visually revisiting slavery, the Middle Passage, Reconstruction, the civil rights era, and on to militant Black power activism, Weems has created images that chart the passion of rebellion and resistance. Commemorative plates remind us of the nature of that journey. Simon called this process "insurgent commemoration" that "attempts to construct and engage representations that rub taken-for-granted history against the grain so as to revitalize and rearticulate what one sees as desirable and necessary for an open, just and life-sustaining future." In the series *Ain't Jokin*, Weems used wit and satire to exorcise the power of racist representation. Referencing racist iconography, as well as highlighting folklore used to perpetuate white supremacy in everyday life, that makes this iconography appear matter of fact, while contrasting these images with narrative statements that problematize, Weems deconstructed these ways of knowing. Throughout her work, she has relied on strategies of deconstruction to challenge conventional perceptions created by our attachment to fixed ways of looking that lead to blindspots.

In the installation *And 22 Million Very Tired and Very Angry People*, Weems created an assemblage of carefully chosen political narratives—the declarative confessions of working-class activists, the lyrical prose of the novelist—and placed them with specific images. No fixed, authentic Black subject is represented in this piece. The common bond is not race or shared history but, rather, an emotional universe inhabited by individuals committed to ending domination, oppression, and injustice around the world; who are linked together across the boundaries of space, time, race, culture, nationality, and even life and death, by a shared commitment to struggle. As this installation makes clear, rage against injustice, as well as the weariness that comes with protracted struggle, is not the exclusive property of Black people. As the image of the globe suggests, it is present wherever oppression and exploitation prevail in daily life.

In this installation, Weems laid claim to a diasporic vision of journeying in search of freedom and strategies of resistance and fulfillment. She has staked her claim by inhabiting the space of Blackness in the United States, but also by refusing to stay in her place and rejecting a narrow identity politics imposed by systems of domination. The radical Black subjectivity mirrored in this installation audaciously unites that particularly with a universal transcendent emotional landscape wherein the desire to be free is the tie that binds and creates continuity in the midst of discontinuity. Within the emotional landscape of this work, the *Sea Islands* series, and the images of *Gorée Island*, Weems established a commonality of longing, of yearning for connection, for home. Here home is not a place but a condition—felt only when there is freedom of movement and expression. It is the seeking that is shared, not what is found.

The will to search out spaces of recovery and renewal led Carrie Mae Weems to Africa. Articulating with satiric wit and contemplative significance of that search in *Went Looking for Africa*, she problematized this dream of exile and return, of homecoming. She found in the Sea Islands African cultural retentions that link Blackness in the diaspora, that create an imaginative world wherein Africa can be represented as present yet far away, as both real and mythic. To distinguish this search for subjugated knowledge from nostalgic longing for the mythical, paradisiacal homeland that is so often the imperialist vision imposed by contemporary Afrocentric Black neonationalism, Weems presented images of specific locations. She arranged these sites to compose a ritual of seduction that evokes an emotional connection between Africans and African Americans, even if that common bond cannot always be documented with visual proof of African cultural retentions in the United States. Her work offers documentary "proof" even as it tells us that this is ultimately not as important as the abiding sense of emotional and spiritual connection that imperialism and colonialism have not been able to suppress.

Within a political context of anticolonialism, Weems positions her work on Africa as a counterhegemonic response to the Western cultural imperialism that systematically erases that connection—that diasporic bond—which links all Black people.

To do this she decenters the West by abandoning notions that reason is the only way to apprehend the universe. This serves to promote alternative means by which we can know what connects us to distant places, to folks we have never seen but somehow recognize in our hearts as kin. Jane Flax challenged progressive thinkers to resist investing "in the primacy of reason," to prevent it from occupying "a privileged place within our subjectivity or political hopes." With her images of African sites, Weems has insisted on rituals of commemoration that can be understood only within the context of an oppositional worldview, wherein intuition, magic, dream lore are all acknowledged to be ways of knowing that enhance our experience of life, that sweeten the journey. When Weems looks to Africa, it is to rediscover and remember an undocumented past even as she simultaneously creates a relationship forged in the concrete dailiness of the present. For example, in the *Gorée Island* series, captivity is evoked by the depiction of spaces that convey a spirit of containment. A cultural genealogy of loss and abandonment is recorded in the words Weems stacked on top of one another: "Congo, Ibo, Mandingo, Togo." These markers of heritage, legacy, and location in history stand in direct contrast to those words that evoke dislocation, displacement, dismemberment: "Grabbing, Snatching, Blink, And You Be Gone." Whereas the *Sea Islands* series marks the meeting ground between Africa and America, the *Gorée Island* images articulate a decolonized politics of resistance. They represent a return that counters the loss of the Middle Passage, the recovery that is made possible because of revolution and resistance, through ongoing anticolonial struggle. Weems is not attempting to create an ethnographic cartography to document diasporic Black connections. Her work does not record a journey to unearth essential, authentic Black roots, even though it will likely be critically discussed and arranged by curators in a manner that makes this

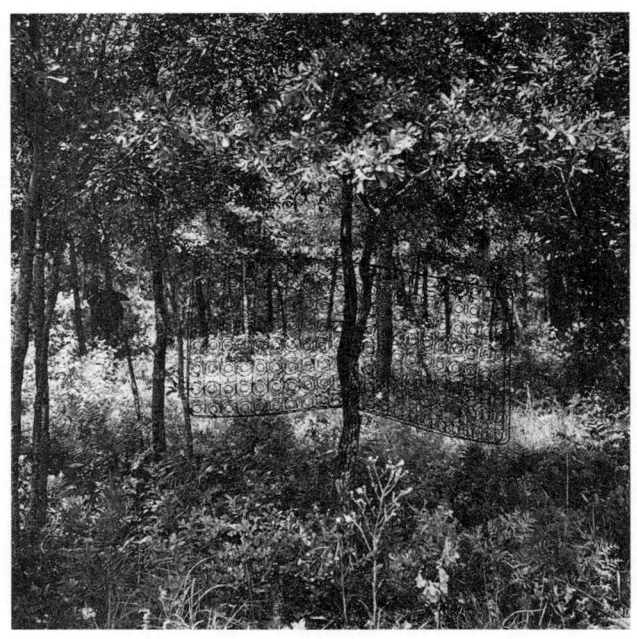

Carrie Mae Weems, Box Spring in Tree, *1992.*
20" x 20". Silver print.© Carrie Mae Weems.
Courtesy of the artist and Gladstone Gallery, New York,
Fraenkel Gallery, San Francisco, and
Galerie Barbara Thumm, Berlin.

appropriative reinscription possible. Weems is most concerned
with ways such knowledge remakes and transforms contemporary radical Black subjectivity. A spirit of contestation that
emerges with the *Went Looking for Africa* series exposes the way
Western imperialism informs the relationship of African Americans to Africa. Yet the failure to embrace a progressive, anticolonial standpoint as the perspective that might enable everyone
in the West, including Black folks, to see Africa differently in
no way delegitimizes the longing to return to Africa as origin
site, as location of possible spiritual renewal. The Africa Weems

visually represented in the *Gorée Island* series is both a site for insurgent commemorative remembrance and a contemporary location that must be engaged on its own terms, in the present.

Weems has centralized architectural images, linking traditional dwellings with modern space. In these images, Africa is both familiar homeland and location of Otherness. Fundamentally, it is a place that awakens the senses, enabling us to move into a future empowered by the previously subjugated knowledge that we cannot allow reason to overdetermine constructions of identity and community. As Bernard Tschumi declared, we have an experience of space that is registered in the senses, in a world beyond words: "Space is real for it seems to affect my senses long before my reason. The materiality of my body both coincides with and struggles with the materiality of space. My body carries in itself spatial properties, and spatial determinations. . . . Unfolding against the projections of reason, against the Absolute Truth, against the Pyramid, here is the Sensory Space, the Labyrinth, the Hole . . . here is where my body tries to rediscover its lost unity, its energies and impulses, its rhythms and its flux." Weems seeks such reunion in her imaginative engagement and remembrance of Africa—past and present. Her visual quest to recover subjugated knowledge is fulfilled in a process of journeying that, as Mary Catherine Bateson proclaimed, makes learning a process by which we come home: "the process of learning turns a strange context into a familiar one, and finally into a habitation of mind and heart. . . . Learning to know a community or a landscape is a homecoming. Creating a vision of that community or landscape is homemaking." In her art practice, Weems imagines a diasporic landscape of longing, a cartography of desire wherein boundaries are marked only to be transgressed, where the exile returns home only to leave again.

Talking Art with
Carrie Mae Weems

bell hooks: Carrie Mae, whenever I see your work I am deeply moved. More than any contemporary photographer creating representations of Blackness, your work evokes the exilic nature of Black people. Everyone forgets that when we talk about Black people living in the diaspora, we're talking about a people who live in exile, and that in some ways, like all other exiles, we imagine home, we imagine journeys of return. We embark on such journeys by first looking for traces—by engaging the palimpsest that reveals the multilayered nature of our experience. Derrida's notion of palimpsest comes to mind as I look at your work. A vision, a journey through time—past, present, and future—to unravel connecting threads is ever-present in your work. There is both the evocation of exile in your work and a politics of dislocation, when, for example, you are charting your family's movement from the South to Portland, Oregon (I think about people often thinking, well, there are no Black people in Portland), and you are on the move. That politics of dislocation in your work makes this new move towards Africa really exciting. Talk about this spirit of journeying, of homeland, about Black people imaging some kind of static, homogeneous sense of our place.

Carrie Mae Weems: In most every Black person's life today, home is where you find it, just where you find it. To me this suggests open possibility—that home can be for me Portland, Oregon, to the same extent that it can be New York or Ghana or Maui or Senegal. It doesn't matter.

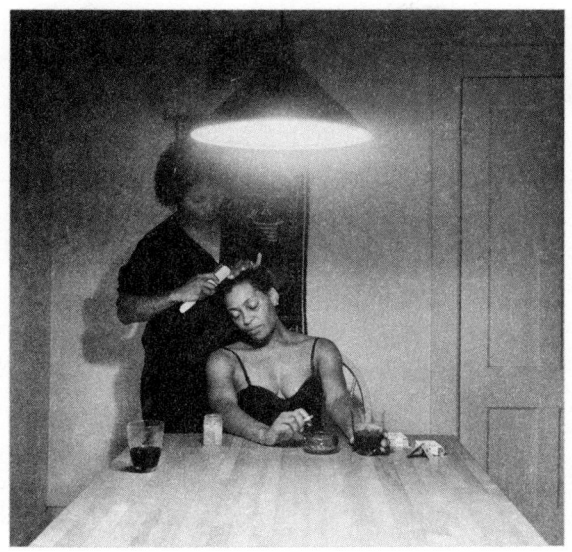

Ccrrie Mae Weems, Untitled (Woman brushing hair), *1990.*
15" x 15". Silver print. © Carrie Mae Weems.
Courtesy of the artist and Gladstone Gallery, New York, Fraenkel
Gallery, San Francisco, and Galerie Barbara Thumm, Berlin.

bh: The specific postmodern deconstructive positionality that interrogates notions of fixed origins, of roots, is not just in this new work that lays claim to Africa as a possible site of home, but in all your work.

CMW: From the very beginning.

bh: It's there in the piece *Went Looking for Africa.* To me, this new work calls to mind Audre Lorde's sense of biomythography. You're not looking to "document" in some scientific, linear, orderly, factual way where we came from, how we got here; you are uncovering these details, but also exploring the gaps, the spaces in the shadows that facts don't allow us to see, the mystery.

CMW: Home for me is both mysterious and mythic—the known and the unknown. My search begins with the *Sea Islands* piece. That initial focus on family folklore was the beginning of my searching out a home place, trying to figure out for myself, that moment in the early 1980s, where I come from, how is that place constructed, what went on there, what was that sort of historical movement about. In any case, the movement of my family, leaving Mississippi, traveling from the South to the North, that kind of migration. I wanted to know how I fit into that as a woman who was already starting to move around, starting to travel, and digging, digging.

bh: There is that archeological dimension to your search expressed in the work. Your journey is intensified by the way in which both race and gender situate you within a cultural context of exile. That is doubly intensified when you embrace oppositional thinking, when you resist the forms of domination that would keep you in your place. It's not like you return "to the South" or go anywhere unproblematically—you return as this person who early in her life embraced feminist thinking in a very existentially self-reflexive way. Your feminist understanding of Black womanness has always inspired your work. That complex feminist sensibility is there in the *Kitchen Table* series. I am always annoyed when I read critics who are so fixated on the Blackness of the images that they ignore the question of gender—of desire and power.

CMW: These images of Black men and Black women should speak on many levels, calling to mind in the viewer a range of issues and concerns.

bh: Your work compels recognition of race and representation even as it moves beyond race to an exploration of gender and power that has universal implications. Many of your images of Black women and men raise issues about the politics of gender in our lives. I am thinking here about the *Kitchen Table* series.

CMW: Right. Well, you know, one of the things that I was thinking about was whether it might be possible to use Black subjects to represent universal concerns. When we watch Hollywood movies, usually with white subjects, those images create a cultural terrain that we watch and walk on and move through. I wanted to create that same kind of experience using my subjects. Yet when I do that, it's not understood in that way. Folks refuse to identify with the concerns Black people express which take us beyond race into previously undocumented emotional realms. Black images can only stand for themselves and nothing more.

bh: Then critics "read" Blackness as signifying confrontation. I think your work is counterhegemonic in that it disturbs—it challenges and contests conventional perception. Contestation is different from confrontation. I think what people want, in a sense, is to see the work as confronting race, because whiteness and white viewers are centralized as the primary audience for the work. Thinking of the work as being about contestation, however, invites any viewer to work with a particular image and place themselves in relationship to the image. In this light, my favorite piece in the *Ain't Jokin* series is the *Mirror, Mirror* piece; that piece challenges me to interrogate my notions of beauty, to situate myself.

CMW: Right. For the most part, there have been only white critics who've been talking about the work. And they talk about the works of Black artists, in general, in ways that centralize race, seeing only this facet.

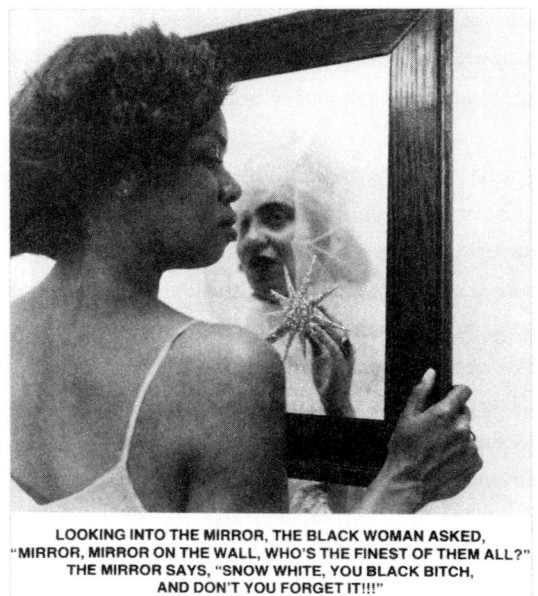

LOOKING INTO THE MIRROR, THE BLACK WOMAN ASKED,
"MIRROR, MIRROR ON THE WALL, WHO'S THE FINEST OF THEM ALL?"
THE MIRROR SAYS, "SNOW WHITE, YOU BLACK BITCH,
AND DON'T YOU FORGET IT!!!"

Carrie Mae Weems, Mirror Mirror, *1987–1988.*
24" x 20". Silver print. © Carrie Mae Weems.
Courtesy of the artist and Gladstone Gallery, New York, Fraenkel
Gallery, San Francisco, and Galerie Barbara Thumm, Berlin.

bh: Well, two issues arise here. There is the work made by the
Black artist and the response to the Black image. That response
is shaped by the politics of location—the standpoint from which
we look. I just wrote a piece for Deborah Willis's new collection of essays on photography, *Picturing Us: African American
Identity and Photography.* One of the things that I wrote about
was how photography has been so central to African Americans.
Nonetheless, more than any other artistic practice, it has been
the most accessible, the most present in our lives. I wrote about
the significance of snapshots, about the ways they enable us to
trace and reconstruct a cultural genealogy through the image.
This critical engagement with images has been consistent in

Black life, but so little has been written about it. If the only critical writing about the work of Black photographers looks at the work in a manner that sees it only through the lens of a colonizing gaze, then the universal, metaphysical dimension of that work will never be discussed.

CMW: Yes. Yes.

bh: You know, when I look at the *Kitchen Table* series what immediately surfaces is a visceral connection with a heterosexual convergence of pleasure and danger, of power and desire. Yes, the individuals are Black, but the issues raised are about sexuality in general, the politics of desire—intimacy and domination.

CMW: Historically, it's been absolutely impossible for the vast majority of critics, of white audiences, and even of Black audiences to come to the work and not first and foremost fixate only on the Blackness of the images. As soon as Blackness becomes the all-important sign, audiences assume that the images are addressing victimization. What is the level of victimization that we're looking at? Black people come to it in a different way, but posing the same question. They might be able to jump past this, or leapfrog past that quickly, but it's still the same issue. It's the issue for everyone, because we so rarely see Black subjects, right?

bh: Most of your earlier work that is often seen as documentary photography isn't about victimization at all.

CMW: No. 'Course not. [*Laughs*]

bh: That's exactly why there has to be a challenge to critics to come back to this early work and reconsider ways of seeing and writing about it. In all spheres of cultural production, work by

Black artists rarely receives sophisticated critical attention from the outset. For example, much of the early critical writing about Toni Morrison's work was terrible. All too often, Black artists must reach a certain prominence before the critical writing about their work stops being shallow and superficial.

CMW: The assumption that our ability as artists is restricted to our only being able to deal meaningfully with the question of race and rage overdetermines critical perception. For instance, I was at a gallery about a year ago, and a white woman was there looking at some of my new pieces, which she bought. Some of the *Ain't Jokin* pieces and earlier works were pulled for her. I was someplace in the building, checking out some other shit, and girlfriend walks in, she looks at the work, the *Sea Islands* piece. She looks at the work, and finally she asks if she can be introduced to me. They bring me over. She walks over to me, she says, "Is the work angry? But this work is not making me feel guilty." She wants me to tell her how to respond to the work because she assumes that the only legitimate response is guilt in the face of perceived rage.

bh: The other, but no less limited, way of viewing your work is to see it as many audiences, particularly white folks, do, as ethnographic documentation.

CMW: Oh, right.

bh: That's still a way of denying the complex cultural landscape presented by the images.

CMW: To see the work as ethnographic deflects away from the seriousness and makes it mostly entertaining.

bh: In much of your work, you centralize Black subjectivity in ways that do not allow whiteness to rewrite itself using the Black face as though it's another frontier, another blank page, which whiteness can conquer and consume. The risk that you take by breaking a certain photographic silence is that your interest, your artistic concerns, will be overshadowed by simplistic, superficial responses to the work. Artistic work that is counterhegemonic always risks cooptation by critical practices that deny, that don't see the radical implications of a particular standpoint. Does documentary photography make these concerns more explicit?

CMW: Documentary as a genre has been very, very interesting to me, and there are aspects about it that I've always been interested in. I started out very early working in that terrain and spent a lot of time in a variety of places photographing in the tradition of Cartier-Bresson. Early on, my artistic practices were shaped by those traditions that said: This is how a photograph is made. These are the elements of a good photograph. This is the way the shit's supposed to be printed. Then you knew that you were working in that mode. And I tried that. I worked with it and there was something appealing about it, the whole idea that you were somehow describing the complicatedness of the human condition. That's what documentary was, or certainly was to me. I think a part of documentary had a lot to do with the notion that you would go into somebody else's backyard and capture it and bring home the ethnic image, as trophy, but, hopefully, once you have captured the ethnic image, in the process of capturing it, you've gone through some harrowing, life-transforming experience—like Eugene Smith, who was beaten in Harlem, or Cartier-Bresson, who was shot in Zimbabwe. In your passion to document you encounter a tragic reality that transforms, so that you can come back even bigger, with your prize, and be praised for that. Well, I started to really understand what documentary was, what it really was, and I understood it even more later. However, when I started to understand it, when I learned that the terrain that I wanted to walk on couldn't be carried forth by straight documentary, my attention shifted. There was something different that I wanted to explore, work that had the appearance of documentary but was not at all documentary. It was highly fabricated work.

bh: Absolutely. Your work engages a process of defamiliarization. You take a familiar image, a familiar frame, and through a series of displacements challenge us to see it in a new way.

CMW: Right, right.

bh: I see your work as profoundly informed by the politics of displacement, where the colonizing gaze has to shift itself. It is this demand that makes the work counterhegemonic. It calls us to interrogate received perceptions. And it is not merely white people who look at the Black image with the colonizing gaze. We have all been taught to look at Black images with a colonizing eye.

CMW: Exactly, though it is often Black folks, and other non-white viewers, who are most eager to shift their gaze—to make the leap and see with new eyes.

bh: Few critics place your work within the discourse about identity, nationality, or postcoloniality. Black artists and critical thinkers in Australia, aboriginal people, are rejecting the term *postcoloniality,* using *anticolonialism.* This is a useful way to frame discussions of your work. The images you create are a form of resistance. Those persons who are most likely to be victimized by the imposition of a colonizing gaze can reach into your work and find the strength that is there. I remember that when I walked into a museum and saw *and 22 Million Very Tired and Very Angry People*, what struck me was the way you used familiar tropes in this alluring, poetic yet profoundly political way. It was so amazing. [*Carrie laughs*] Walking into that exhibit was almost like entering a Buddhist temple, calm and compassion-surrounded. The work articulated our experience as exiles in the diaspora, for one thing, in its wandering. Such border-crossing work, combining the idea of Gramsci with Stuart Hall. There is no one-dimensional construction of Blackness or of revolution in the work. Instead, it problematizes the whole notion of turning, of what we are turning toward. And yet you are constantly insisting that we cannot simply assume that what we are turning toward is—

CMW: —is better than what you're turning away from.

bh: Absolutely. [*Carrie laughs*] This is the power in the work that I think has to be called out more by critics.

CMW: I've been thinking about ways of forcing the issues, when it comes to the way in which the work gets talked about in the world. You know, I feel I can't sit back anymore and just allow people to do whatever the fuck they want to do around the work, particularly when it becomes truly disinformation.

bh: Also, Carrie, I think of you as a cultural critic, a theoretical peer. When I hear you talk about the work, you do so with a level of theoretical sophistication. Not all artists can talk about their work, placing it within theoretical frameworks—not everyone has that skill. At times the playfulness in the work may lead audiences to overlook its extreme seriousness. Wit and serious deconstruction go together. "In-your-face" contestation is an aspect of satire, irony. It ain't just funny for the sake of making folks laugh. It's saying something about the multiple ways that we approach a subject. I just finished writing about the *Ain't Jokin* pieces, the image of the Black man in the window.

CMW: It's called *What are the three things you can't give a Black person?*

bh: You have a tension within the piece itself. On one hand you have the construction of a Black person, and yet you also give us the image of a type of Black male body that we rarely see represented in this culture.

CMW: Very rarely. That's right. That's right.

bh: And what is this image doing?

CMW: For me the vast majority of the *Ain't Jokin* series is constructed in that way—so there will always be this kind of tension between what you see within the photograph and what you see beneath it, with the text always cutting through. Hopefully, then, for the viewer, there would be a curious pull between what you see and the way this subject has been flipped and undermined by the power of humor, of the racist joke. For the most part, I think that that works. For example, if you look at the image of three baboons which I show in a photograph—you see a fabulous piece, a gorgeous photograph, right? And then you have a context: We would have that up on our wall and we would say, "That that's a beautiful Black family," right? The moment this description is made of three baboons, and that assertion is made by the text and the language that describes who they are, then something else is called into question in a very, very, very good way.

bh: In his essay "Reflections on Exile," Edward Said talks about contingency and what it means to be in a contingent world. Well, part of what it means to be in a contingent world is that meaning is constantly being reworked—that images will not always have the same meaning. And some images won't always work; earlier, we talked about the way the Black artists are "blamed" if there are images that don't work.

CMW: . . . don't work, or fail.

bh: Where the very nature of artistic practice is rooted in a philosophy of risk, the fact that there are sometimes images which do not work is part of the process.

CMW: That's right. That's right.

bh: In fact, let's say there are times when Black people, individual Black people, have seen those images and have felt crushed or humiliated by them. Is that a failure of the work, or is it simply that, because of contingency, because of circumstance, how *they* see what they see hurts?

CMW: That's right. It could be both.

bh: Absolutely. This possibility of failure is part of a deconstructive element in your work, in the sense that much photography does not require people to think about audience while your work does. And that's part of its genius and power. So much photography doesn't lead people to think deeply about the work, to interrogate it. And the value of most prominent white photographers is not determined by audience response to their work. Yet folks will tell me, "Well, I'm troubled by Carrie Mae Weems's work, because it doesn't work with the audience."

The assumption is that there is one correct response, rather than multiple responses.

CMW: Which is much more of what I'm interested in at this point.

bh: Absolutely. But that's also the fundamental critical challenge in your work to contemporary notions of the subject. I mean, there's a fundamental postmodern quality to your work that I think is often overlooked because the images are structured in a manner that appears simple, straightforward. In actuality, the meanings of the images are altered by the text. People may initially assume that these images are familiar, even ethnographic, but your use of text displaces, subverts, and changes meaning. For example, I was looking at the *Mirror, Mirror* piece, asking, "Who's really looking?" Is it the white face gazing out at the Black face? Is it really the hope on the part of millions of white women in America who have anxiety about their beauty and their seductive powers, who are the ones who actually need to look in that mirror and affirm their primacy—to affirm that Black women can never be more beautiful than they themselves are. Looking at this piece from diverse standpoints changes its meanings. I've seen individual Black women respond to it—I see their discomfort, and I think, "God, part of what this piece does is remind us of the politics of location that is operating in all our lives." The piece displaces that sense of fixed location, because the meaning depends on the direction from which you gaze at the piece. It mirrors the postmodern emphasis on the fragmented sense of self.

CMW: After thinking about postmodernism and all this stuff about fractured selves, and so on, when I was constructing the *Kitchen Table* series, Laura Mulvey's article "Visual and Other

Pleasures" came out, and everybody and their mama was using it, talking about the politics of the gaze, and I kept thinking of the gaps in her text, the way in which she had considered Black female subjects.

bh: That's exactly what I was thinking, though you and I didn't know each other at the time. Her piece was the catalyst for me to write my piece on Black female spectators, articulating theoretically exactly what you were doing in the *Kitchen Table* series.

CMW: All the pieces in the *Kitchen Table* series highlight "the gaze," particularly the piece where the woman is sitting with a man leaning against her, his head buried in her neck, a mirror placed directly in front of her, but she looks beyond that to the subject.

bh: Go, girl.

CMW: At the audience, right?

bh: Hm-mmm. Yes.

CMW: You know, just using that as the beginning and the turning point to flip all that shit around, and to start creating a space in which Black women are looking back, right?

bh: Right.

CMW: Looking back, and challenging all of those assumptions about gaze, and also questioning who is in fact looking. How much are white women looking? How much are Black men looking?

bh: Your work immediately challenges our sense of Blackness.

CMW: Oh, yes.

bh: Right now so much in popular culture defines Blackness as Black urban experience. And, to some extent, I find your focus on the South so powerful—its evocation of our concern with return. In so many ways your work can be talked about as linked to psychoanalysis, particularly the issue of recognition and memory.

CMW: Oh sure, oh sure.

bh: We need to acknowledge that there are other complexities of Blackness that are not emerging from—from the urban scene. When I think of a piece like *The Mattress Springs* [Sea Islands series].

CMW: That was so bad!!!

bh: We can talk for days about the multilayered textuality within that piece, because on one hand you have the notion of country and city, of primitive longing and the desire for progress.

CMW: Yeah. That was so bad, I can't even believe I made it.

bh: I know, and I think people should not look at that piece and reduce it to something simple about the South and how the folks do creative shit with trash.

CMW: Right, right, right.

bh: In *The Mattress Springs* we have this notion of the place of technology in agrarian Black life. What Black people do with it. And where is this sign of modern life, the mattress spring, that becomes the backdrop in a natural, pastoral world, where it appears in union with nature—not against, but a part of nature.

CMW: Right, it's linked to a whole belief system. You know, we have to make art work for us within the context of our own individual belief systems. I've often thought about this. How do you do this with photography? How do you describe complex experiences in a photograph? What are the sights of it? What should it have to look like? What does it have to challenge? To whom is it challenging? You know, who's it for? All those kinds of questions are constantly shifting for me. The moment that I think that I have it locked down is the moment in which it flips; you can't talk about the pros without talking about the cons. You can't talk about the "positives" without talking about the "negatives." And you can't talk about the truths without talking about the untruths.

bh: Well, let's say we talk about that picture of the slave quarters. The first thing that should jump out at people with that picture is that these slave quarters are made of brick—that this is not wood and that we have to think of the creativity and expressive genius of these enslaved people, working with brick. The image invites us to ask, "What do slaves and brick have in common?" You know, I kept thinking about that in relation to the whole Afrocentric focus now on ancient Egypt and kings and queens and the pyramids. And I also kept thinking about the slaves. I keep saying to people, "Well, what about the slaves who were hauling that brick?" You know, I mean there's something else going on here besides simply the narrative of kings and queens.

And there's something in the work you're doing around space and housing that speaks to culture and class—raising questions of how we inhabit space, about architecture.

CMW: Well, how you inhabit space and how you construct it, as well as how you construct the architecture of your life, is the issue: How do you do that? What will it look like? And within this context, let's say the *Sea Islands* image, within this world, how will you construct the space you inhabit to make it work for you, even when it was not meant to?

bh: It's funny, because I was thinking of your work as I was reading Bernard Tschumi's new book, which is the most exciting book I've read lately: *Architecture and Disjuncture.* And I was thinking about how your photographs interact with one another to create this sense of disjuncture, starting points where you don't end up where you start off, endpoints that don't come from this logical move from A to B to C.

CMW: No, they're not, they're not linear at all. They construct something that feels on the surface to be very linear, and, as you said, simple in their construction.

bh: Tensions arise when folks look at your work, especially your new images that highlight returning to Africa, and they tell me they've talked with "real" Africans who don't see anything particularly "African" about this work. And I remind them of how many "real" Africans there are. If a few individuals don't see something in a creative work, does that mean this thing doesn't exist? Are we still stuck within some kind of Western, metaphysical, either/or dualism, where we can recognize ourselves in Africa only if African people grant us that right? This is not about ownership. That's exactly what this work in its movement, its refusal to be fixed, is asserting: that there is no owner-ship of Blackness.

CMW: Right, and the thing that's really interesting is that the ideas that ground the work emerge from my critical reflections about stability and from ideas of wholeness. You see, wholeness has all kinds of fracture in it. It has all kinds of ruptures in it, but it is a wholeness nonetheless. For example, the wholeness might be not having a true and complete sense of Africa. Rather, we might have a sense of a construction of Africa, as seen through the eyes of one person who is on some mythical journey in search of a place she might be able to call home.

bh: That sensibility, which is what we began talking about, is what this recent work evokes. This is the spirit of exile—really, the emotional politics of exile. When Cornel West and I were preparing our book, he spoke often of the exilic nature of Black people, of why the Old Testament has been so important to Black believers. Everything Black people in America have seen or experienced has been filtered through that primal experience of exile, and that includes a longing to return to "the promised land."

CMW: Only the promised land isn't there.

bh: It's so multifaceted—there are many promised lands.

CMW: That's right, but it's not there.

bh: It is a creation. And it's the hint of that creation that your work moves us toward. What is that homeland that we jour-ney toward? Is it a homeland of the mind or of the emotion-ality, in a sense, where one—where one's longing is what ties things together. And it's interesting, because I think this is the subtextual emotional universe of your work that is often overlooked, overshadowed by the focus on race as its central metaphor and not in fact the emotional universe. And yet it's that emotional landscape in your work that gives it force and passion. The *Kitchen Table* series often makes me think of the blues. Like how a blues song may say something in words that you may not even like, you know, you may never even get all the words, but the sensibility is what takes you somewhere. I was listening to one of my favorites, Muddy Waters, and there's this line where he says, "I've had my fun if I don't get well no more." And I was saying to somebody that that is a deeply meaningful song for our time, as so many diseases such as cancer, AIDS, all these things, really disrupt our experience of pleasure. So now, here's a song that we know emerges out of a concrete specificity within Blackness and that shows this complex emotional field of choice in relation to pleasure and danger evoked in this line: "I've had my fun if I don't get well no more." Your work has a similar broad scope, deeply embedded in our culture and identity. I disagree with one of the critics who said that your work "takes us beyond abstract ideas." I thought, actually, no, her work takes us to the abstract complexity within Black identity that has been denied, and that has been denied not merely by politics of race but by a politics of culture, and particularly that of vernacular culture in opposition to high culture. In part as a response to high culture's attempt to reduce vernacular culture. No one writes about the place of vernacular culture in your work, in the images.

CMW: It's not just vernacular culture—it's class. The work is very, very class-based. It is working class–based; I think that reality shapes the pictures—the way the images are constructed. I'm very interested in ideas about blues and jazz, that expressive musical culture. That's where I function. That's where I get my shit from, my impulses from. If it's not in that, I'm generally not interested, right? But how do you again use that, how do you, you know, listen to Muddy Waters, to Bessie and Billie, and begin to construct a visual world that this music is played in, that's generated by the culture that the music creates. So in doing the *Kitchen Table* piece, it was always about how you construct it. How do you make a blues piece? What does that look like? And because of the emotional response you're talking about, that emotional sensibility is embedded in the work.

bh: Like in my favorite piece, *Jim, If You Choose.* . . .

CMW: You understand what I'm saying!

bh: Absolutely. I wrote about that photograph in terms of the Black male body, speaking about the sensibility underlying that piece. I couldn't find a single person who had written about technology in relation to this image, yet the reference that immediately came to my mind was "Mission Impossible." If you think of white patriarchy as the framework within which Black men are asked to construct an identity, and that there has been a capitulation that Black maleness has made to that system, then your subversive image says, "You have a choice, Black man . . ."

CMW: That's right. That's right.

bh: To resist—

CMW: —this bullshit.

bh: That gender crisis you articulate with this image is there in blues music, yet is not talked about. The kind of music that Skip

James sings, "Devil Got My Woman," and that whole sense of the male who is caught up in a politics of emotional vulnerability. Now, what your piece says is "Ha! Aha, world, the emotional vulnerability may not be of the Black man in relation to the Black woman. It may be of the Black man in relation to the white man"—and the gaze, then, is really about these men looking at one another. I recently gave a paper called "Doing It for Daddy: Representing Black Masculinity as Unrequited Longing for White Male Love." And there we have it in that portrait of Jim, that sense of anguish. What is the anguish that he is feeling? And also there's the double tragedy that we can live in a world where someone can see that image and not see that anguish, and only think of it as having something to do with Black men and Black women. That reduces the elegance and grace of that image to the mundane.

CMW: It's not just the image that's reduced. It's our historical situation.

bh: And your process as an image-maker changes too. Because in order for people to think of these images differently, they have to think differently about the people who make these images. We all have to rethink and take another look to see that we are no longer talking about Black people in a state of colonization trying to come to some primitive subjectivity. We are talking about image-makers like yourself who are engaged in ongoing processes of decolonization and reinvention of the self, whose work cannot be understood deeply because we lack a critical language to talk about contemporary radical Black subjectivity.

CMW: You have given us this critical language in your work. Why is it so impossible for more critics to follow that example?

bh: Well, I think for many other writers there needs to be a demand for critical growth and change, a repositioning of the self in relation to the "other" that only comes through the politics of demand. This is what Frederick Douglass meant when he said, "Power concedes nothing without demand."

CMW: We have to challenge simplistic, traditional, fixed notions of what criticism is and develop a new vocabulary and language. And until that happens we will continue to have little understanding of how to approach the Black subject. We certainly don't have any understanding of how to talk about there being aesthetic variation, what that might mean in the construction of the photographic image.

bh: More folks who are theoretical need to write more or to speak and document that speaking. I think it's an unusual historical moment, because we usually presume that artists and critics are not the same, but these days there are individual artists who are able to discuss work in a critically aware manner. More and more artists will do more of what we conventionally have thought of as the work of critics, and that artificial separation may have to be completely and utterly disrupted.

CMW: Also, I think that something else has to happen, and I think that, you know, a part of it has to do with the way in which we're educated about images. It's as simple as this, bell. I don't know how much you know about photography and various aspects of photography and the technical aspects of photography, but we have something in photography that's called a zone system.

bh: Right, right.

CMW: Well, the zone system is completely constructed around what makes white people look best. It is our system and our theory—photo theory—for understanding what a good print is, and it is based on white skin. So the very base of photography and the way that photography has been developed in the West as a science, because that's what most of it is, is based on ideas of whiteness. What would have happened, for instance, if photography had been developed in Japan? Not just cameras, but the means of photography, had been developed in Japan? The images would look very different, and what is theoretically impossible or even practically acceptable would be very, very different as well.

So in terms of artists being critics, I think they are not necessarily always the same people. I'm not a critic. You're like a brilliant woman, a fabulous woman with this incredible sensibility. And you use incredible language and so forth and you're a gifted writer. I am not a gifted writer. I'm an artist trying to figure out how to do this shit. So, though it's true that I'm talking a whole lot, and actually I'm very good on my feet when I'm up and talking, I want to use my time to make art—not to write. Yet I want to hear critics talk about work in a way that makes sense.

bh: Oh, I do agree. When I was doing more art, I was not writing.

CMW: There just needs to be more critical discussion of what we're doing and what it is we are looking at, because for the most part, not only are we coming to Black images made by Black artists, but we're also coming to a different kind of artistic and visual and aesthetic terrain that is just not understood.

bh: We're looking to a future where there have to be more collaborations. There has to be more dialogue. And, let's face it, there have to be alternative journals—spaces that don't simply pipe us all through the mainstream, because different ideas will not be welcomed there. If art is to be talked about differently, artists cannot rely on traditional frameworks of image making, or on institutional frameworks where image making is talked about.

CMW: Right, and who was doing the talking? Right? Who was doing the talking?

bh: The exciting thing is that work like the work you're doing makes this demand. It contests in a way that means it will no longer allow for the kind of criticism that has happened. You know, it's a process. That's why we are talking now. I began as someone who watched your work from afar, but who felt outside the loop of those critics who write about it. After we just talked, I thought, "No, I have to resist exclusion through omission and/or disregard, and enter that loop of people who write and think about Carrie Mae Weems's works." Collaborations like this dialogue will make a difference.

CMW: I'm excited when my work is talked about in a serious manner—not because it's the work of Carrie Mae Weems, but because I think there's something that's important that's going on in the work that needs to be talked about, finally, legitimately, thoroughly.

bh: We have to create a kind of critical culture where we can discuss the issue of Blackness in ways that confront not only the legacy of subjugation but also radical traditions of resistance, as well as the newly invented self, the decolonized subject.

CMW: Yes. That is the critical issue for now and for the future.

Facing Difference:
The Black Female Body

Lorna Simpson's photograph *Waterbearer* was reproduced in 1987 in one of the early issues of *B Culture*, a progressive Black newspaper of arts and culture that was fresh beyond all belief. For a brief moment in time *B Culture* was the expressive space for everything radical and Black—it was on the edge. Of course, it disappeared. But not before publishing a full-page reproduction of *Waterbearer*.

After carefully pressing my newspaper copy with a hot iron, to remove all creases, I taped this page on the wall in my study, awed by the grace and profound simplicity of the image: a Black woman with disheveled hair, seen from the back, pouring water from a jug and a plastic bottle, one in either hand. Underneath the photograph were the subversive phrases.

> *She saw him disappear by the river*
> *They asked her to tell what happened*
> *Only to discount her memory.*

Subversive because it undoes its own seeming innocence, Simpson's portrait is reminiscent of Vermeer's paintings of working women—maids standing silently by basins of water in still poses that carry no hint of emotional threat. Yet Simpson's language brings a threat to the fore. It invites us to consider the production of history as a cultural text, a narrative uncovering repressed or forgotten memory. And it declares the existence of subjugated knowledge.

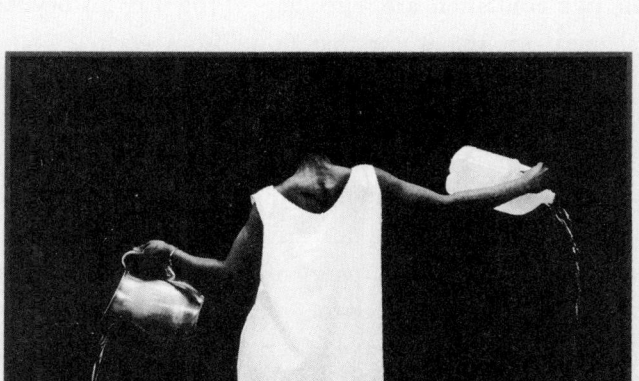

SHE SAW HIM DISAPPEAR BY THE RIVER,
THEY ASKED HER TO TELL WHAT HAPPENED,
ONLY TO DISCOUNT HER MEMORY.

Lorna Simpson, Waterbearer, *1986.*
Silver gelatin print, vinyl lettering. Ed. of 1 + 1 AP.
Overall: 53 ½" × 82" × 2 ¼" (135.9 × 208.3 × 5.7 cm).
Framed print: 41 ¾" × 79 ¼" × 2 ¼" (106 × 201.3 × 5.7 cm).
Lettering: 14" × 82" (35.6 × 208.3 cm).
Courtesy of the artist.

Here in this image the keeper of history, the griot, the one who bears water as life and blessing, is a Black woman. Her knowledge threatens, cannot be heard. She cannot bear witness. She is refused that place of authority and voice that would allow her to be a subject in history. Or so the phrases suggest. Yet this refusal is interrogated by the intensity of the image, and by the woman's defiant stance. By turning her back on those who cannot hear her subjugated knowledge speak, she creates by her own gaze an alternative space where she is both self-defining and self-determining.

The two containers are reminders of the way history is held and shaped, yet the water that flows from each is constant, undifferentiated, a sign of transcendent possibility, a reminder that it is always possible to transform the self, to remake history. The water flows like a blessing. Despite changes, distortions, misinformation symbolized by its containers, the water will continue to sustain and nurture life. It will redeem. It is the water that allows the Black woman figure to reclaim a place in history, to connect with ancestors past and present.

The Black woman in the photograph understands that memory has healing power. She is not undone, not in any way torn apart by those dominating gazes that refuse her recognition. Able to affirm the reality of her presence—of the absent him whose voice, unlike hers, might be listened to—she bears witness to the sound of the water and its meaning for her life. Hers is a portrait of serenity, of being, of making peace with oppositional history.

Few contemporary American artists have worked with images of the Black female body in ways that are counterhegemonic. Since most Black folks in the United States are colonized—that is think about "Blackness" in much the same ways as racist white mainstream culture—simply being a Black female artist does not mean one possesses the vision and insight to create groundbreaking revolutionary images of Black females. Simpson's reimagining of the Black female body not only presents these images in a new way, she does so in a manner that interrogates and intervenes on art practices in general. To do this, she turns her back, in a manner not unlike that of the figure in *Waterbearer*, on art practices that have been traditionally informed by racist and sexist ways of thinking about both the female image and Blackness.

Living in white-supremacist culture, we mostly see images of Black folks that reinforce and perpetuate the accepted, desired subjugation and subordination of Black bodies by white bodies. Resisting these images, some Black folks learn early in life to divert our gaze, much in the same way that we might shield a blow to the body. We shield our minds and imaginations by changing positions, by blocking the path, by simply turning away, by closing our eyes.

We learn to look at the images of Blackness that abound in the popular cultural imagination with suspicion and mistrust, with the understanding that there may be nothing present in those images that is familiar to us, complex, or profound. Our eyes grow accustomed to images that reflect nothing of ourselves worth seeing close-up. As a survival strategy, aware Black folks often cultivate a constructive disregard for the power of the image. Some of us just dismiss it.

Given this cultural context, we are often startled, stunned even, by representations of Black images that engage and enchant. Creating counterhegemonic images of Blackness that resist the stereotypes and challenge the artistic imagination is not a simple task. To begin with, artists have to engage in a process of education that encourages critical consciousness and enables them as individuals to break the hold of colonizing representations. Once that process is completed, they then have a space to map a new terrain—one that can emerge only from an imaginative inventiveness since there is no body of images, no tradition to draw on. Concurrently, even after the images are in place the art world may lack a critical language to speak to the complexities these images evoke. To see new and different images of Blackness is to some extent shocking. Since images that are counterhegemonic are necessarily provocative, their seductiveness, their allure lie in the freshness of insight and vision. They fulfill longings that are oftentimes not yet articulated in words: the longing to look at Blackness in ways that resist and go beyond the stereotype. Despite the tenacity of white supremacy as a worldview that overdetermines the production of images in this society, no power is absolute to the imagination. The practice of freedom in daily life, and that includes artistic freedom, is always a liberatory act that begins with the will to imagine.

Lorna Simpson's images of Black female bodies are provocative and progressive precisely because she calls attention to aspects of Black female identity that tend to be erased or overlooked in a racist sexist culture. Her work counters the stereotype. In the accepted version of Black female reality that predominates in mainstream images there is no subtlety to our experience. We are always portrayed as lacking in complexity, as transparent. We are all surface, lacking in depth. Within mainstream art photography the vast majority of images representing Black females are full frontal views of face or body. These images reaffirm the insistence on transparency, on the kind of surface understanding that says to the viewer, "What you see is what you get." Simpson's images interrogate this assumption, demanding that the viewer take another look, a closer look.

When I look at images of the Black female body in Simpson's work, I see recorded an understanding of Black female presence that counters racist/sexist stereotypes through the pronounced rejection of the fixed static vision of our identity that exists in the popular imagination. Yet Simpson's concern is not to simply interrogate, set the record straight. She wants us all to look again, to see what has never been seen, to bear witness.

Beginning with the understanding that common racist and sexist stereotypes of Black female identity insist that our reality can be easily understood, that we are not mysterious, we confront images, in Simpson's work, that defy this norm. In general, in this culture, Black women are seen and depicted as down to earth, practical, creatures of the mundane. Within sexist racist iconography, Black females are most often represented as mam-

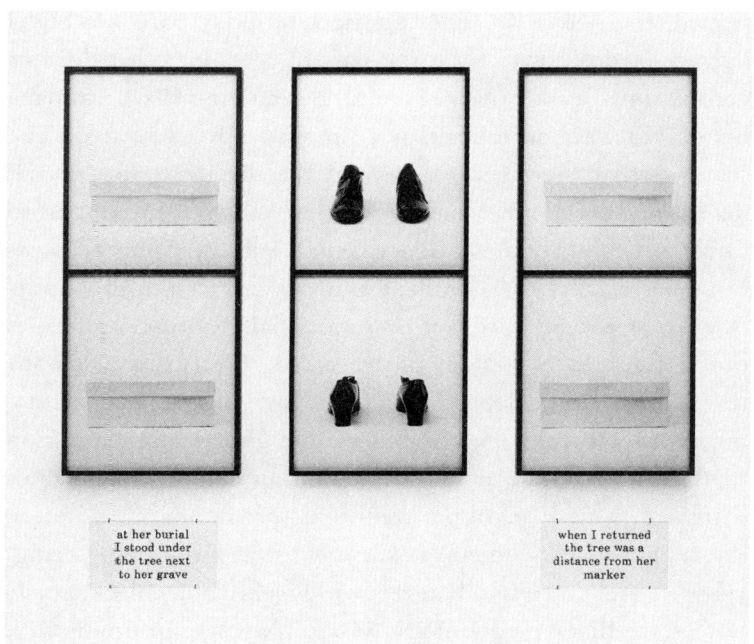

at her burial
I stood under
the tree next
to her grave

when I returned
the tree was a
distance from her
marker

Lorna Simpson, Magdalena, *1992.*
6 dye diffusion color Polaroid prints, 2 engraved plastic plaques.
Overall: 63" × 78" (160 × 198 cm).
Courtesy of the artist.

mies, whores, or sluts. Caretakers whose bodies and beings are empty vessels to be filled with the needs of others. This imagery tells the world that the Black female is born to serve—a servant—maid—made to order. She is not herself but always what someone else wants her to be. Against this backdrop of fixed colonizing images, Simpson constructs a world of Black female bodies that resist and revolt, that intervene and transform, that rescue and recover.

Her images of Black female bodies are initially striking because so many of them are not frontal images. Backs are turned, the bodies are sideways, specific body parts are high-lighted—repositioned from the start in a manner that disrupts conventional ways of seeing and understanding Black woman-hood. This shift in focus is not simplistically calculated. The intent is that viewers look beyond the surface, ponder what lies beyond the gender and race of these subjects. Inviting us to think critically about the Black female subject, Simpson posi-tions her camera to document and convey a cultural genealogy based not on hard but on emotional realities, landscapes of the heart—a technology of the sacred. Whereas female bodies in this culture depict us as hard, low down, mean, nasty, bitchified, Simpson creates images that give poetic expression to the ethereal, the prophetic dimensions of visionary souls shrouded in flesh. Evoking traditions that honor the goddess, she depicts Black women in everyday life as if our being brings elegance and grace to whatever world we inhabit. Black female bodies are Black madonnas in Simpson's work. In union with the earth, in touch with ancient properties, they embody the sacred. Charlene Spretnak contends in *States of Grace: The Recovery of Meaning in the Postmodern Age* that "When we expe-rience consciousness of the unity in which are embedded, the sacred whole that is in and around, we exist in a state of grace. At such moments our consciousness perceives not only our individual self, but also our larger self, the self of the cosmos." This perfect union of body and spirit is there in the photo-graph *You're Fine*, where the Black female body is surrounded by medical terminology and labels that define her as subordi-nate, that reduce her to disembodied parts as though she were subhuman. Yet the image that accompanies this text shows a Black female reclining with an aura of serenity and repose in the midst of dehumanization. This flesh transcends the limits of domination and oppression which would confine and con-tain it.

Often Simpson playfully and ritualistically juxtaposes images of Black females that interrogate the stereotypes by overtly naming them, imagistically, while conveying more radical disruptions at the same time. While series like *Five Day Forecast* and *Three Seated Figures* overtly articulate the mundane terrorism of racist objectification, images like the one presented in *Necklines* contextualize this dehumanization by addressing the history of slavery—a continuum of domination that moves.

Though commemorating and re-membering the past, reconstructing a useful legacy for the present, many of Simpson's photographs articulate the convergence of public and private reality. In *Time Piece* a Black woman dressed in Black is framed from behind, her story suppressed by the omnipresence of death. The litany that stands alongside this image tells us that death continues, that it is inevitable, that the specifics of Black female death matter to few, that the details are not important. The recovery of meaning to Black female death is enacted by the photographer, by she who wills recognition.

This abiding sense of memory and sustained grief is present in the series of photographs *Magdalena*. Here it is an empty shoe box, an image of shoes that bear witness. They are the everyday artifacts, left behind, that trace the dead back to the living. These artifacts converge and overlap with the reality of death and dying recorded in the text that bears witness: "at her burial I stood under the tree next to her grave." Yet this memory is juxtaposed with a second narrative that records a different reality: "when I returned the tree was a distance from her marker." In trying to gather the evidence to name Black female experience, the reality and diversity of lives, the facts are muddled, our memories unclear. How to name accurately that which has been distorted, erased, altered to suit the needs of other?

Simpson's photographs name that which is rarely articulated —a technology of the sacred that rejoins body, mind, and spirit. The plain white shifts worn by various Black female figures in Simpson's work, like the simple garments worn by monks, are a repudiation of materiality. It is the spirit that matters, the soul flesh shrouds and hides. Beyond the realm of socially imposed identity, the limitations of race and gender, one encounters the metaphysical. Transcendent experiences, like death and dying, put into perspective the finite nature of human activity, the limits of human will and power. Despite all that is imposed on Black female flesh, no coercive domination is powerful enough to alter that state of grace wherein the soul finds sanctuary, recovers itself. Simpson's work offers us bodies that bear witness. Through these images subjugated knowledge speaks—remakes history.

Talking Art as the Spirit Moves Us

In her critical book *Radiance from the Waters*, art historian and critic Sylvia Ardyn Boone theorizes the aesthetic understandings that shape ideals of beauty in Mende art. While the subtitle to this work implies a central focus on the "feminine," in actuality Boone begins with the standpoint of Mende women to lay the foundation for a complex reading of art, aesthetics, and philosophical assumptions in Sierra Leone. Again and again in her book, Boone shares a popular proverb in Mende society that declares: "There is a thing passing in the sky; some thick clouds surround it; the uninitiated see nothing." Explaining to those who do not intimately grasp the significance of these words, Boone states: "This proverb presents the idea of *initiation as a condition of seeing*, as personal enlightenment. Everything is out in the open; nothing is purposefully hidden. Seasons change; flora and fauna go through their life cycles; people move about, interact, handle objects; events take place; things 'happen.' Initiates have their eyes opened, so they have 'eyes to see.' These 'eyes' are metaphysical: an informed intellect, a widened vision, a deepened discernment." This proverb easily applies to the way in which art created by African Americans is looked at and talked about. All too often the "uninitiated see nothing."

This cultural inability to recognize the complexity of vision that informs the work of African American artists cuts across boundaries of race. Painting in the 1940s, Romare Bearden found that Black folks were often freaked by the images in his work: "To many of my own people, I learn, my work was very disgusting and morbid—and portrayed a type of Negro that they were trying to get away from." Now that Bearden's work has become an accepted part of the canon, it is seen differently by Blacks and whites alike. Edward Lucie-Smith's book *Race, Sex, and Gender in Contemporary Art* is a prime example of the way in which art by African Americans continues to be regarded with contempt and suspicion. While one opens this book and sees a marvelous red page displaying a work of art that includes the text: "Art is the greatest possible rationalization of our deepest fears, joys, and instincts as human beings. Visual artists should seek to explain life metaphorically and poetically . . . the aesthetic dimension is the carrier of hope." Despite this auspicious beginning, Lucie-Smith, a self-proclaimed generalist, like his more serious counterparts, is unable to access the aesthetic dimensions of the work he writes about, which he simply labels "minority" art. While seeking to "pimp" that visual culture and critical audience that is concerned with issues of difference, Lucie-Smith simply mirrors the white-supremacist patriarchal colonizing mind-set. In his introduction, he tells readers that "minority" art is gaining prominence because markers of artistic merit "such as quality of workmanship . . . are now largely disregarded." And he draws the conclusion "that the work of art is no longer seen as something which truly represents its time and is important to it, unless it challenges the norms of that time." Of course, Lucie-Smith does not engage any critical thinking about what constitutes norms, just as he does not presume that, as a white male, he has any biases that blind and bind him, limiting and constricting his critical vision. Yet the biases are so blatant in this work as to require little critical analysis. Throughout his book Lucie-Smith makes evident that, in his eyes, the only really important works of art by people of color are those created by individuals who reject progressive identity politics to engage in that conservative version of identity politics where the person of color disidentifies with her or his ethnicity or race in order to gain reward in the eyes of whites. This is white-supremacist identity politics. The inability of unenlightened critics and artists who have not divested themselves of white-supremacist thinking to accept that an individual may engage the particular in relation to race, gender, or class while simultaneously evoking an aesthetic that transcends these categories continues to be the standpoint that overdetermines the critical reception of art created by people of color. Any work by these artists that overtly articulates and calls attention to these concerns is automatically seen as "political" and lacking in appreciation for aesthetic concerns. Yet no artist from any marginalized group has ever suggested aesthetic merit is not relevant.

Edward Lucie-Smith's book reflects the dominant culture's attempt to block the interrogation of racist biases through art work by perpetuating the notion that any such attempt really is masking the failure on the part of marginalized groups to understand the importance of aesthetics. There are many individuals in the mainstream art world who would insist that Lucie-Smith is irrelevant precisely because he is a generalist, clearly not a critical thinker. Yet his large book, with its provocative and compelling title, interests me because it is marketed in the direction of a mass audience. It relies on the interest in race, sex, and gender generated by the resistance struggles of the very groups Lucie-Smith writes about with ignorance, disregard, and contempt. It represents a perfect gesture of colonization and appropriation. Yet the note on the dust jacket of this book tells readers that "works by African Americans, feminists, homosexuals, and Latino-Hispanics—once considered marginal—have come to transform contemporary art," a statement that few critical thinkers about art would disagree with. However his insistence that "minority" art has become "our most major concern" is ludicrous. Lucie-Smith carefully and strategically assumes the false posture of objective neutrality. He claims that the discourse of difference is "deliberately obfuscating" and "constantly shifting" because its purpose is to exclude generalist critics such as himself, who "can then be dismissed as racists." While racism, as overt exploitation and oppression on the basis of skin color, is not something one can trace in Lucie-Smith's book, his critical standpoints unabashedly reflect white-supremacist patriarchal biases. The extent to which Lucie-Smith arrogantly displays his ignorance about marginalized groups and the art we produce is shocking. Since the intent of the book is to insist that most such art is not relevant, that it is a mere imitation of "great" art no doubt created primarily by white men in the West, Lucie-Smith ends with the statement: "The main conclusion must be that the minority visual arts, though on the surface often an expression of revolt against contemporary western society and its social and economic structures, are in fact completely dependent on that society." Contrary to this assertion, most artists from marginal groups would not choose "revolt" as the defining characteristic of their work.

Significantly, this insistence on "revolt" as the quintessential marker that distinguishes works of art produced by artists from marginal groups, especially people of color, is a standpoint rooted in the politics of domination. Often it is only the anger and rage expressed by marginal groups that is "seen" by white folks, that can garner their attention. This is as true of the liberal and progressive white gaze as it is of the conservative right. It then becomes the totalizing ethos. Without any mainstream precedent, the 1993 Whitney Biennial Exhibition highlighted works by artists from marginal groups to intervene and challenge the politics of domination in the art world. Yet it failed in this intention because it indiscriminately framed all the work within the context of revolt. That framing was imposed the moment one arrived at the museum and confronted a large billboard-size blowup of a really intense, provocative photograph of apparently hostile young Black males taken by the artist Pat Ward Williams. The graffiti-like text on the image was an in-your-face confrontative declaration: "WHAT YOU LOOKIN AT." In actuality, the vast majority of work in this Biennial Exhibition, particularly pieces that were not specifically commissioned and created for the show, were not concerned with revolt. Much of the work did not evoke narrow notions of identity and essence but, rather, reflected concerns with cultural hybridity, border crossings, and constructive cultural appropriations. That expansive and diverse artistic scope was subsumed by the imposition of a totalizing curatorial ethos privileging revolt—reacting to white supremacy. Ironically, even though the African American curator Thelma Golden suggests in her catalog essay "What's White . . .?" that "artists in the nineties have begun to fully deconstruct the marginality-centrality paradigm" because "the center is increasingly undefinable and perhaps irrelevant," that very paradigm of margin and center usefully describes the underlying assumptions informing the curatorial process of this show. By situating all the work of these diverse artists as a gesture of revolt against mainstream culture and its values, whiteness was not decentered, it was constantly the point of departure. The center had not been disrupted. Foregrounding work from the "margins" was not transgressive or transformative precisely because that work was reappropriated and positioned to serve the dominant culture's need to see the margins as always and only in revolt.

Inclusion, without any disruption of the status quo, usually reinscribes, in a different form, the very patterns of domination that have been critiqued and interrogated to make an opening. A major dilemma faced by all marginal groups suffering exploitation or oppression in this culture and by our allies in struggle is the struggle to resolve, in a constructive way, the tension between reformist work that aims to change the status quo so that we have access to the privileges accorded the dominant group and the more radical project of resistance that seeks to dismantle or transform the existing structure. All too often the price of the ticket for inclusion is that we are subordinated in new and different ways. Clearly, this has happened in the art world. When works of art by people of color are highlighted in an essentialist way, not because of the nature of the work but more because of the dominant culture's newfound interest in the "other," then certain stereotypes and assumptions about tokenism are simply reinforced. This was certainly the case with the Whitney Biennial. Even so, the show had positive implications and effects. It positively highlighted the work of individual artists in a setting that accrues status and attention and is visited by a large number of people. The response to the show by mainstream white culture exposed the extent to which white supremacist biases continue to inform critical reception of work by artists from marginal groups, especially when that work does not directly reflect the interests and concerns of the conservative white majority. In this sense, the show served as a painful "wake-up" call, reminding us that a politics of domination remains in place in the art world, unchanged by resistance struggle. Not only, then, must the struggle continue, the strategies for challenge and transformation must be constantly changed, reevaluated, reenvisioned.

Before the Whitney Biennial, many progressive artists, critics, and art audiences really believed that the work of unlearning racism and other biases was being effectively accomplished. Many of us believed that liberal individuals of all races had come to new understandings about difference. Yet negative reactions to the Whitney show, fiercely hostile to this attempt to redress past biases and deeply contemptuous of both the project and the work, came from all sides of the political spectrum. And the most negating polemical responses came from critics.

Although critics are often seen as not really important when it comes to the making of public policy about art and the creating of spaces for cultural production and curatorial display, it is more than evident that a major revolution must happen in the areas of both traditional art criticism and new critical writing about art emerging from various intellectual locations and standpoints if we are to transform art practices in ways that interrogate, challenge, and alter in a lasting way politics of domination. At the same time, our insightful critiques of white-supremacist capitalist patriarchy (which includes a challenge to heterosexism) cannot be made only in an intellectual or academic subculture lest elitism merely take on a new form. Indeed, if progressive artists and critics from diverse locations want to make critical interventions that reach wide audiences, we need to value generalist work as much as we do work that is more specific. We need to express our views more often in popular mass media—in magazines, newspapers, etc. Much of the negative critical attention that focused on the 1993 Biennial Exhibition had its origins in the popular press. The discourse of difference, then, does enter the everyday lives of the masses, but rarely in a way that is at all constructive.

As a cultural critic, I began writing about art because I saw an absence of progressive art criticism in both traditional and popular settings. I wanted to respond to gaps and blindspots. When I first began to read and study critical work about African American art, I was truly appalled by the lack of complex thinking. As both a writer and an artist, I continue to feel a tremendous sadness that there is not a large body of critical writing about art by African Americans that truly addresses the aesthetic dimensions of that work in its diversity and complexity. Unfortunately, when the rare white critic pays attention to art by Black artists, (s)he tends to be rewarded no matter what the content of the criticism is. Oftentimes, after all, individual artists are just so grateful to be the recipients of even a small measure of regard. Often a hierarchy emerges within critical writing about African Americans where any work by a white critic deemed liberal and progressive is held in such esteem that it is difficult for nonwhite critics to interrogate that work without censor. When we critique and challenge the critical writings of our progressive white peers, we are often admonished for not recognizing the "good" they do. It is the missionary ethic of colonialism all over again. To give an example. Several years ago I engaged in a critical conversation about art with Amalia Mesa-Bains at the San Francisco Art Institute. We were critical of Lucy Lippard's book *Mixed Blessings*. While we both prefaced our critique by acknowledging the book's value, some individuals in the audience, rather than hearing the ideas raised and grappling with them, heard our comments only as a personal attack. To them Lippard represented, and rightly so, a meaningful ally. Yet being an ally should not mean that any work one produces cannot be engaged dialectically, critically. Concurrently, people of color tend to be reluctant to critique one another. We are fearful of losing comrades, connections, or of just adding to the stress that our peers are already facing. To produce a body of excellent, sophisticated, diverse critical writing that addresses art by African Americans and people of color in general, we must collectively embrace rigorous dialectical exchange. We must be willing to listen to one another, to read work carefully, and to engage it critically. Much of the marvelous critical writing on African American art is emerging from cultural critics who have not been traditionally trained in academic disciplines focusing on art. In the future we will hopefully see compelling critical work from a variety of locations.

Of all the critical writing I do, my work on art, though personally fulfilling, garners the least amount of attention and reward. It also requires tremendous effort both to produce and to disseminate. If we fail to privilege critical writing about African American art that emerges from a progressive standpoint, we will not see a change in how that art is critically received in mainstream culture. Critical writing must be valued by artists and audiences of color if we are to create a cultural context where more critical thinkers will choose to do that writing.

Sylvia Ardyn Boone, who was my senior colleague and friend when I taught in the African American Studies department at Yale University, was a brilliant progressive thinker and writer about art. We had many conversations about the fact that art magazines almost never sought to print her work, that symposiums on art held by foundations and universities did not seek to hear her voice. Her book *Radiance from the Waters*, mentioned at the beginning of this essay, has rarely been referenced or talked about in critical writing on art. Boone often felt silenced. She felt that her voice could not be heard above the clamor created by better-known white peers receiving widespread attention and acclaim. Rarely did these critics call attention to her work. Though we no longer have the opportunity to "hear" her voice speak about art, fortunately we can still read and appreciate her work. Yet I cannot close this essay without lamenting the loss of Sylvia Ardyn Boone, whose critical perspective challenged me to grow as a critic, who often initiated me, guiding me so that I would look more closely at a given subject, so that I would see deeply. Boone believed wholeheartedly that the aesthetic dimension of Black life needed our critical attention and regard—needed to be witnessed. To sustain this critical legacy, African American critics and our allies in struggle must dare to courageously speak our minds, to talk about art as the spirit moves us.

Critical Genealogies: Writing Black Art

When I first begin to talk with folks cross-class about the place of art in our lives, I was surprised by the number of folks who just did not think about it. Contrary to stereotypes, class, though important, was not always the major factor determining quality of interest, appreciation, and engagement. Some of the individuals I spoke with, who have tremendous access to art through family members (some of whom were or are well-known artists), were as uninterested in an engaged relationship with the visual as those individuals who have no art in the intimate spaces of their lives. Certainly a distinction must be made between having access to art and being willing to engage the visual on an experiential level—to be moved and touched by art. Many of us see art every day without allowing it to be anything more than decorative. The way art moves in the marketplace also changes our relationship to it. Often individuals who collect art spend more time engaged with issues of market value rather than experiencing the visual.

Class politics definitely inform the way we think about aesthetics, the way we respond to art. Shaping how we see what we see when we choose to look at art, class often overdetermines our relation to art—while talking about race and gender in relation to the art world has become more acceptable. Class is still a taboo issue, although it is often the subtext in many discussions about art practices. Issues of class are most evident in the realm of critical thinking and writing about art. While individuals from marginal groups—from nonmaterially privileged backgrounds—often find a way to make art, writing about art continues to be the domain of those who have some degree of class privilege. Rarely are there public discussions about the way in which class informs which Black artists, critics, etc., will receive attention both in segregated Black cultural spaces and in the dominant culture where such spaces are most often controlled by non-Black individuals.

So much attention has been focused on the relationship of Black artists to the mainstream white art world, in ways that highlight the relative disenfranchisement of these individuals in that sphere, that no attention is accorded to the politics of class as it shapes and informs the work of African American artists and critics. Often the Black people who receive a degree of attention in the mainstream art world—whether as artists, critics, or both—come from privileged class locations within their ethnic groups. Among Blacks, as among other groups in this society, class standing is not determined solely by material possession; it is informed by family background, education, values, geographical location, and so forth. For example, the politics of racial apartheid in relation to housing has meant that poor and privileged Black folks often live in close proximity to one another, in locations that an outsider might perceive as low-income or ghettolike. Yet inside these segregated neighborhoods, a class structure remains intact that often mirrors the dominant culture and influences both who makes art and who will write about art.

Privileged individuals within these segregated locations, who control cultural locations where artistic production is encouraged, are often as hierarchical and dominating when relating to poor and working-class folks of their own race as are their white counterparts in the mainstream art world. Throughout the history of postslavery African American art making, class hierarchies both within and outside Black communities have shaped the nature of art practices, controlling the way art by African American artists is critically considered. The standards of valuation used in white-dominated art circles were and often still are applied in segregated Black culture. As a consequence, the Black poor and working class did not and do not have a primary voice in shaping Black aesthetics. Even when Black liberation movements of the 1960s and early 1970s extolled the virtues of laboring classes, the folks who defined what our relationship to art and aesthetics should be were still primarily the Black bourgeoisie.

Autobiographical writings by the critic Michele Wallace document her experience growing up in Harlem surrounded by artistic Black people, many of whom were her relatives. Their aesthetics were often informed by mainstream notions of high culture. Faith Ringgold, Wallace's mother and a celebrated modern artist, confronted racism and sexism every step of the way as she pursued her commitment to making and teaching art. While race and gender were factors that impeded her development, class positionality positively mediated her relation to art making. She was raised in a family where art was valued. Wallace's autobiographical work and her insightful critical pieces provide a unique perspective because she starts from a critical standpoint that examines the interplay of race, gender, and class. Similarly, the African American artists Emma Amos and Lyle Ashton Harris both speak about coming from families in which class privilege informed their relation to art. Though generations apart, these two artists both draw on the work of elder family members who make or made art. By focusing on these legacies, their intent is to establish a cultural genealogy where aesthetic traditions that have been shared generationally are passed down, remembered, noted, and documented. This documentation serves to counter that form of racial tokenism and cultural stereotyping that almost always represents Black artistic talent and genius as residing solely in a lone individual who, against the odds, strives to create. Like Wallace, both Amos and Harris write and speak about growing up in solid middle-class backgrounds where they were immersed in a world that deemed art important.

African Americans coming from poor and working-class backgrounds have usually relied solely on schools to teach and legitimize our interest in art. In segregated Southern schools art has traditionally been taught from a perspective informed by the class and racial biases of Eurocentric traditions. This is an accurate description of the way art continues to be taught in many predominantly Black schools, including colleges and universities. Usually African American scholars who focus on art are trained in both predominantly Black and white institutions to think about art solely in Eurocentric terms. As a consequence, African American art critics, both inside and outside the academy, have made few progressive critical interventions that fundamentally change the way work by African American artists is critically received.

Significantly, the recent *Time* magazine cover story "Black Renaissance: African American Artists Are Truly Free at Last" (October 1994) assessed the development and public reception of works by Black artists without engaging, in any way, the ideas and perspectives of African American scholars who write about the visual arts. The blatant absence of this critical perspective serves to highlight the extent to which Black scholars who write about art, specifically about work created by African American artists, are ignored by the mainstream. Ironically, the insistence in this essay that the "freedom" of Black artists can be measured solely by the degree to which the work of individual artists receives attention in the established white-dominated art world exposes the absence of such freedom. And, of course, no efforts were made in this piece to critique or challenge the pervasive racism in the mainstream art world, the way it constructs a system of exclusion and inclusion that not only limits the career development of African American artists but also fosters a system of tokenism that pits individuals against one another. The progress of African American artists in contemporary society cannot be measured solely by the success of individuals. It is also determined by the extent to which this work is critically considered.

An overall examination of the way in which work by African American artists is critically received would reveal a tremendous lack. Much of the critical writing on the work of African American artists is limited in vision and scope. Black academics writing about art within a conservative educational hierarchy that is deeply mired in white-supremacist thinking about aesthetics and art practices often choose traditional ways of approaching the work of African American artists. As a result, little critical work from a more progressive standpoint emerges. Outside the academy, the world of art criticism continues to be dominated by the voices of white males, many of whom come from economically or educationally privileged backgrounds. There are very few Black critics writing about art who are not academics. Since art criticism is certainly not a moneymaking enterprise, such writing is usually done by individuals who have some degree of class privilege. Even though race can now be considered in contemporary writing about art, there is still a lack of progressive critical writing by African Americans.

Often individual progressive white critics have taken the lead in making necessary critical interventions that disrupt conventional ways of seeing and thinking about the work of Black artists in the diaspora. Certainly the terrain of cultural conservatism and Eurocentric chauvinism, particularly in relation to African and African American art, was powerfully disrupted by the work of the art historian and critic Robert Farris Thompson. While it was certainly less threatening to the art estab-

lishment for a privileged white male scholar to challenge the
system, Thompson's willingness to challenge Eurocentric biases
set a powerful example.

Like many readers, I was thrilled by my initial encounter with Thompson's work, especially *Flash of the Spirit: African and African American Art and Philosophy*. Many of the ideas
of progressive Black critical thinkers, who questioned Eurocentric biases in all disciplines, were mirrored in Thompson's work.
It was more than evident that, within the context of white-
supremacist capitalist patriarchal culture, a privileged white
male professor's "take" on "the Black Atlantic world" (Thompson was one of the first scholars in the United States writing
about art to use this term) would have a greater chance of receiving academic validation than that of insurgent Black thinkers. It
is useful to focus on Thompson's work when thinking critically
about the absence of a large group of African American critics
writing about art, because Thompson's visibility is, in part, a
reflection of the way that systems of race, gender, and class privilege continue to create a social context in which it is difficult
for Black critics to gain visibility and regard. Concurrently, the
combination of race, class, and gender privilege often makes it
more acceptable for white male scholars to successfully transgress boundaries.

I first met Robert Farris Thompson when I went to teach
English and African American Studies at Yale University.
Fondly called Master T. because of his administrative role as
head of Timothy Dwight College, Thompson was also in the
African American Studies department. His role as "critical diva"
of African and African American culture must be critically
interrogated in light of new progressive thinking about issues of
cultural appropriation, about race, gender, and class hierarchies,
and in light of our growing awareness that we need to create
a cultural context that will allow more critical writings about

the work of Black artists in the diaspora to emerge, and that will allow the voices of African American critics to be heard. In his classes at Yale, Robert Farris Thompson is the incarnation of Norman Mailer's "white Negro." Thompson's teaching style turns on its head Malcolm X's assertion that Black people love white people more than they love themselves. Thompson's love affair with Blackness was and is far more passionate and intense than that of most of his Black academic counterparts. Unlike them, he has been willing to let his passion change his pedagogical practices.

Thompson attempts to make the diasporic connections in the Black Atlantic world come to life in the classroom. His teaching is performance art. Whether imitating Black vernacular speech, percussive style, or style and response, Thompson attempts to engage students. To critical onlookers, Thompson's work may appear to be just another minstrel show, another way of "eating the other"—a conventional white ethnographic mode of cultural appropriation. At times such criticism is justified. A critique of Thompson need not diminish the fact that he brings to any discussion of art and aesthetics in the Black Atlantic world a wealth of knowledge and experience.

When he began this work, Thompson's standpoint was unique in the mainstream academic world. The African American art critic Rick Powell has said that he went to study at Yale after hearing Thompson lecture in 1977. Powell recalls that the lecture was "ostensibly on Haitian art, but he discussed people like Ntozake Shange and Gwendolyn Brooks." To the young student onlooker, Thompson's approaching Black creativity in a holistic manner was fascinating. From Powell's perspective as a student, this white male art professor was "the only scholar with whom [he] would have some simpatico in terms of thinking about Black culture in a broad way." Most professors and critics who worked with Thompson when they were students are reluctant to critique his work because he has been so helpful to them. It is unfortunate that criticism is often seen as negative. Constructive critical interrogation can enhance and illuminate our work.

While I found Robert Farris Thompson to be an ally as a colleague, I also observed that he functioned within the concrete hierarchy of Yale like most other senior white male professors, particularly in relation to gender issues. I mention this because it is not a radical disruption of racism and racial hierarchy, of sexism and gender hierarchy, when white and/or male scholars, in general, whose own careers are well served by their focus on Black and/or gender issues, do not also work at changing their habits of being in ways that repudiate domination. Many white males in the academic context in which Thompson and I worked, particularly those individuals who focused their attention on marginal groups, acted as though their theory and practice should not be critically interrogated. Not only were they rarely critical or self-reflective, they usually acted punitively toward individuals who dared to raise critical questions. It was the norm that these men (as well as men of color who occupied similar positions of power and authority) did not regard women as peers, did not value our thoughts or opinions, or did not acknowledge our intellectual commitment and seriousness.

I was reminded of this recently when I was asked to participate in a project, jointly organized by the San Francisco Art Institute and the Fine Arts Museum of San Francisco, called "The Global Presence of African Spirit in Contemporary Art." One of the conference planners had been informed that I probably would not want to share a panel with Thompson because I "did not like him." I countered that all my personal interactions with Thompson had been positive, that I appreciate his work, and that although I am critical of his theory and practice, this did not mean that I did not like him. I share

this anecdote because it exposes the extent to which intellectual and academic communities in the United States are often
unable to distinguish between a critique of ideas and a personal attack. The fear of being perceived as personally attack-
ing colleagues, or of making personal enemies, effectively
censors meaningful critique and closes off the possibility that
there will be meaningful, dialectical, and critical conversation
and debate among colleagues. These critical dialogues must
take place if progressive commitment to ending domination
on the basis of race, gender, and class within the academy is
to become a reality on all levels, in our teaching, our writing,
and our working relations.

Indeed, a major absence in Thompson's work is any indication that he engages in ongoing critical exchange with Black
critical thinkers who find his work and/or pedagogical practices
problematic. Within the academy, Thompson was challenging
Eurocentric biases long before the age of multiculturalism and
the age of postcolonial and anticolonial cultural studies. He is
to be praised for breaking new ground back in the day when
certain standpoints were deemed unacceptable. Yet this praise
should not usurp the place of meaningful critique. The theory
and practice that inform Thompson's work should be rigorously
and critically interrogated. For example, Thompson rarely talks
about the behind-the-scenes labor and investigation that inform
his work, his relation to sources, the impact of his white male
presence and all the privilege that embodies. As the Black male
critic Greg Tate, a self-proclaimed fan of Thompson's, attests:
"He never deals with his own alienation in the material—alienation from Black folks. He does not deal with himself as a white
man in his work." The point of dealing with himself in this
way would not be purely confessional but, rather, a sign of progressive critical engagement with the issues of white supremacy,
cultural appropriation, and the new politics of anticolonialism.

Those of us who have had the opportunity to engage in private dialogues with Thompson know that he does deal with the hard political issues and that he is willing to discuss these issues: I'd like to see more of this exchange in the work. Critically discussing issues of power and access in relation to race, gender, and class politics within the art world is all the more crucial at a time when narrow nationalism, fundamentalism, and fascism are gaining new momentum. When I asked Robert Farris Thompson about the experience of being one of the first white male scholars to break with racist conventions and engage in a critical decentering of the West, the groundbreaking intellectual border crossings on African and African American art that his work affirms, he replied: "I feel like it's a struggle and I can't let my guard down. I have a smile on my face and a militant posture."

Many white critics feel their position of "authority" challenged as more people of color claim a critical voice. All too often these individuals are defensive when asked to discuss issues of cultural appropriation or to talk about the way in which the existing social structure creates a cultural context where what white people have to say about Blackness continues to be deemed more relevant than other voices speaking on the same issues. Concurrently, it is crucial that progressive white critics be vigilant both in the critical interrogation of their work and in the way that work is represented. For example, the paperback edition of Thompson's *Flash of the Spirit* carries a one-sentence endorsement from the *New York Times Book Review*: "Convinces the reader there is a real and important significance in the term *African American*." This quote is not counterhegemonic. It does not decenter the West. It reaffirms Eurocentric thinking and, as a consequence, perpetuates white-supremacist biases. Given Thompson's astute critical facilities, it would be counterhegemonic for him to critique the way this quote undermines his antiracist standpoint. While it is always a useful and necessary intervention for white scholars to address issues of race and creativity, of art and aesthetics in the Black Atlantic world, if that work is merely providing yet another way for white folks to "eat the other" (i.e., appropriate nonwhite cultures in ways that diminish) structures of racist hierarchy and domination remain intact. This work then becomes part of the colonizing apparatus. Concurrently, when individuals in power represent that they have divested themselves of any allegiance to racism, while clinging to the desire to be uncritically accepted and affirmed in a manner that blocks and censors critique, the process of decolonization is incomplete. Bluntly put, as long as white scholars feel that they are doing Black folks a favor when they critically engage Black culture or that they necessarily know more than any Black could ever know, then racism remains unchanged.

Issues of appropriation and standpoint as they relate to neocolonialism are addressed more directly in discussions of ethnography and anthropology than in critical scholarship on art and aesthetics. In *Radiance from the Waters*, the art historian and critic Sylvia Ardyn Boone is openly critical and self-reflective about her positionality as an American Black woman seeking to learn from the Mende people. Subverting those racist conventions within an art history that repeatedly acts as though the issue of aesthetics is relevant only to white culture, Boone simultaneously interrogates this assumption and counters it by offering a detailed interpretation of the relationship between art and philosophy in this Third World community. Significantly, her work has only recently begun to receive wide recognition and attention. Although her approach to African art and philosophy mirrors and at times surpasses Thompson's, it is rarely evoked, even by scholars and critics who draw on it. In other essays I have written in detail about the ways structures of racism, sexism, and class elitism function in the academy to minimize, if not to obscure entirely, the work of individuals from marginalized groups. This is especially true for Black women.

In our many conversations about the art world, Sylvia Boone and I talked about the way in which the interplay of race, class, and gender hierarchies work to ensure that the critical voices of individuals from marginal groups are always subordinated to those of their white peers. Frequently, our talks were orgiastic celebrations of the concrete ways Black folks in the diaspora subvert strategies of neocolonialism both in our art-making practices and in critical writing. These conversations were clarifying moments when subjugated knowledge surfaced with elaborate critical excavation. They prompted me to critically reexamine issues of aesthetics in the everyday life of the segregated Black communities where I lived as a child. In that world, art was always offered as a marginal location where issues of race, gender, and class were subordinated to the mystery of talent or genius. Our aesthetics were informed by religious experience. Within our all-Black churches we were taught to value talent, what old folks called "the gift." We were taught that no matter the circumstance, class, gender, or race, if the divine spirit had given one the "gift"—the capacity to create art—then one had to yield, to surrender to that calling. In *The Gift*, Lewis Hyde reminds us "that the task of setting free one's gift was a recognized labor in the ancient world." Within those racially segregated, mostly poor and working-class communities of my childhood, spaces of oppositional cultural intervention were formed to make a place for the creation of art. Yet there was no recognition of the need to create spaces for the affirmation of critical thinking and writing about art.

The will to honor one's artistic gifts or the gifts of others was maintained despite dire circumstances of exploitation and oppression. It was believed that the soul suffered irreconcilable loss if gifts were not developed, used, shared. Hyde contends: "The genius of daemon comes to us at birth. It carries with it the fullness of our undeveloped powers. These it offers to us as we grow, and we choose whether or not to accept, which means we choose whether or not to labor in its service." No doubt it was this recognition of the gift that compelled enslaved Africans to express their artistry, their capacity to make pictures and elaborate designs, even as they constructed instruments of punishment or torture that would be used against them or their brethren. When I first encountered such objects, adorned with carvings, in a museum, I stood in awe, weeping. Crying in the face of a will to make art so intense as to lose oneself in a rapture of forgetfulness. How to imagine the mind of the artist then—how to articulate the aesthetic beliefs informing this creativity? To be bound and yet not bound—this was the paradox: the slave liberated for a time in the imagination, liberated in that moment of creative transcendence.

The culture of white-supremacist capitalist patriarchy seeks to remove all traces of this subjugated knowledge. It seeks to contain art and suppress the will to create in the interest of neo-colonialism. In such a context the poor and underprivileged are meant to have no relationship to art practices, to the art world. More than at any other time in our history, African Americans embrace notions of victimhood that deny the power of the imagination, that block our capacity to create. No wonder, then, that this is a time when our collective interest in art wanes. To counter this threatening cultural genocide, artists in all groups marginalized by structures of domination must engage in ongoing acts of resistance to form oppositional spaces where art can be made, where we can gain and sustain visibility, where progressive critical thought about art can emerge.

This culture of resistance must be manifest in critical writing. Unless there is collective recognition that there is an ongoing need to create contexts where more Black folks from diverse class backgrounds are able to think and write about art, not enough African Americans will receive the critical consideration their work merits.

Beauty Laid Bare:
Aesthetics in the Ordinary

Growing up in conservative working-class and poor Southern Black communities, I had no notion that Black folks were inherently more radical or "cool" than any other marginalized or oppressed group. While the folks I lived amongst were often militant in their condemnation of racism, they were pretty much in agreement with many of the other values that trickled down from the worlds of the conservative ruling classes, from the white or Black bourgeois world. When it came to materialism, across class it was clear that success in diverse Black communities was measured by having nice things. Whether or not something was perceived as "nice" depended on one's social environment.

One of the intense pressures I experienced as an adolescent was caused by my longing to cultivate my own style and taste, clashing with the pressure to conform to set bourgeois standards. Sarah Oldham, my mother's mother, was the "style radical." Her aesthetic sensibility was grounded in a more traditional appreciation for the natural world, for color and harmony. As a quiltmaker she was constantly creating new worlds, discovering new patterns, different shapes. To her it was the uniqueness of the individual body, look, and soul that mattered. From her I learned the appropriateness of being myself.

The example of personal freedom and creative courage set by my grandmother was constantly challenged by the bourgeois aspirations of my mother, whereby she insisted on conformity, on imitating acceptable appearances and styles. To my mother, "nice things" were not the earth, the sky, the eggs in the hen-house, a fishing worm uncovered in dark, moist dirt, the sight of a tomato growing on a vine; "nice things" were the objects seen in advertisements, on the screen, and in catalogues.

My grandmother and her daughter, my mother, did agree on the basic principle that beautiful objects enhanced life, even if their aesthetic standards differed. Although we came from a poor and working-class background, from a history of squatting, sharecropping, and working in white folks' houses, among the traditional Southern Black folks I grew up around there was a shared belief in the idea that beautiful things, objects that could be considered luxurious, that were expensive and difficult to own, were necessary for the spirit. The more downtrodden and unfortunate the circumstances, the more "beauty" was needed to uplift, to offer a vision of hope, to transform. When it came to the issue of desiring and longing for the beautiful object, whether it was a house, a car, furniture, clothing, shoes, etc., everyone agreed, across class, that folks needed to be in touch with beauty. When I was a child, this did not seem to be a radical idea. It was such a common way of thinking about life it seemed "natural." There was never a need to make someone feel guilty when he or she did without the basic necessities of life in order to acquire an object deemed beautiful, healing to the spirit. At times those objects were luxury items, not intrinsically aesthetically beautiful, but desired because the culture of consumerism had deemed them lovely symbols of power and possibility. Even though folks sometimes laughed at the individual who bought a shiny car bigger than the wood frame shack he or she lived in, underneath the mockery was the understanding that this symbol of luxury was a balm to a depressed and wounded spirit. This stance was in every way oppositional.

The Black elders in our community, like Sarah my grandmother and Gus my grandfather, believed it was better to seek beauty in a world that was not subject to monetary exchange. For Sarah, beauty was there in the growing of flowers in her elaborate garden, or in the making of her quilts. Alice Walker, in her insightful essay "In Search of Our Mothers' Gardens," acknowledges the way poor Black women expressed their concern with beauty in the growing and arranging of flower gardens. Offering the example of her own mother, Walker declares: "Her face, as she prepared the Art that is her gift, is a legacy of respect she leaves to me, for all that illuminates and cherishes life. She has handed down respect of the possibilities—and the will to grasp them." This legacy had been handed down through generations in traditional Southern Black folk culture. These were notions of beauty and wealth grounded in a worldview that was in opposition to excessive materialism.

Southern Black males who had an oppositional aesthetic were often economically deprived but rich in spirit. When the forces of white supremacy and capitalism denied them access to meaningful work, they cultivated ways to care for the soul that sustained them. For my grandfather Daddy Gus, the will to create was life-sustaining. To him beauty was present in found objects, discarded objects that he rescued and restored because, as he put it, "spirits lived there." His room—a luxurious, welcoming place for us as children—was full of "treasures." Entering that sanctuary of precious "beautiful" objects, we were embraced by an atmosphere of peace and serenity. In *Shambala: The Sacred Path of the Warrior*, Buddhist monk Chogyam Trungpa teaches that we create this atmosphere by expressing gentleness and precision in our environment: "You may live in a dirt hut with no floor and only one window, but if you regard that space as sacred, if you care for it with your heart and mind, then it will be a palace." This caretaking promotes "awareness and attention to detail." There can be a sacred place in everyone's life where beauty can be laid bare,

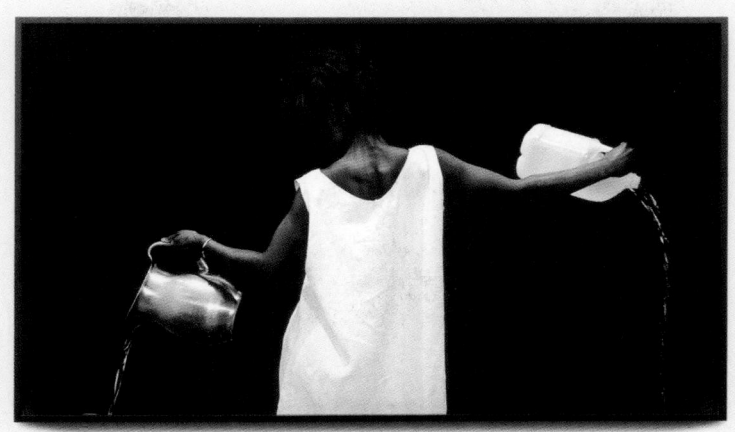

SHE SAW HIM DISAPPEAR BY THE RIVER,
THEY ASKED HER TO TELL WHAT HAPPENED,
ONLY TO DISCOUNT HER MEMORY.

Lorna Simpson, Waterbearer, 1986.
Silver gelatin print, vinyl lettering. Ed. of 1 + 1 AP.
Overall: 53 ½" x 82" x 2 ¼" (135.9 cm x 208.3 cm x 5.7 cm).
Framed print: 41 ¾" x 79 ¼" x 2 ¼" (106 cm x 201.3 cm x 5.7 cm).
Lettering: 14" x 82" (35.6 cm x 208.3 cm).
Courtesy of the artist.

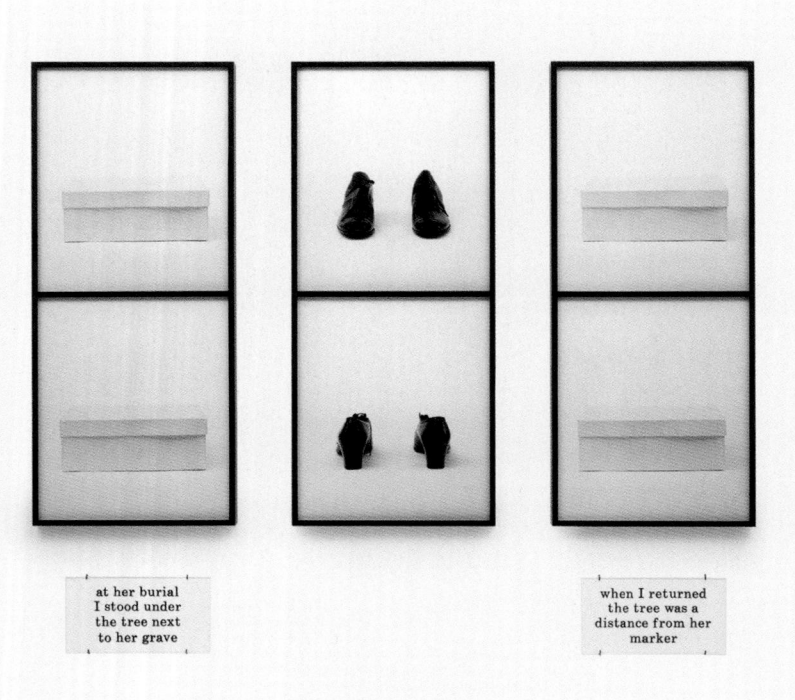

Lorna Simpson, Magdalena, *1992.*
6 dye diffusion color Polaroid prints, 2 engraved plastic plaques.
Overall: 63" x 78" (160 cm x 198 cm).
Courtesy of the artist.

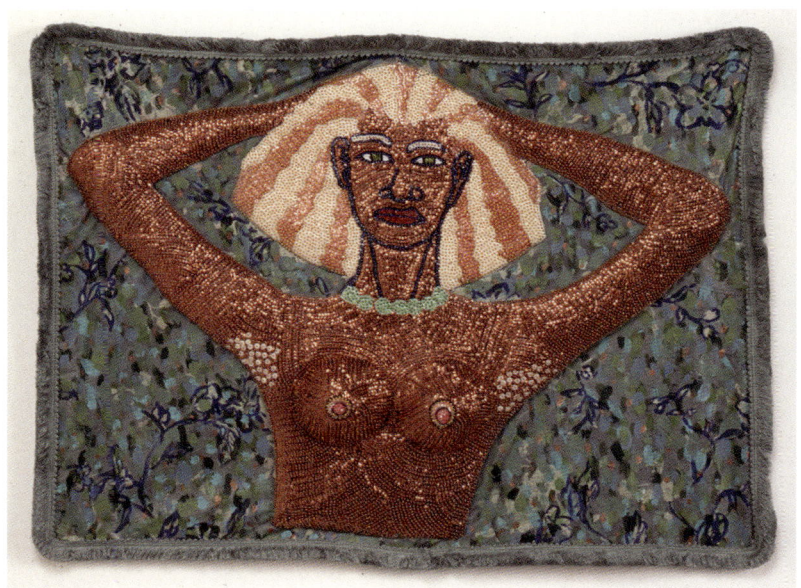

Alison Saar, Sapphire, *1986.*
Beads and Sequins. 25" x 34".
© Alison Saar.
Courtesy of L.A. Louver,
Venice, CA.

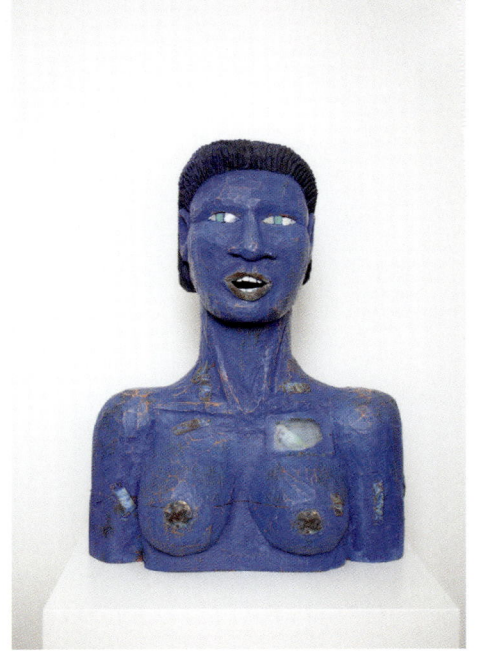

Alison Saar, Diva, 1988.
Wood, tin, paint.
25" x 17" x 9"
(63.5 cm x 43.2 cm x 22.9 cm).
Collections of the Jordan
Schnitzer Family Foundation.
© Alison Saar.
Courtesy of L.A. Louver,
Venice, CA.

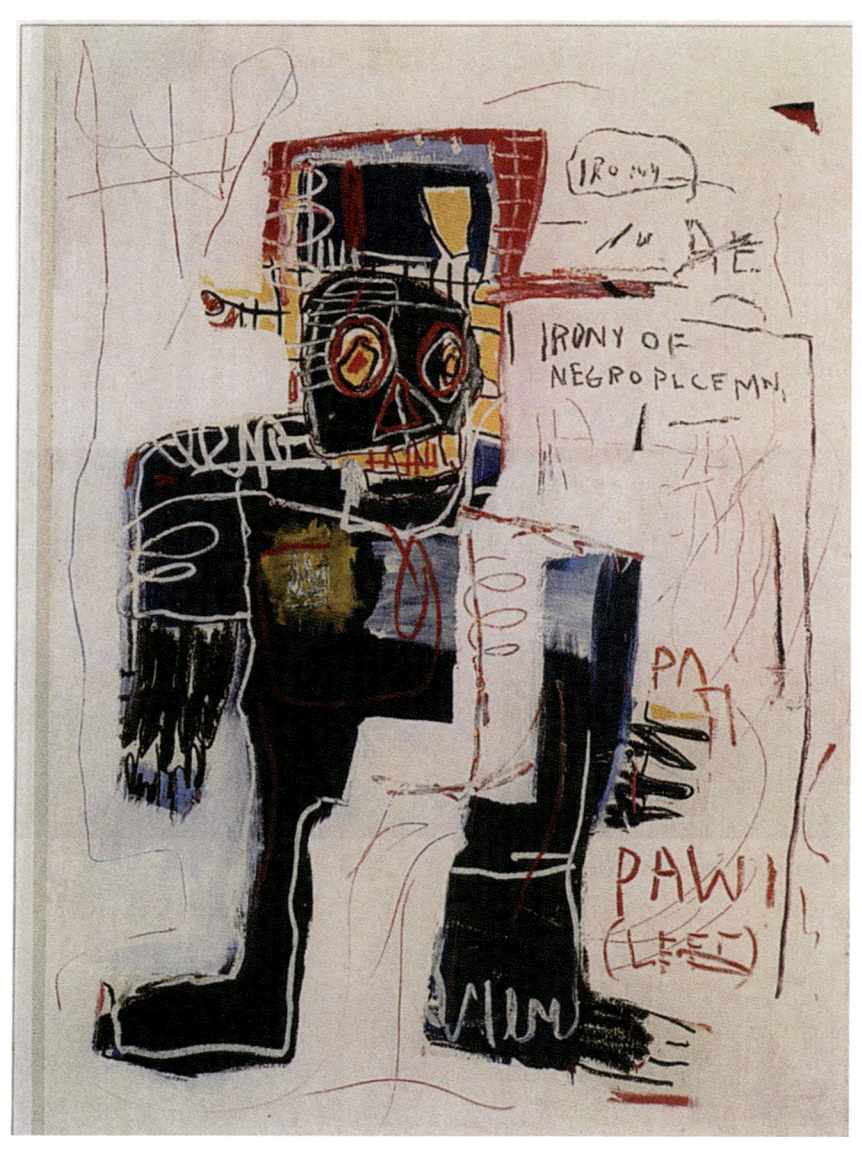

Jean-Michel Basquiat, Irony of a Negro Policeman, *1981.*
Acrylic and oil paintstick on wood. 72" x 48".
© *Estate of Jean-Michel Basquiat. Licensed by Artestar, New York.*

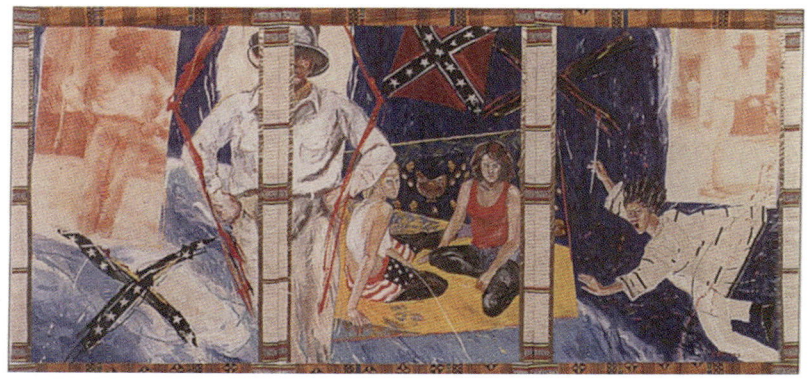

Emma Amos, The Overseer.
Acrylic on canvas with photo transfer, hand made weaving by the artist and African fabric borders. 84" x 168".
© [2024] Emma Amos / Licensed by VAGA at Artists Rights Society (ARS), NY. Courtesy of RYAN LEE Gallery, New York.

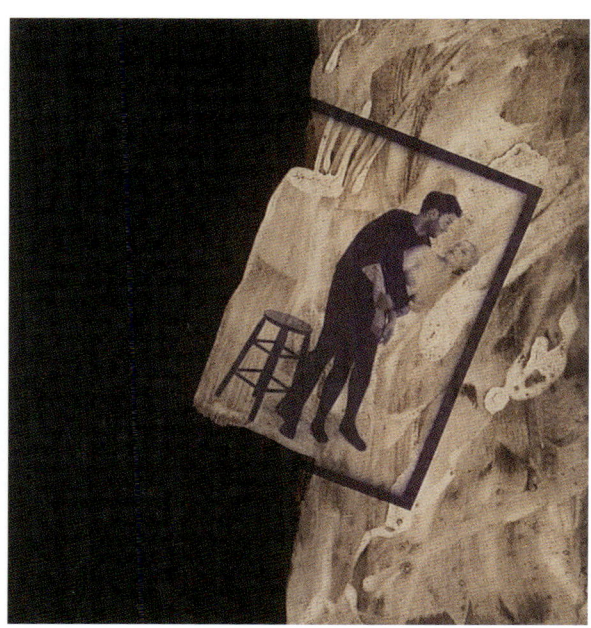

Emma Amos,
Lucas's Dream,
1994.
Photo transfer with silk collagraph. 22" x 19".
© [2025] Emma Amos / Licensed by VAGA at Artists Rights Society (ARS), NY. Courtesy of RYAN LEE Gallery, New York.

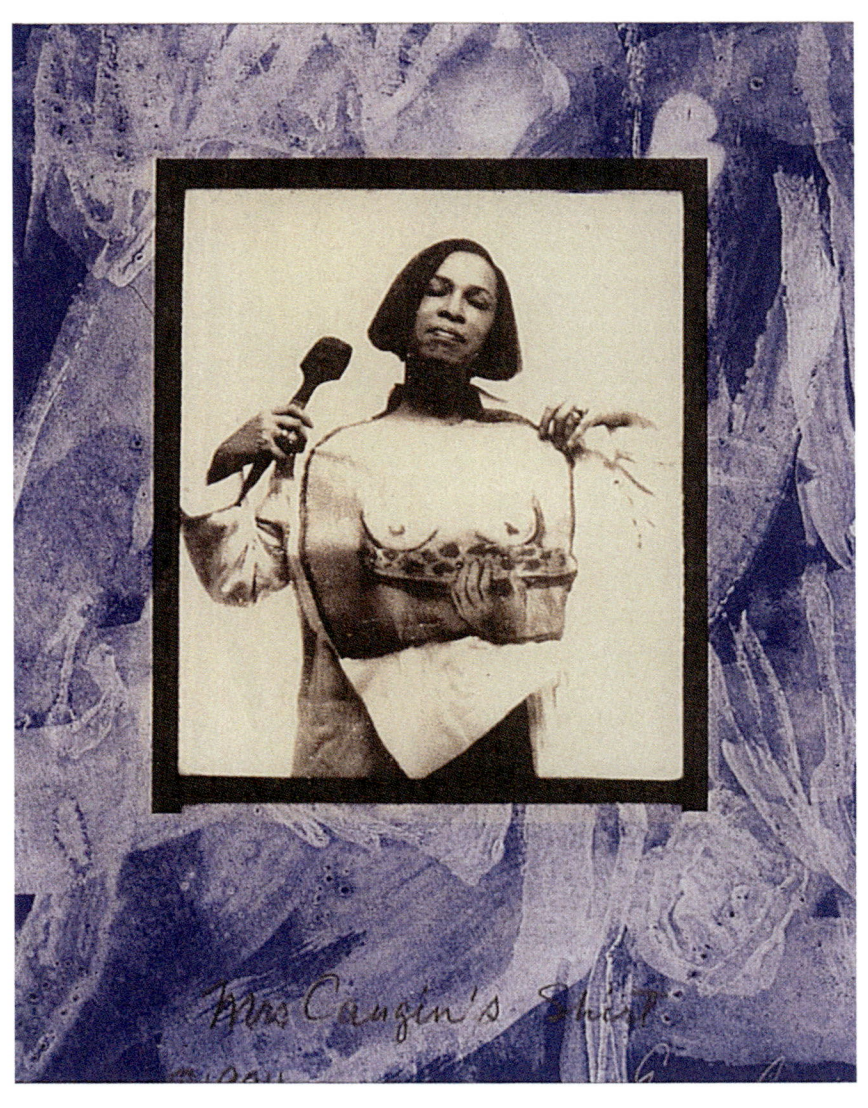

Emma Amos, Mrs. Gauguin's Shirt, *1994.*
Photo transfer with silk collagraph. 12" x 9".
© [2025] Emma Amos / Licensed by VAGA at Artists Rights Society (ARS),
NY. Courtesy of RYAN LEE Gallery, New York.

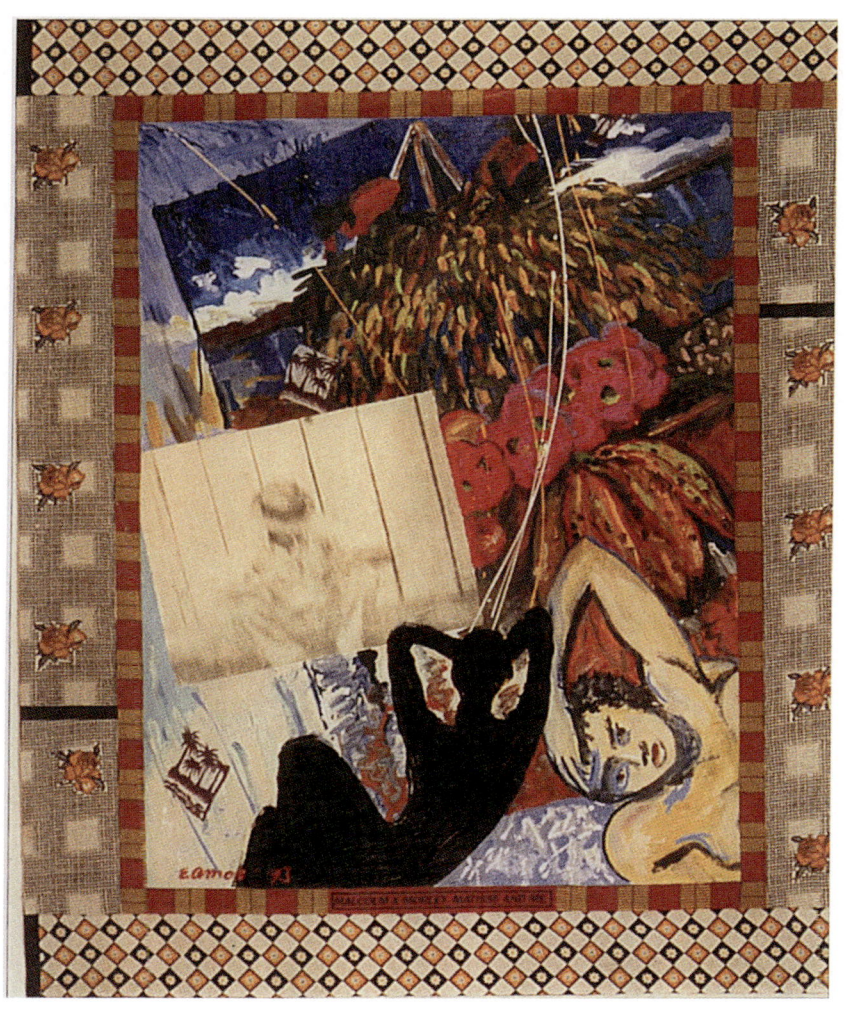

Emma Amos, Malcom X, Morley, Matisse and Me, *1993.*
Acrylic on canvas with photo transfer, hand made weaving by the artist and
African fabric borders. 74" x 61".
© [2025] Emma Amos / Licensed by VAGA at Artists Rights Society (ARS),
NY. Private Collection, DE; Courtesy of RYAN LEE Gallery, New York and
Art Finance Partners, New York.

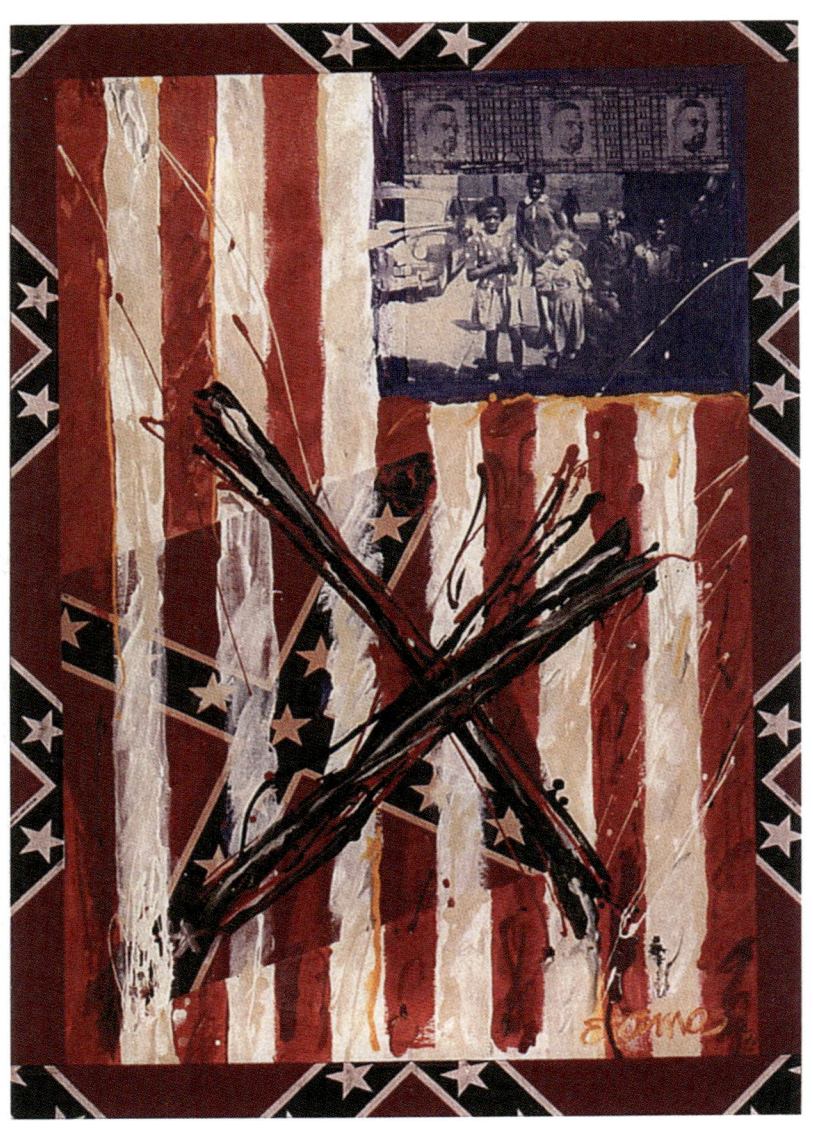

Emma Amos, X–Flag, 1992.
Acrylic on canvas with photo transfer, handmade weaving by the artist and
African fabric borders. 58" x 40". © [2025] Emma Amos / Licensed by
VAGA at Artists Rights Society (ARS), NY. Collection of Meredith Harper,
New York; Courtesy of RYAN LEE Gallery, New York.

where our spirits can be moved and lifted up by the creation and presence of a beautiful object.

When I first began to travel to different continents, I was fascinated by how, in most parts of the world, especially in places that the United States designates as "Third World," no matter how poor the surroundings, individuals create beautiful objects. In the deserts of North Africa, beautiful woven rugs were present in every abode, no matter how humble. In countries where folks are ravished by genocidal war and famine, suffering, anguished bodies shroud themselves in beautiful cloth. Indians in Mexico and the United States, living in various states of impoverishment, make clay pots that reveal artistic skill and vision.

In contrast, in the United States, contemporary African Americans have been increasingly socialized by the mass media to leave behind attachments to the oppositional worldviews of our elders, especially to those having to do with beauty, and to assimilate into the mainstream. Hedonistic consumerism is offered as a replacement for healing and life-sustaining beauty. Unlike the global nonwhite poor, who manage to retain an awareness of the need for beauty despite imperialist devastation, the vast majority of the Black poor in the United States do not harbor uplifting cultural objects in their homes. This group has been overwhelmingly encouraged to abandon, destroy, or sell artifacts from the past. And this destruction has brought in its wake the loss of an aesthetic sensibility that is redemptive. For example, today's concrete state-designed and -operated homogenous housing for the poor takes away the opportunity for creativity that was characteristic of the rural shack, its porch and gardens.

Black liberation movement has not addressed the issue of aesthetics in everyday life. Militant Black power movements in the 1960s and 1970s did not encourage a reclamation of attitudes about beauty common in traditional Black folk culture. While

obsessive materialism has been consistently critiqued in antiracist movements, as well as by radicals on the left, the issue of
aesthetics has not received much attention, nor has the relationship between the desire for beauty and the longing for material
goods.

At the outset of the contemporary feminist movement there
was significant interrogation of consumerism, of women's addiction to materialism, and of the issue of money, both its distribution along gendered lines and its use. Early feminist anthologies
such as *Women in Sexist Society*, edited by Vivian Gornick and
Barbara Moran, included discussions of consumerism and beauty
in relation to appearances. An anonymous "red-stocking sister"
made the useful point that feminist discussions of female obsession with consumerism would be useful if they began from a
standpoint that depicted Americans as mere dupes of patriarchal
advertising culture, "oppressed" by an infatuation with goods.
She suggested: "The consumerism theory is the outgrowth of an
aristocratic, European-oriented antimaterialism based on upper-
class *ressentiment* against the rise of the vulgar bourgeois. Radical
intellectuals have been attracted to this essentially reactionary
position . . . because it appeals to both their dislike of capitalism
and their feeling of superiority to the working class . . . Oddly,
no one claims that the ruling class is oppressed by commodity
choices; it seems that rich people consume out of free choice."
As was the case in Black liberation struggles, there was no discussion of aesthetics, of the place of beauty in everyday life,
within feminist debates about materialism, money, etc. Progressive feminist thinkers are more likely to critique the dangers of
excessive materialism without discussing in a concrete way how
we can balance a desire for beauty or luxury within an anticapi-
talist, antisexist agenda.

As revolutionary and radical feminism becomes less visible,
and as more reformist thinking, such as Naomi Wolf's *Fire with*

Fire, prevails as the feminist order of the day, there is hardly any discussion among feminists about the politics of materialism or money. Contemporary feminists, myself included, can receive more financial rewards for feminist work than has ever been possible, yet we remain relatively silent about these issues. Wolf is not silent. She advocates a brand of "power feminism" that sees nothing problematic about both pursuing and achieving wealth and opposing patriarchal domination. Certainly there is a distinction to be made between the processes by which material privilege can be acquired and wealth accumulated.

Most radical or revolutionary feminists continue to believe that living simply, the equitable distribution of resources, and communalism are necessary to the progressive struggle to end sexism while ending class exploitation. All too often in the past, living simply was made synonymous with a vulgar antimaterialism or anti-aestheticism that privileged living without attention to beauty, to decoration, either of one's person or one's space. Although nowadays the tendency seems to be toward the other extreme, toward indulging to excess, some radical feminists, myself included, grapple with the place of beauty in revolutionary struggle, with our materialism and with our longing for luxury. Just as my Southern Black ancestors recognized that in the midst of exploitation and oppression suffering could be endured if transforming encounters with beauty took place, many revolutionary feminists recognize that we need these same values within the progressive feminist movement. Since it is so easy for those of us with material privilege to hoard resources, to have an attachment to wealth or privileged class power, we need to be vigilant in creating an ethical approach to consumerism that sustains and affirms radical agendas for social change.

Rather than surrendering our passion for the beautiful, for luxury, we need to envision ways those passions can be fulfilled that do not reinforce the structures of domination we seek to change. Hopefully, feminist thinkers will begin to engage in more discussion and theorizing about the place of beauty in revolutionary struggle. Many of us who have a degree of material privilege find that sharing resources, sharing objects we find beautiful that enhance our lives, is one way to resist falling into a privatized, hedonistic consumerism that is self-serving. Those of us who engage in barter, conscious gift giving, tithing, sharing of living space and money, celebrate the luxurious if that which we deem luxurious is not acquired by harming others.

Females in white-supremacist patriarchal society are most often socialized to consume in an unmindful manner. We are encouraged to value goods, especially luxury goods, over our well-being and safety. Many women remain in domestic situations where we are being hurt and even abused by sexist men because of an attachment to material wealth and privilege. While there are many poor women who remain in abusive households because they plainly lack the economic means to leave, there are also some women who remain in such settings because they fear leaving behind material abundance. This kind of thinking is life-threatening and must be challenged.

Beauty can be and is present in our lives irrespective of our class status. Learning to see and appreciate the presence of beauty is an act of resistance in a culture of domination that recognizes the production of a pervasive feeling of lack, both material and spiritual, as a useful colonizing strategy. Individuals who feel constant lack will consume more, will submit more readily. As feminist thinkers construct feminist theory and practice to guide us into a revolutionary, revitalized feminist future, we need to place aesthetics on our agenda. We need to theorize the meaning of beauty in our lives so that we can educate for critical consciousness, talking through the issues: how we acquire and spend money, how we feel about beauty, what the place of beauty is in our lives when we lack material privilege and even basic resources for living, the meaning and significance of luxury, and the politics of envy. Interrogating these issues will enable feminist thinkers to share certain strategies of resistance that will illuminate the ways we can create a balanced, harmonious life where we know the joy of collective, progressive struggle, where the presence of beauty uplifts and renews the spirit.

Women Artists:
The Creative Process

I am a girl who dreams of leisure, always have. Reverie has always been necessary to my existence. I have needed long hours where I am stretched out, wearing silks, satins, and cashmeres, just alone with myself, embraced by the beauty around me. I have always been a girl for fibers, for textiles, and for the feel of comforting cloth against my skin. When I have adorned myself just so, I am ready for the awesome task of just lingering, spending uninterrupted time with my thoughts, dreams, and intense yearnings, often the kind that, like unrequited love, go unfulfilled. Lately, in the midst of that solitude, I find myself writing, spinning words together in my head so as not to lose or forget the insights, the sharp moments of clarity that come during this quiet time, that surface amid the luxurious smells of expensive French lemon verbena soap and fruity perfume, a book in my hand.

More often than not I end up breaking the reverie to reach for pen and paper, to write. Writing for me is never a moment of reverie; it's always work. Writing is my passion. But it is not an easy passion. It does not shelter or comfort me. Words try me—work me as though I am caught in a moment of spirit possession where forces beyond my control inhabit and take me, sometimes against my will, to places, landscapes of thoughts and ideas, I never wanted to journey to or see. I have never been a girl for travel. Always one wedded to the couch, the back porch, the swing, I want to see the world standing still. My thoughts are movements, my ideas, my adventures. If I travel somewhere, it is often just too much; I feel bombarded, too many sensations, overloaded, I break down. "Girl," I tell my sweetest friend, who often worries about how much time I spend shut away, confined, in the midst of solitude, "I understand Emily [Dickinson]: she stayed home to collect her thoughts—to work undisturbed."

I think often and deeply about women and work, about what it means to have the luxury of time—time spent collecting one's thoughts, time to work undisturbed. This time is space for contemplation and reverie. It enhances our capacity to create. Work for women artists is never just the moment when we write, or do other art, like painting, photography, paste-up, or mixed media. In the fullest sense, it is also the time spent in contemplation and preparation. This solitary space is sometimes a place where dreams and visions enter and sometimes a place where nothing happens. Yet it is as necessary to active work as water is to growing things. It is this stillness, this quietude, needed for the continued nurturance of any devotion to artistic practice—to one's work—that remains a space women (irrespective of race, class, nationality, etc.) struggle to find in our lives. Our need for this uninterrupted, undisturbed space is often far more threatening to those who watch us enter it than is that space which is a moment of concrete production (for the writer, that moment when she is putting the words on paper, or, for the painter, that moment when she takes material in hand). We have yet to create a culture so utterly transformed by feminist practice that it would be common sense that the nurturance of brilliance or the creation of a sustained body of work fundamentally requires such undisturbed hours. In such a world it would make perfect sense for women who devote themselves to artistic practice to rightfully claim such space.

Long after the contemporary feminist movement stirred up questions about great art and female genius, compelling folks to rethink the nature of gender and artistic practice, to look at women's art with respect and full recognition, we still must confront the issues of gender and work with respect to the politics of making space and finding time to do what we women artists do. Most artistic women I know feel utterly overextended. We are working to make money (since we have all long abandoned the notion that men would support us while we make art—if we ever thought that—or that patrons would recognize the inequities of history and make reparations granting us time and material support), to take care of ourselves and our nonpatriarchal families. We spend inordinate amounts of time doing the political work (both theoretical and practical) to keep in place those changes brought about by the feminist movement that are enabling more women than ever before to do artistic work. And we spend much time trying to figure out how to use our time wisely. We worry about not giving enough of our care and personhood to loved ones. Many of us still labor with the underlying fear that if we care too much about art, we will be companionless, alone. And some of us who have companions or children make sure that when we come home there are no visible signs of our artistic selves present. Many women artists clear workspace, do not display work, so as to erase all signs of their passion for something so transcendental as art. Despite feminist thinking and practice, women continue to feel conflicted about the allocation of time, energy, engagement, and passion. Though important, it is not overly reassuring that some of us have managed to fit everything into the schedule. Because of this, we now know that making everything fit is no guarantee that we will mature as artists and thinkers. Some of us fear that all of this tightly controlled scheduling is also constricting and limiting our imaginations, shutting down our dreams and visions, so that we enter a different psychic imprisonment. No longer bound by sexist, racist, or class constraints that tell us we cannot be artists, cannot create great and compelling work, we remain bound by limitations on our imaginations.

It has not been my experience that I can dream, think, and create my best when weary, overworked, and stressed out. Many years ago I decided that if I wanted to know the conditions and circumstances that led men to greatness I should study their lives and compare them with the lives of women. I read the biographies of men across race, class, and nationality whom our culture has declared great or significant creative thinkers and artists. I found that folks in these men's lives (parents, friends, lovers, etc.) both expected and accepted that they would need space and time apart for the workings of the everyday to blossom, for them to engage in necessary renewal of spirit. For the most part, their biographies and autobiographies revealed that these men did not have to spend an inordinate number of hours justifying their need for contemplation, for time to be alone, to revel in quietude, to work undisturbed. Adrienne Rich comments on the need for this time in her compelling book *What Is Found There: Notebooks on Poetry and Politics*, and she emphasizes that such time is often "guiltily seized." She continues: "Most, if not all, of the names we know in North American poetry are the names of people who have had some access to freedom in time—that privilege of some which is actually a necessity for all. The struggle to limit the working day is a sacred struggle for the worker's freedom in time . . . Yet every work generation has to reclaim that freedom in time, and many are brutally thwarted in the effort. Capitalism is based on the abridgement of that freedom." Most women artists, including myself, are also salaried workers in areas not directly related to their art. I still dream of the day when I can stop teaching and devote time to writing and making art. Most women artists are still struggling to find time. Even though the feminist movement led to the opening of class opportunities that have enabled individual successful women to claim this time, these opportunities are still rare. These lone individuals were and are often well situated by their class, race, upbringing, education, or milieu to receive the benefits of these opportunities.

I grew up in a large working-class Southern Black patriarchal family, with many sisters and one brother, and my experience of emerging from that context as a potentially gifted artist/creator has always served as the groundwork of my consistent consideration of the impact of class, race, and gender on female creativity and artistic production. Most women I encounter (with the exception of a privileged few) feel that we are still struggling against enormous odds to transform both this culture and our everyday lives so that our creativity can be nurtured in a sustained manner. Respect for the intensity of that struggle must lead us to continue to make a public context for discussion, debate, theorizing, and for the institutionalization of strategies and practices that continue to critically interrogate female creativity and artistic production from a feminist standpoint. These days I am often asked by women, particularly women of color, how it is I find the time to write so much. I find time by sacrificing other involvements and engagements. Living alone without children helps makes that sacrifice possible. Like many women who have been passionately devoted to artistic practice, I find that devotion is often seen by others as "suspect," as though the very fact of writing so much must mean that I am really a monstrous self, hiding some horrible disaffection for life, for human contact. Sexism generates this response to women who are passionately devoted to work. We are all impressed by men who devote their lives to artistic practice. I recall the wonder with which I first took the male German poet Rilke to be one of my artistic spiritual mentors and guides. His confessional writing made solitude seem like a necessary ritual for artistic self-actualization. When I read writing about him, literary criticism, biography, the thoughts of other writers whom his work had inspired, no one seemed to find his devotion suspect. It was seen as a sign of his genius, essential to the cultivation of brilliance. His devotion to artistic practice was never viewed as suspect or monstrous, but simply, as essential to his growth and development.

Growing up Black, female, and working-class without the guidance of many well-meaning grown-ups, I chose my mentors from those individuals whose work touched my spirit. Naively unaware of the politics of gender in the world of culture, I felt I could be as faithful to the examples set for me by white male writers/artists as I was to those of Emily Dickinson, Lorraine Hansberry, or James Baldwin. My only longtime companion, whom I left years ago, continues to write and publish poetry. A professor of literature, he brought into my life an awareness of the importance of discipline and devotion. We were both poets, sharing a mutual fascination for works by white male poets of the Black Mountain School. We pored over the writings of Charles Olson, William Carlos Williams, and Robert Duncan. Through his research he developed a friendship with Robert Duncan. White, male, gay, Robert and his lover Jess represented for me an ideal relationship. They placed art at the center of life and structured a mutually satisfying relationship around it. I learned from their example. They gave themselves "time" to create and were supported by patrons and admirers. Jess, who still works alone in his studio, was my primary mentor. He was the one who often shut himself away from an interfering world, enclosed himself in a world of art. Seeing Jess gave me a courageous and constructive example. He never seemed to care what others thought of him or his work. Unlike Robert, who occasionally mocked my devotion to artistic practice in the typical sexist manner, Jess always reassured me that I could fashion for myself a world in which I could create.

Given the politics of race, gender, and class, it is not surprising that so many of the models of artistic discipline I drew upon to guide my work were white and male. I knew that I needed guidance because of the difficulty I had constructing a confident identity as an artist. In my younger years, I found myself struggling with an inability to see projects through to their end. I habitually abandoned art work before it was done, never quite finishing pieces I was writing. Discipline was an important issue. I had to find a way to break through the barriers that were leading me to abandon work, had to learn to complete it. I practiced discipline by following the example of chosen mentors. Long before Frida Kahlo became the pop cultural icon that she is today, I was fascinated by her relationship to painting—the way she continued to work even when she was in great physical pain. As is the case with contemporary artists such as the Afro-Caribbean American painter Jean-Michel Basquiat, Kahlo's relationship to art risks being submerged by the cannibalistic, voyeuristic obsession with her personal life, the details of her love affairs, and her abuse of alcohol and drugs. While I, too, am drawn to the hedonistic passion that colored her relationship to daily life, I remain most fascinated by her relationship to work, by the young woman who, after suffering intense surgery, could proudly declare, "I haven't died and I have something to live for: painting." Perhaps there will come a day when Kahlo's hedonistic lifestyle will be talked about as merely a constructed backdrop, a mask or persona she created to hide the intensity of a woman driven by love of art. Intuitively, and then later politically, she must have understood how monstrous and threatening she might have appeared to sexist cultures everywhere had she made it more evident that art was always the driving obsession, always the primary longing, the primal quest.

From the example of Kahlo, I saw the necessity for sustained work. Learning from artists from diverse cultural backgrounds and experiences, I was determined to create a world for myself where my creativity could be respected and sustained. It is a world still in the making. Yet each year of my life. I find myself with more undisturbed, uninterrupted time. When I decided to accept a smaller salary and teach part-time, it was to give myself more time. Again, this choice required sacrifice, a commitment to living simply. Yet these are the choices women artists must make if we want more time to contemplate, more time to work. Women artists cannot wait for ideal circumstances to be in place before we find the time to do the work we are called to do; we have to create oppositionally, work against the grain. Each of us must invent alternative strategies that enable us to move against and beyond the barriers that stand in our way. I often find that other women are among that group of people who see female devotion to work as suspect. Whether such women speak from positions of repressed rage or envy, it is clear that we need to do more feminist consciousness raising about the importance of women affirming one another in our efforts to construct uninterrupted undisturbed spaces wherein we can contemplate and work with passion and abandon.

Consciousness-raising groups, gatherings, and public meetings need to become a central aspect of feminist practice again. Women need spaces where we can explore intimately and deeply all aspects of female experience, including our relationship to artistic production. Even though most feminists these days are aware of issues of race, class, and sexual practices, of our differences, we tend to confront these issues only superficially. Women have yet to create the context, both politically and socially, where our understanding of the politics of difference not only transforms our individual lives (and we have yet to really speak about those transformations) but also alters how we work with others in public, in institutions, in galleries, etc. For example: When will white female art historians and cultural critics who structure their careers focusing on work by women and men of color share how this cultural practice changes who they are in the world in a way that extends beyond the making of individual professional success? When will they speak and write about how this work changes how they interact with people of color? When will all of us interrogate issues of race and racism in relation to our notions of artistic excellence, looking at the ways we think about color, how we use images in works? How many artists truly politicize difference by interrogating their choices? Working alone in her studio, the African American painter Emma Amos strives to critically interrogate the way in which race, racism, and white supremacy actually determine what colors we choose to use in paintings, the colors we make human bodies. Issues of class are raised by works such as Eunice Lipton's *Alias, Olympia*. To what extent does her privileged class and nationality affect how she interprets the life and history of a white working-class woman? These are the types of discussion that must emerge if we are to understand the complexity of our differences, if are to create a cultural context where meaningful solidarity between women artists can be strengthened. When such strengthening occurs, the art world in which we work will expand and become more affirming.

Many folks assume that feminism has already changed the social context in which women artists produce work. They mistake greater involvement in the marketplace with the formation of a liberatory space where women can create meaningful, compelling, "great" art and have that art be fully recognized. The "commodification" of difference often leads to the false assumption that works by people of color and marginalized white women are "hot" right now and able to garner a measure of recognition and reward that they may or may not deserve. The impact such thinking has on our work is that it often encourages marginalized artists to feel we must do our work quickly, strike while the iron is hot, or risk being ignored forever. If we write, we are encouraged to write in the same manner as those who have made the big money and achieved the big success. If, say, we take photographs, we are encouraged to keep producing the image that folks most want to see and buy. This commodification for an undiscerning marketplace seeks to confine, limit, and even destroy our artistic freedom and practice. We must be wary of seduction by the superficial and rare possibility of gaining immediate recognition and regard that may grant us some measure of attention in a manner that continues to marginalize us and set us apart. Women must dare to remain vigilant, preserving the integrity of self and of the work.

As women artists expressing solidarity across differences, we must forge ahead, creating spaces where our work can be seen and evaluated according to standards that reflect our sense of artistic merit. As we strive to enter the mainstream art world, we must feel empowered to vigilantly guard the representation of the woman as artist so that it is never again devalued. Fundamentally, we must create the space for feminist intervention without surrendering our primary concern, which is a devotion to making art, a devotion intense and rewarding enough that it is the path leading to our freedom and fulfillment.

Being the Subject of Art

To transgress I must move past boundaries, I must push against to go forward. Nothing changes in the world if no one is willing to make this movement. Everyone I know talks about border crossing these days, as though it were a simple matter not to stay in one's place, not to stand still. All this talk does nothing to change the reality that there are so many barriers blocking the paths that would lead us to any space of fulfillment that it is impossible to go forward if one lacks the will to transgress. And yet most of us seem to carry this will. It comes to us early in life, when we are really little beings and just learning a relationship to space. And we are taught over and over again that the only way to remain safe is to stay within fixed boundaries. Most often it's the boundary of family, community, nation. Before we face even these boundaries, it is the body that is the first site of limitation. The body is the boundary most of us are unable to move against to recover the dimensions of self lost in the process by which we are made to behold to fixed locations, by which we are bound in conformity against our will in many facets of our daily lives. The fact that the word *transgress* appears most often in discussions of the sexual is an indication that the body is the fundamental boundary of self. To transgress we must return to the body.

To return to my body I must be willing to face
indeterminacy, contingency, the reality of dying.
The body has its limits. To know death is to
transgress. It is to violate the taboo understanding
that death is the subject we cannot speak of, the
closeted possibility, that which is shut away and not
remembered—the location of one's desire. When I
learn to look at death, to see someone dying and not
turn away, I am a young girl living in a moment of
transgression. I am a witness. To be intimate with
my body I must like to be close to death. I must be
willing to tell what I've seen. I must bear witness. I
must transgress.

The discourses of death and dying, unlike the
discourse of sexuality, do not lay claim to the word
transgress. Though never spoken, death is the silent
witness, waiting to see if any of us want to live
fully, want to be so fiercely alive that we will not
deny death. To refuse denial is to transgress. The
politics of denial, like the culture of shame, keeps us
in our place. Without fear of exposure, transgression
might become an everyday action. Every moment
someone might be willing to change something
about themselves, the world they live in, if they
were not so afraid of loss, of being confined to states
of ongoing aloneness, states of nonrecognition. To
recognize is to transgress. Withholding recognition
strips us of our power to interrogate, to intervene
on, to act. We are afraid of not being seen. We do
not know the truth that to be seen and not known
is the ultimate abandonment. We refuse to know
each other. In pain there is also the possibility
of connection. It is easy to dominate that which

you see and never know. To want to know is to
transgress.

Knowing my body and its limits, I am able to
sacrifice belonging. If the fear of death is all that
keeps us away from one another, then I willingly
embrace death to reach you, to stand by your side.
If you see me dying then you too are a witness.
You have crossed the boundary. You transgress. In
transgression is the possibility of pleasure and danger,
of redemption and violation. To transgress is to
claim the right to choose. There is no one to blame,
no need to regret. I am moving against to move
toward. Your body lying next to mine cannot remain
silent. We speak to desire together—letting out the
secrets and lies that keep us within fixed boundaries.
Your body inside me violates the limits of flesh. We
cannot go any further. The only pleasure beyond
this moment where the self can be lost in another is
death. Someone, anybody, must remain alive to be
the witness. To tell the truth is to transgress.

I write these passages for a book in which each critical
thinker who was asked to contribute chose a word that moved
them. I chose the word *transgress*. To me these passages speak
about the body. They say nothing about the image—about
representation. Reading them, I hear in these words a will to
transgress—the longing to move across boundaries, against the
norm. That commitment is challenged when I am invited to let
my body be the subject of art: Writing about art, making art, is
not the same as being the subject of art.

When Shu Lea Cheang asked me to participate in the installation *Those Fluttering Objects of Desire*, I was willing. My task
was to be a disembodied voice on the phone speaking about

desire, saying whatever I wanted to say, whatever was on my heart. I journey to New York to read a love letter I have written to the young Black man who is my lover at the time. I arrive in New York confident that I will have no trouble participating in this work of art, being part of its subject. Yet when I stand alone in the studio reading this letter, knowing that it will be taped and later heard on red telephones whenever unknown heads dial 1-900-DESIRE, I am suddenly vulnerable, feel naked— exposed. I cannot disguise the trembling of my voice, the sadness that brings tears. I am suddenly ashamed that strangers will hear my passion. That the people I do not know who are taping this session can see me this way, can hear the way I was then.

Suddenly all my desire to transgress the boundaries of public and private is lost. Even though he agreed to the sharing of these intimate words in a world beyond us, would he withhold agreement if he were hearing, feeling them now in this public place? I am not ready to share these feelings without shame. I am not ready to cross the boundaries of public and private. I fear no one will understand these words. We stop the taping. We begin again. I want to resist this self-imposed shame. It is not natural. It is the product of public and private pain—the outcome of separation.

I begin to read again, surrendering myself to the intimacy of the words. Months later I will stand before the red phones, unable to dial 1-900-DESIRE even after I am told again and again that the intimacy of this disembodied voice touches the listeners, speaks to them heart to heart. A man called me wanting a copy of the poem he thought I was reading as he listened on the red phone. I had to repeat over and over again before he heard: It was not a poem. It was a letter I wrote to my lover. I was hurting at the time. He never called back. Writing about art, making art, is not the same as being the subject of art.

When I went to do a series of lectures at Cal Arts, there were signs about video classes on a wall in bold letters: "Open your heart and expose." I use this as the heading for my class. In that class I meet a young Black male photographer, Lyle Ashton Harris. We talk theory, desire, transgression. He shows me slides of a show that contains many images of his body naked. Sometimes he is alone in the pictures, sometimes he is with his male lover. He has no shame.

Later, when we are together at the San Francisco Art Institute, he stays in my tiny one-room apartment with me. When I awaken in the morning, he has camera in hand, he is taking photos of me. Writing about art, making art is not the same as being the subject of art. At this moment the camera pushes against my boundaries, transgresses, violates. I make a fuss. I am sick. My body is in pain. I ache all over. I did not sleep well. *No,* I tell Lyle. *No pictures. I do not feel well.* I resist the camera because I do not want to see myself this way. I do not want to be seen trapped in a body that is letting me down again and again. Trapped. The camera traps me. I hear in my saying *no* the fear of confronting an image of a sick body, a body in pain. He shoots again and again. I let the camera take aim against the shame that invades me, against my fear of not being perfect.

Lyle says these snapshots will not be shown without my consent; I never see the images he produces. More than a year later, on the Friday night before his show "The Good Life" opens at a SoHo gallery, Lyle calls to tell me I am in the show. He hangs a picture of me that I have not seen. I want to know if I have my clothes on. He does not respond truthfully. I am disturbed by the secrecy, by the absence of consent. Writing about art, making art, is not the same as being the subject of art.

When I go to the show I walk past posed family portraits, the stylized images of Lyle and his friend Ike, images of Lyle naked with his brother, and find myself. I am naked. It is the image of my body in pain. I am anointing it with oil after washing. My morning ritual. The image is so mundane. It is out of place on the gallery wall, in this show of fancy posed figures. My trust has been violated. The red walls on which the images hang are an inner sanctuary where transgression is sanctioned. Violation is a transgression. Betrayal can make a boundary where there has been none.

I would not have offered this image to anyone, not even to myself. The image I see is no longer familiar to me. Since this photo was taken, my body has been opened up—parts of it removed. Life-threatening illness violates the limits of flesh. I am no longer my body. In the face of death, I long for life. I am without shame. To see this image here in public, away from private sorrow and grief, I transgress—move against the boundaries of shame. Will they look beyond this naked flesh and see pain there, impending sorrow? Will they see the vulnerability, the fear of loss?

Shame about the body that is not perfect, that is not well, that is full of disease is a boundary I want to transgress. I want to move past this shame to embrace flesh on its own terms—to let the body fall into various states of sickness and decay without regret. We are all strangers here. None of us knows how to keep death away, how to make ourselves be well always and forever.

To be naked without intimacy, without privacy, without consent calls out memories of violation, of lying in rooms without the will to say *no*. When I go under the knife that will wound and violate me, I am hearing lyrics from *Porgy and Bess*. Lines that say, "Don't let them touch me—don't let them handle me with their hot hands." I will be touched anyway. I will be touched against my will. And I will not remember. I will wake up slowly and feel the coldness of coming close to death and coming back to life. My body will be changed forever.

Before this moment in the unfamiliar gallery room with Lyle and his art, there was no image—no record—of my uncut body. Pushing past my shame, I embrace the documentary image— my naked body uncut, without wound or scar. That is the body I will not see again. It is by now already unfamiliar flesh. On this red wall hangs the image. It does not speak. It has no story to tell. It does not shout out to those who stand staring, *Don't look at me this way. No pictures.* This image has its own destiny. My flesh moves in a history of its own making.

I am without shame. This image cannot wound or hurt me. Violation is an act of betrayal. There is no picture of this moment—no way to articulate separation, loss. To transgress one boundary and make another leaves us nowhere, unable to move forward. There is no way to take a picture of this moment. To tell the truth is to transgress. Writing about art, making art, is not the same as being the subject of art.

Workers for Artistic Freedom

In a democratic society art should be the location where everyone can witness the joy, pleasure, and power that emerges when there is freedom of expression, even when a work created evokes pain, outrage, sorrow, or shame. Art should be, then, a place where boundaries can be transgressed, where visionary insights can be revealed within the context of the everyday, the familiar, the mundane. Art is and remains such an uninhibited, unrestrained, cultural terrain only if *all* artists see their work as inherently challenging to those institutionalized systems of domination (imperialism, racism, sexism, class elitism, etc.) that seek to limit, coopt, exploit, or shut down possibilities for individual creative self-actualization. Regardless of subject matter, form, or content, whether art is overtly political or not, artistic work that emerges from an unfettered imagination affirms the primacy of art as that space of cultural production where we can find the deepest, most intimate understanding of what it means to be free.

In the cultural marketplace, art is never simply a site for freedom of expression but, rather, an arena in which opportunistic forces interact to promote a dynamic of competition that makes art a place where these institutionalized systems of domination are mirrored in art practices on every level, whether it is through the development of canonical works that allow the formation and representation of starring lineups made up of teams of white males; through the dismissal of overtly political work, especially when created by individuals from marginalized groups (particularly people of color or folks from poor backgrounds); in funding choices; in the production and dissemination of art criticism; or even in the seemingly "innocent" clinging to a fixed, static, overdetermined notion of "great" art.

Ironically, those individuals who are most mired in perpetuating coercive hierarchies often see themselves as the sole champions of artistic freedom. To truly champion artistic freedom we must be committed to creating and sustaining an aesthetic culture where diverse artistic practices, standpoints, identities, and locations are nurtured, find support, affirmation, and regard; where the belief that individual artists must have the right to create as the spirit moves—freely, openly, provocatively—prevails. Fundamentally, artists who work individually or collectively bear witness to this truth with the art we make and with our habits of being. Until this expansive vision of the role of the artist in society is embraced as the necessary aesthetic groundwork for *all* artistic practices, freedom of expression will be continually undermined, its meaning and value lost.

Were this progressive vision of artistic practice shaping the nature of funding, funders would need to be ever mindful that we must work to create diverse contexts for the public, across class, and must be educated about the importance of art, about aesthetics. This education must take place on a national and community-based level. Ideally, in a wealthy democratic society, government would recognize the importance of art and form the cultural offices necessary both to stimulate awareness about art, its meaning and significance (this would mean funding programs in elementary schools, making sure really great artists have residencies in schools), and to support artists on all levels. While all of us who celebrate the importance of art in the making of culture must continue to lobby to create a government that responds fully to these needs, we must also work to garner the support of funders.

It might be possible for grant givers to support more art education in the schools, to buy, barter, and, when possible, donate spots on television, or invent any number of cultural strategies that would seek to share with everyone the lived understanding that art enriches life. Concurrently, gifted children, especially those from underprivileged marginalized groups, need to be supported while they are young, when their talent is first emerging. For too long in this society it has been assumed, most often by those classes of folks who are materially privileged, that nonprivileged folks who are gifted will somehow prove their mettle by how well they manage to triumph over limiting hardships and deprivations and still remain committed to doing art. Such thinking is the kind of false consciousness that seeks to cover up informed understanding about the conditions under which any artist works freely. As long as these sentiments prevail we will never see an abundance of truly significant art emerging from marginalized groups (note that the key word here is *abundance*). A continuity of affirmation and support from all possible fronts is important for artistic development.

There is no artist deemed "great" by the art establishment who has not received affirmation, whether given by a family member, a friend, or a patron. If a cultural climate of support is established at the outset of a young artist's commitment to doing art work, there is much greater likelihood that this work will develop and mature. We all know how many times funders and patrons approach the work of an aspiring adult artist from an underprivileged background only to make the critique that the work may be good but lacks maturity or needs to develop more slowly. Artists from marginalized groups, especially those who come to doing art in a committed way late in life, often feel that they lack the time to develop slowly. They create with stressful urgency and, of course, this impacts the work. For this reason alone it would be a tremendous intervention to support the development of children who have reached a stage where they have a disciplined commitment to the practice of art.

Funders can discover gifted children who lack the means to pursue their work by sending artists, paid as consultants, to schools. These artists could establish working contact with teachers and students and then act as liaisons between children and funding agencies. I am not talking here about the giving of large sums of money to individuals. I am talking about buying paint and paper for a child for a number of years. Growing up in a large working-class household where I longed to develop as a painter, I confronted parents who felt that they just could not take the money away from primary needs to buy paint and paper. Had a donor provided it, my parents would have undoubtedly supported me in pursuing this passion. Concurrently, while many students from marginalized groups can apply for scholarships to attend graduate school, and in some cases to attend prestigious art schools, doing art while in school is not the same as having long stretches of unoccupied time both to educate oneself fully about art and to practice. More funders could play a role in this respect than already do.

Artists from all groups (whether or not disadvantaged or marginalized) need time. Although throughout the United States funding sources are currently in place to select talented folks and award them sufficient funds to set aside some months or even a year just to work, often the same individuals enter and reenter the grant-receiving loop and are rewarded by several sources. This limits the number of individuals who can receive support. It would be exciting to see the emergence of more diverse types of funding that would be on a simple scale (grants that would provide rent and/or food and supplies). New big bucks can be acquired only by the few. A granting process in the arts that is differently scaled opens up the possibility for more folks to benefit.

Artistic production would be enriched in our culture if grant givers would create a system of inter-art relations that would reward discussion and engagement—the sharing of knowledge, information, and skills across boundaries of race, class, gender, age, etc. Many of those of us who have developed a mature artistic practice testify that meeting certain individual artists and learning from them was crucial to our development. Often these meetings are serendipitous, happen quite by chance. When I was young, I had a boyfriend who wrote his dissertation on the poet Robert Duncan. My friend's development of a working friendship with Duncan led to my meeting one of the more influential role models for my life—the white male painter Jess, Duncan's lover. Both men were more than forty years old when we met them. Even though Robert died a few years ago, and my contact with Jess has diminished over the years, when we met regularly I was able to talk with him about art practices, to learn from his wisdom. I mention his being white and his age because these two factors might have prevented us from ever making contact or from establishing the kind of contact where sharing of knowledge and information could occur, given the nature of social relations in a white-supremacist capitalist patriarchy. Celebratory rhetoric about multiculturalism aside, it is not easy for folks to bond across differences in this society. From Jess I learned how to become a disciplined artist. This was an invaluable lesson. Were it not for the wonder of chance, our meeting might never have happened.

In view of the growing nationalism and mounting xenophobia in our society, meetings that cross the boundaries of class, race, sexual preference, gender, age, etc., are becoming increasingly unlikely. Were such meetings arranged and funded by an organized body, they would facilitate not only meaningful contact and exchange but would spread the message that being an artist is not simply a matter of possessing the gift to create. To truly mature in one's artistic practice it is important to learn about art, to see art from everywhere and everyone, to study, to interact with others. Currently, there is so much emphasis on production, on the making and selling of art as a product, on the packaging of careers, that this type of nurturance of artistic spirit is not promoted. And it is definitely not materially rewarded. Yet the development of organized artistic communities is essential to the making and sustaining of a democratic artistic culture.

To create an aesthetic culture that promotes diversity, it is necessary that established artists from all backgrounds be encouraged to expand the scope of their knowledge and interactions. It is tragic that so many mainstream artists or folks seeking to enter the mainstream wrongly imagine that they are keeping art pure when they devalue the importance of diversity, policies of inclusion, artistic support that prioritizes marginalized groups. These artists should be able to undo the kind of socialization that inhibits their capacity to see that "all" artists who believe in artistic freedom create work that challenges domination. Grants that would allow them to interact with critics and artists so that they could develop a more expansive vision would be useful.

To date, much of our cultural emphasis on diversity has been narrowly orchestrated so that all too often it has created divisiveness between those artists who see themselves as preserving art as a sacred sphere uncontaminated by politics and those artists (many of whom are from marginalized groups) who rightly understand that political critiques in various contexts are needed if we are to disrupt and change the existing structure. It is crucial that we face the fact that artists can create work having a progressive vision about the development of community, using artistic practices that are more inclusive. Only education that encourages critical consciousness will create a climate where thinking can change and paradigms can shift.

The phrase *marginalized groups* is useful because it is not limited to one category. It can be used to refer to all groups of individuals (including groups of white males) who have been systematically denied access to the resources that make artistic production possible. Members of some groups have been historically oppressed or exploited in ways that concretely deprive them of resources—knowledge, information, access. These groups rightly deserve the support of everyone who would like to promote a truly democratic artistic culture in our society. Given the ongoing reality of sexism, the institutionalization of patriarchy, women certainly remain a marginalized group. Yet we have to add to that knowledge the understanding that, due to race and class distinctions, some groups of women are more marginalized than others, and some have greater access than others to the spheres of power. Anyone involved in the grant-receiving, grant-giving process on any level (and that includes observers) can see that often it is individuals, irrespective of race or gender, from privileged backgrounds (and here we must be willing to acknowledge that higher levels of education are a privilege) who are best able to utilize existing funding agencies. A major new agenda for funding agencies should be the effort to envision diverse ways of sharing information and to formulate means of providing support that do not require massive amounts of paperwork. Many artists have not had the opportunity to develop the kind of critical literacy that is often needed to navigate a journey through the funding process. Even someone with a Ph.D. might never apply for funding because the process seems too formidable. Rather than rigidly assuming that everyone can adapt to the existing patterns and that everyone knows not only how to apply for funding but how to fill out forms, we could collectively begin to imagine and institutionalize simpler processes. What would it be like to establish a framework where all one needed to do to apply for funds was to have an oral interview with a board of selected folks? Private funders willing to try a process as radical as this could serve as a model for other agencies. Failure to interrogate existing processes of funding means that everyone, whether we want to or not, ends up reproducing the status quo with a few little differences that appear to integrate an unchanging same. Finally, working as both artist and critic, I know that the development of an insightful, sophisticated body of criticism addressing diverse art practices is necessary for work to be given sustained serious regard. Efforts at inclusion that lead to the formation of more open spaces (a prime example would be the recent Whitney Biennial) will never be fully successful if they do not coincide with the production of a body of critical written work that creates an intellectual climate where the importance of these interventions can be articulated and understood, where the value of the art represented can be illuminated. As a member of a marginalized group who writes art criticism, who longs to see more work by African American thinkers, especially women, and by other groups as well, I would be among the first to testify that one can bring in very little income with this type of work and that indeed it helps to have a good supplementary job. Perhaps the day will soon come when grant-giving agencies will establish constructive liaisons between critics and artists, materially rewarding both groups of individuals so that the work of marginalized artists may be given the sort of critical attention that ensures that its value will be sustained through time; that the knowledge and appreciation of the significance of such work will not wane with passing trends.

Like artists, public funders also need education that encourages critical consciousness. More forums and small conferences are needed that create a context for dialogue, for the working through of differences, for the airing of ideas that are not yet fully understood. This requires the will and imagination to break with the ways in which information has traditionally been shared. How many of us have attended conferences where there were small group sessions and one-on-one encounters with significant visionaries and thinkers? All too often we structure conferences in such a way that conflicting viewpoints cannot be worked through or even explored. We are desperately in need of new models. Ultimately, new agendas can be set and successfully implemented by funding agencies only if the individuals working within these spheres of power embrace the spirit of change that calls us all to deepen our awareness, to intensify our commitment to art as the practice of freedom.

Black Vernacular: Architecture as Cultural Practice

Designing the house of my dreams in a high school art class, I did not think that any decisions I made were political. Indeed, every thought I had about the aesthetics of this project was rooted in imaginative fantasy. Beginning with the idea of a world of unlimited freedom where space, and in particular living space, could be designed solely in relation to "desire," I greatly wanted most to move away from concrete "political" realities, such as class, and just dream. When we were given the assignment—to build a dream house—our art teacher encouraged us to forget about dwellings as we knew them and to think imaginatively about space, about the link between what we desire, dream about, and what is practical.

We were to design, as I understood it, a dwelling place of dreams. I began this assignment by making a list of all the aspects of a house I found most compelling: stairways, window seats, hidden nooks and crannies. On paper, my house exposed and revealed my obsessions. I was a constant reader, living with a huge family, in small space. To me, reading was a deliciously private experience, one that allowed me to be secluded, walled in by silence and thought. In my dream house there were many places designed to enhance the pleasure of reading, places for sitting and lying down, places for reading and reverie. Every bit of space was shaped to be subordinate to these desires. Thus, there were endless stairways, window seats, and small rooms everywhere. On paper, in structure and design the house I imagined was a place for the fulfillment of desire, a place with no sense of necessity.

Although I have no clear memory of where this design ended up, I know this assignment affected me deeply. More than twenty years later, I can close my eyes and see the image of this house as I drew it. Loving flowers, I had designed the different floors to be like petals. It fascinates me now to think about why a white male Italian immigrant high school art teacher in the segregated South would encourage students to think of artistic practice solely in relation to fantasy and desire. In retrospect it is clear that this was precisely the kind of assignment that was meant to deflect attention from political realities, from the class, race, and gender differences that separated and divided us from one another. Through this sort of a project, we could work harmoniously, focusing on dreams; we could see ourselves as connected—as the same.

This would have been a radically different assignment had we been encouraged to think critically about the actual spaces we inhabited, the neighborhoods and houses that were our world. Had we been given such an assignment, we would have learned to think about space politically, about who controls and shapes environments. This assignment might have compelled recognition of class differences, the way racial apartheid and white supremacy altered individuals' space, overdetermined locations and the nature of structures, created a sense of entitlement for some and deprivation for others. Doing this assignment, we might have come face to face with the politics of property, not only who owns and controls space but the relationship between power and cultural production.

We were not given such an assignment because it not only would have disrupted and subverted the idea of artistic endeavor and creative expression as politically neutral acts, it would have at the same time fundamentally challenged the idea of art as a site for transcendence, of art as emerging from an unfettered free zone of the imagination. Even though I did not see myself as thinking politically then, the very fact that I designed my dream house to counter the experience of growing up in small overcrowded space, a circumstance that reflected my families' economic standing, meant that undergirding my dreams, my fantasies and desires, were class-based longings. This dream house, then, was not solely the outcome of abstract musings about dwellings; it was equally rooted in a concrete acknowledgment of my reality. Despite its limitations, this assignment did teach us that, irrespective of our location, irrespective of class, race, and gender, we were all capable of inventing, transforming, making space. It would have been exciting to have designed this dream house, then to have done another assignment in which we worked on designing space to meet concrete needs within the limitations of our lived experiences.

Had we done an assignment that required us to think critically and imaginatively about our homes and neighborhoods, those of us from nonprivileged backgrounds would have had an opportunity to think about architecture and design in relation to our lives both in the present and in the future. Growing up working-class and Black in the South, I do not remember any direct discussion of our architectural realities. If our earliest understanding of architecture was that it exists only in the location of dream and fantasy, of "impossibility," it is no wonder then that many children of the working class and poor tend not to grow to maturity understanding architecture as a professional and cultural practice central to our imaginative and concrete relationship to space.

Although the dream house I designed had no direct connection to the dwellings in my community—which were separate, distinct, segregated spaces inhabited by the Black working and nonworking poor—the link between that fantasy place and the actual world I lived in was grounded in generations of concern with space, with the shaping and construction of environments. Poor Southern Black folks were often land rich. Owning land, they were concerned with the use of space, the building of dwellings. Many narratives of resistance struggle from slavery to the present share an obsession with the politics of space, particularly the need to construct and build houses. Indeed, Black folks equated freedom with the passage into a life where they would have the right to exercise control over space on their own behalf, where they would imagine, design, and create spaces that would respond to the needs of their lives, their communities, their families.

Growing up in a world where Black working-class and "po' folk," as well as the Black well-to-do, were deeply concerned with the aesthetics of space, I learned to see freedom as always and intimately linked to the issue of transforming space. I have chosen to write about this concern with space in order both to acknowledge the oppositional modes of psychic decolonization that marginalized, exploited, and oppressed Black folks envisioned and to document a cultural genealogy of resistance. This project is distinct from those forms of nostalgic remembering of the past that simply appropriate colorful touristic images of "the darkies way back then." Framing this cultural genealogy of resistance in relation to space is necessary for the "cognitive mapping" Fredric Jameson speaks about when he insists that "it is at least empirically arguable that our daily life, our psychic experience, our cultural languages, are today dominated by categories of space rather than categories of time." It is my conviction that African Americans can respond to contemporary crises we face by learning from and building on strategies of opposition and resistance that were effective in the past and are empowering in the present.

It is empowering for me to construct, in writing, the continuum that exists between the exploration of space and architecture that was a fundamental aspect of poor Black rural Southern life even though it was not articulated in those terms. When my father's father, Daddy Jerry, a sharecropper and farmer, talked in concrete terms about his relationship to land, his longing to own and build, he spoke poetically about working with space so that it would reveal and mirror the texture of his longings. I never understood how Daddy Jerry "came by" a piece of land; that was the way folks talked about it then. The phrase could define a number of transactions. It could mean that he bought, traded, inherited, or exchanged work for land. On this land Daddy Jerry built a house. I can still remember the way he and my father would sit on the porch and have deep discussions about that house; their talk evoked a poetics of space, the joy of thinking imaginatively about one's dwelling. And I can recall my disappointment when I finally saw the small square brick house that he built. In my childhood imagination this space seemed so utterly closed and tight. Had I understood the interconnected politics of race, gender, and class in the white-supremacist South, I would have looked upon this house with the same awe as I did my favorite house.

My awe was reserved for the house of my mother's father, Daddy Gus, and her mother, Baba. An artist/quiltmaker, Baba shaped this house to meet her needs, those of her husband of more than seventy years and the extended family that stayed or visited there. Like Toni Morrison's fictional character Eva Peace in *Song of Solomon*, Baba's wood-frame dwelling was a place where rooms were continuously added in odd places, racked on, usually to accommodate the desires of the individual who was destined to inhabit that space. At Baba's house there was always an excitement about space—a sense of possibility. There dwellings were seen as in a constant state of change. Significantly, the absence of material privilege did not mean that poor and working-class Black folks (such as my grandparents) did not think creatively about space. While lack of material privilege limited what could be done with one's surroundings, it was nevertheless always possible to make changes.

My grandmother's house was not unlike the small shacks that were the homes of many Southern Black folks. Her place was just a bigger, more elegant shack. Wood-frame dwellings that were fragile or sturdy shaped my sense of meaningful vernacular architecture. Many of these structures, though fragile and therefore altered by time and the elements, remain and offer a wealth of information about the relationship of poor and working-class rural Black folks to space. African American professor of architecture LaVerne Wells-Bowie highlights in her writings the significance of architecture created by folks who were not schooled in the profession or even in the arts of building. She offers the insight that "vernacular architecture is a language of cultural expression" that "exemplifies how the physical environment reflects the uniqueness of a culture." Little railroad shacks in the South were often peopled by large families. When I was a child, I entered the home of an elderly Black woman who lived in a lovely shack and was most impressed and delighted by the small cot-size beds placed here and there. I carry in my memory the serenity this woman's utterly neat and sparse place evoked. This experience helped shape my relationship to interior design and dwellings.

Often the rural Black folks who lived in shacks on the edges and margins of town conceptualized the yard as a continuation of living space. Careful attention might be given to the planting of flowers, the positioning of a porch or a rope-hung swing. In the recent autobiography of the more-than-a-hundred-year-old Delaney sisters, they describe their migration north, their purchase of a small house, and the amazement of white folks that they wanted to add on a porch. Reading this, I recalled overhearing the conversations between my father and his dad as they sat on the porch and shared thoughts, ideas, dreams. Often, exploited or oppressed groups of people who are compelled by economic circumstance to share small living quarters with many others view the world right outside their housing structure as liminal space where they can stretch the limits of desire and the imagination.

Recording these memories seems absolutely essential, because in today's world we are led to believe that lack of material privilege means that one can have no meaningful constructive engagement with one's living space and certainly no relationship to aesthetics. I am often disturbed when folks equate a concern with beauty, the design and arrangement of space, with class privilege. Unfortunately, so many poor people have been socialized by the mass media and the politics of consumerism to see themselves as lacking "taste and style" when it comes to issues of architecture and aesthetics that they have surrendered their capacity to imagine and create. They explain this surrender as the unavoidable consequence of poverty. Yet lack of material privilege need not be synonymous with poverty of spirit or imagination. Significantly, in the past, even during the most dire circumstances of oppression and exploitation, African Americans could find ways to express their creativity—to display artistry. They dared to use their imagination in ways that were liberatory.

Few critics have attempted to look at poor and working-class Black folks' relationship to space. We need studies of housing that talk about the way in which the construction of "projects" —state-owned and -designed dwellings for the economically disadvantaged—brought an end to the dwelling in shacks that allowed for individual creativity and an assertion of aesthetic engagement with space and one's environment. The state-built dwellings erase all chances for unique perspectives to shape living space and replace these with a blueprint of sameness—everyone's place structured similarly. Clearly, these structures inform the ways poor folk are allowed to see themselves in relationship to space. No matter how poor you were in the shack, no matter if you owned the shack or not, there you could allow your needs and desires to articulate interior design and exterior surroundings. Poverty could not be viewed as a circumstance that suppresses creativity and possibility, for all around you were expressions of unique sensibility. Standardized housing brought with it a sense that to be poor meant that one was powerless, unable to intervene in or transform, in any way, one's relationship to space. In many areas of the rural South the shack still remains as a dwelling that counters and subverts the messages of this dehumanization of the spatial imagination of folks who are not materially privileged.

Mapping a cultural genealogy of resistance, we can see ways poor African Americans used their imaginations to transcend limits. This history increasingly becomes subjugated knowledge as Black folks embrace notions of victimhood that suggest our reality can be defined only by the circumstances of our oppression. In the essay "Race and Architecture," the philosopher and cultural critic Cornel West suggests that "the major challenge of a new architectural historiography is that its conception of the 'past' and 'present' be attuned to the complex role of difference—nature, primitive, ruled, Dionysian, female, Black and so on." To rise to this challenge, spaces must exist for us to think and talk about, and theorize architecture as it reflects and informs culture.

In this expansive and more inclusive understanding of architecture, the vernacular is as relevant as any other form of architectural practice. This perspective allows critics to theorize Black experience in ways that promote documentation of our historical and contemporary relationship to space and aesthetics. Few scholars theorize Black experience from a standpoint that centralizes the perspectives of poor and working-class folks. Yet to ignore this standpoint is to reproduce a body of work that is neocolonial insofor as it violently erases and destroys those subjugated knowledges that can only erupt, disrupt, and serve as acts of resistance if they are visible, remembered. Documentation of a cultural genealogy of resistance invites the making of theory that highlights the cultural practices which transform ways of looking and being in a manner that resists reinscription by prevailing structures of domination. Subversive historiography connects oppositional practices from the past with forms of resistance in the present, thus creating spaces of possibility where the future can be imagined differently—imagined in such a way that we can witness ourselves dreaming, moving forward and beyond the limits and confines of fixed locations.

Architecture in Black Life: Talking Space with LaVerne Wells-Bowie

bell hooks: LaVerne, we are both incredibly excited about the politics of space. What interested you initially about architecture and the more expansive idea of design and space?

LaVerne Wells-Bowie: I did my graduate work in architecture. But before I went into architecture, I was a textile designer for about thirteen or fourteen years. My undergraduate degree was in textile design. In designing textiles, I would tell stories that were related to what I felt was an important cultural resource, African folk tales. They were a good source for storytelling, and storytelling was a good mechanism for designing cloth. Anyway, I decided that I wanted to do more than just design the fabric that would appear in people's houses as an expensive commodity, as home furnishing items; so I went to architecture school. When I was in architecture school, I began to recall things, to remember my childhood—like going to South Carolina, to Charleston, which is where my mother's people are from and where I was born, even though I never lived there. Charleston was a place I visited frequently during my childhood. That connection has stayed with me. But it was the formal study of architecture that crystallized these experiences. I remember going to Charleston and seeing lifestyles and cultures change as the landscape changed. It changed because of development. I was reminded of this recently reading a commentary on Africa which made the insightful point that development can be played out as a game of spatial discrimination. Well, as a graduate student, I didn't know how to articulate it in that way, but I knew how to draw these little diagrams that showed where people's houses were located, where different relatives lived. I could map our journeys into the country, and could illustrate the location of those houses to each other. The way space was designed shaped relationships and interactions. Children, for example, could eat at any house, or sleep at any house in a neighborhood. In those days I thought these social relations were what everybody's life was like, that everybody had spaces like this where they could recall and remember themselves. It wasn't until I really studied architecture that I started to put all those ideas together and to understand that I'd been thinking about space as cultural geography.

bh: It is interesting that you use the phrase "recall yourself." I think a great deal about racial memory. When I see a film like Trinh T. Minh-ha's *Naked Spaces: Living Is Round,* the architecture shown there allows me a visual record where I trace a continuum between traditional African ways of thinking about architecture and space and some of the ways of thinking that you see in the diaspora. This is especially true of the architecture I grew up seeing. In my childhood, I saw Black people who were land rich, but who did not have money, design and build dwellings for themselves out of a real spirit of creativity and a sense of space, and an excitement about that. There was a real sense of aesthetics in Southern working-class and poor Black life that emerged from agrarian history and plantation life. That continuum of cultural concern with space is what you see as deeply structured into the roots of Black experience in a place like Charleston.

LW-B: Yes, Black cultural connections to spaces is what I'm talking about. I agree with what you are saying about Trinh

T. Minh-ha's work, but I think that there is a difference in the way that she and Jean-Paul Bourdier approach African architecture, and the standpoint we are talking about, which is rooted in actual cultural experience and racial memory.

bh: Well, exactly. I did not mean to suggest that Minh-ha is consciously concerned with that continuum. I wanted to emphasize that African Americans seeing those dwellings can see a continuum, can see the links between those dwellings and the ones we grew up in. One advantage of a film like *Naked Spaces: Living Is Round* is in the way that it visually allows us to see those dwellings, so that then we can go back to those tiny little shacks that Black folks built in the United States on marshes, on the edges of towns, and see those shacks in a new way. I'm a lover of shacks. I believe that there are marvelous things to be done aesthetically with the shack. And we see more examples of that in the Caribbean, how people have taken the wood-frame shack and redefined it, shaped it in ways that reverberate with past and present African architecture—for example, the structures of the Ndebele—or with other kinds of relationships to dwellings in the African diaspora. I don't know if Minh-ha intended to make this explicit in her film, but I bring this awareness to the film through the poetics of racial memory.

LW-B: You're right. The ability to see in that way comes from our cultural genealogy. This is akin to my perception that these thoughts were in my head, and even sketched out as a child, even though I didn't know about architecture.

bh: Say more about why you chose architecture.

LW-B: In my high school yearbook it said that LaVerne Wells "will be an interior designer." This is what I thought I would do. And that's because I didn't know that I had an option to be an architect. I really didn't. I remember building tents, and shaping small spaces as a child. The whole idea of intervening in a space, building a tent inside of a room so that you had a space inside of a space, and understanding what spatial boundaries were, was powerful then. But it wasn't until I was a textile designer and began to be very much exposed to interior design that I saw that interiors were not my forte. Now I did not actually major in interior design when I was in undergraduate college, because it was boring to me. It was about the technical way to do perspective drawing and match colors and all of that. It was the connection of textiles to culture, changing something from literature to an image, that made me start to realize that I wanted to work with space. When I decided to study architecture, I also decided that I wanted my relationship to space to evoke architecture as it is informed by the humanities, not architecture simply as a technical art.

bh: You were fascinated by architecture as I am. And, in fact, when you and I first met, one of the things I shared with you is that in a very different kind of world I would have been an architect. I designed my first house in high school. But because I was from a poor working Black family in the South, folks didn't say to me, "Oh, you should be an architect." I remember receiving praise in class for the house that I designed. Yet this was not seen as a sign that I should think about a career in architecture. I don't even think *architecture* as a word was in my cultural consciousness. It is that fascination which motivates me to theorize the relationship to space that has shaped the cultural imagination of Black working-class and poor folk. I'm talking about Black people like Daddy Jerry, my paternal grandfather, who was a sharecropper, but who, when he came by his bit of land, built himself a house. It was a small brick house that reflected his aesthetic sensibility. On one hand we have a Southern Black man with very poor reading and writing skills, a man who has been working the earth all his life, and yet he had a strong sensibility that led him to create a space, and to dream and plan that space so it would reflect the essence of his soul, so that it would speak to his spirit. It was exciting when I heard you talk about reading my work and thinking that I could be an architect. I think that this strong tradition that I was born into, that legacy of Black sensibility about the visual and the aesthetic, has shaped and informed my work. The only reason I didn't pursue this career was my class background. No one felt it was worth pointing me in those directions.

LW-B: No one valued your ability to be such a master of manipulating the physical world that you could actually design and build things—that's what it was. I think that it is not simply a question of class. The reality also is that there aren't a lot of Black people who go into architecture. And the reality beyond that is that there are not a lot of women. And there really are not a lot of Black women.

bh: Oh, absolutely. I was dismayed when I read *Architecture: A Woman's Place*, because it was written as though Black women don't exist. The only discussion of African American people in relation to architecture is the discussion of Charleston and the architecture in Charleston that the white woman philanthropist works to preserve. And even though we are told she utilizes the artistry of African American craftspeople, she devalues their artistry in her own reclaiming and appropriating of that space. Acts of appropriation and exploitation are among the reasons so few Black folks articulate a concern with space, with architecture. That is why this kind of collaborative conversation is so crucial. It serves to document in print our concern with space.

We want to speak to architecture as a cultural practice in ways that say to all Black people: This work can be a dwelling place for your spirit. Architecture is a dwelling place for your spirit. And you can claim it rightfully, and claiming it is not to claim something white, or something that is distant from who you are as a Black person.

LW-B: We need to remind one another that architecture is not something mysterious and beyond reach . . .

bh: That's why I think it is so useful to think about architecture as a cultural practice, rather than solely as a professional one. If we look at the history of architecture as a profession in this society, and that is the way most marginalized people learn to look at it, Black folks will constantly think of it as something distant and out of reach. Because a particular kind of mainstream, white male-dominated architecture is still, in some ways, out of our reach, particularly if we come from working-class and poor backgrounds. But the kind of architecture we are talking about is really architecture as a cultural practice, because that sense of architecture acknowledges diversity of location, that wherever folks are dwelling in space, they can think creatively about the transformation and reinvention of that space, about design, about housing, public institutions, etc.

LW-B: That's true. I really like to think about architecture as a cultural practice—because architecture is so informed by culture. That's the most important thing. Before architecture was this bastion that it is now, architecture was something that was very much informed by how people lived their lives, what their belief systems were, how they related to one another, their social and economic circumstances, another available technology in the most minimal kind of way. It is important that this conversation affirm the reality that architecture as a cultural practice is not beyond the realm of people who are not architects, and that people need to think of architecture in a broad and expansive way. That's the most important thing. I've used your work as a way of sensitizing my students at the second-year level of their schooling, when they're really beginning to learn building design, because I feel that if they can look at how someone else evokes feelings about spatiality, descriptions, smells, sights, all kinds of ways that we sense space, then they will be able to look inside of themselves and remember some of those feelings that they've had and understand that those locations provide standpoints that they can draw on when they design.

bh: To relate space to intimate experience is crucial. I recently saw the exhibition of spirit houses curated by Robert Farris Thompson in the Museum of African Art in SoHo, New York City, the museum that Maya Lin designed. In art circles, I'm often asked to comment on the fact that she was chosen to be the designer, and not an African American architect. I think that she created a very mysterious and fascinating, beautiful, and powerful space. And I am more interested in the standpoint she connected with when creating than in the issue of her "right" to do this space. I admire the work she did. At the same time, I am aware that choosing a non-Black person reinforces the idea of the absence of Black people both in architecture and in general, and of Black females in general. I love the work she did, and I also think it would have had a different, and potentially more compelling and powerful message had a young Black female architect designed that space. For everyone who entered that space would know who designed it—who created it, who reinvented it, transformed it. That knowledge teaches. If a Black architect, female or male, had worked with that space, then every Black person, every person of any other ethnicity who entered there would have to be reminded of our place in a world where we think about space. This cannot happen if we are not given that opportunity or when people do not understand the importance of thinking critically about the choice of ethnicity in relation to who the architect is. I'm not an essentialist. I don't think that just because one is Black and an architect that person can create a space that engages African Americans' relation to space (because we both know there are Black architects who could not bring any special sensibility per se). But there are many Black architects who are grounded in just the kinds of traditions we are talking about, who have a unique and distinctive perspective to offer. Their presence needs to be acknowledged and valued. There is a new book about Paul Williams and his architecture in Los Angeles. Although he was the type of architect in a traditional white world who did assimilate in some ways and who did not want his architecture to have any mark of Blackness, his presence matters to us. We need to know he existed, to see his work. And it is so interesting to think of that moment when we will be able to open up books and read about architects who are Black or who have been inspired by African American experience and love of Blackness to see how that love informs how we think and talk about space. And I think people don't want to acknowledge now that emotionality and feeling determine how we see what we see and how we make what we make.

LW-B: Right. There is also Jack Travis's book on African American architects. It is very informative. It lets people know that African American architects exist, but it is basically about the *practice* of architecture. Jack is doing a second book now (to which I'm contributing a theoretical piece on gender and culture)—one which engages our aesthetic interests.

bh: Absolutely, not the aesthetics.

LW-B: Right.

bh: The discourse of aesthetics, of theorizing about artistic practices, continues to be seen as a privileged domain from which Black voices can be excluded. We often exclude ourselves from these conversations. You and I want to bring an end to that exclusion from the location of Blackness and femaleness. In fact, from the location of Black femaleness.

LW-B: Exactly. Many women bring to architecture a willingness to see the way our entire being, feelings, and thoughts help us to understand and look beyond the surface of a structure. But just as women's cultural backgrounds vary, their seeing differs.

bh: Absolutely. And I think that when male architects, both white and nonwhite, write about this kind of emotive relationship to architecture, their thoughts are often much more privileged than when feminist thinkers and women thinkers in particular approach architecture in this way. Because if a man is theorizing it, especially if he is white and male, then somehow it has credibility, it has academic legitimacy in a way that some people would say to you, But what does bell hooks's essay "An Aesthetic of Blackness" have to do with architecture? I think we tend to be silent because we have been socialized to think we have no right to speak about these issues.

LW-B: And I do have a right to interact with architecture as a phenomenological subject, not merely as a person who is able to make decisions. And I have a right to articulate how architecture feels and what makes it manifest. To be able to experience and relay architecture beyond the object of someone else's examination and beyond a traditional academic perspective. To simply place my experience at the center and use that location for seeing and understanding affirms that I have much to offer the discipline of architecture.

bh: Also acknowledging that the world we are living in is one where space is becoming smaller and smaller really calls for a rethinking of architectural cultural practices. We need work that is inspired by "prophetic aesthetics." The cultural critic B. Ruby Rich uses this phrase, drawing on the work of Cornel West. A prophetic aesthetic calls us to talk about what it means to raise generations of architects with a multicultural sensibility who will think about architecture not just as a profession but who will think about spaces that everyday people inhabit and about our accountability toward making those spaces wonderful and inhabitable space. I mean, all my life my concern with space, with the dwellings we lived in, began in my critical engagement with those shacks—with little wood-frame houses on the wrong side of town. Mine is a geography and an architecture that grew out of the experience of racial apartheid and class exploitation.

LW-B: That also reminded you of the primordial hut.

bh: I had the pleasure of coming into your environment and seeing how you have used your visual and aesthetic sensibility to create a home place that is exciting, visually moving. One of the things that I was so awed by was realizing how so many homes that Black people live in today, especially poor Black folks, reflect only our relationship to consumerism, to a notion of someone, something, some catalog outside of ourselves telling us what is desirable. Hedonistic consumerism, which includes a desire even for things which are cheap and ugly, threatens to consume our relationship to the aesthetics of space—to home. That is why we must recover the oppositional aesthetics that have shaped our relation to space historically. Black people must recover the awareness that poverty does not mean that you cannot have an aesthetic sensibility.

LW-B: I think also that we have to be sure that, as we recover, we continually emphasize that architecture really is informed by culture. Something is made and becomes architecture in the true sense because it becomes a spirit, so to speak, with the person who is dwelling in it. That whole notion of dwelling that Headier writes about is a notion that is now used in architectural writing as a kind of intellectual high point in order to talk about space and the way that spaces feel. But when it comes to dwelling, and dwelling in the ordinary way African Americans generally do, all too often there doesn't seem to be anything in these understandings that is thought of as something that should be used as a resource. Black folks need to know that we have visionary cultural practices that must be cherished and treasured. Paule Marshall reminds us of this in *Praisesong for the Widow* when she writes about all that has been lost, declaring: "[We] behaved as if there had been nothing about [ourselves] worth honoring."

bh: Memories are a cultural legacy we must honor. By continuing to perpetuate the creative relationship to space particular to the African diaspora, we acknowledge our history, its particularity and urgency. This also means that it is our task as insurgent Black intellectuals and critical thinkers to articulate these relationships theoretically and analytically so that they will be documented in a way that allows them to be sustained in print. This practice means that Black people won't have to constantly reinvent this knowledge orally to convince a world outside ourselves that we have had and have a complex relationship to space, to architecture, and to the politics of the visual.

LW-B: bell, those concerns are motivating me, at this stage in my adult academic architecture career, to examine anew Gullah architecture. I call it an architectural language of intercultural processes. In our thinking, dreaming, and planning of place, we give recognition to dance, to language, to cooking, to all kinds of different cultural phenomena. Yet we don't give that same credit to architecture. Right now I am continuing to explore my cultural background and using that personal experience and my studied knowledge of Gullah dwellings to theorize about architecture. This is just like linguists' arguments that in a Creole language there is a deep structure and then there's the vocabulary and the lexicon. Well, to me, the architecture of the Gullah and all areas of the African diaspora have a "deep structure" that must be critically examined. I just finished doing intense work in the Caribbean, and I spent this past summer in East Africa. I find that in all areas where there are communities of people of African descent, there is a deep structure. There are commonalities in the way we use and shape space. We like outdoor spaces. And in our essential kind of lifestyles, the one that you recall from your father and your grandfather, and the one that I recall from summers in the Sea Islands and in the Charleston area, the inside of those was an area for storage and for sleeping. And as much as possibly allowable by climate, the outside was also a place shaped for living. We fashioned that space outside, too. And we married the outside to the inside to mitigate the hot climate and to accommodate needing more space. And we made a place outside to accommodate our need for communal space, a space where everyone could come to.

bh: That's interesting, because in the piece I am now writing about space I talk a lot about the yard—extending the idea of space beyond internal structures—particularly in talking about my grandmother's house and her architectural thinking about her house and the adding on of rooms, her inclusion of the yard. The yard was seen as just as crucial to the fashioning of that space. Making the yard a private space was important, and folks worked to decide where to build porches or to hang swings. These were the outside meeting places. And, once again, no matter how poor you were, you still thought very deeply and in a complex way about positioning swings, determining whether it would give you a view of certain things and people, including your neighbors. That kind of spatial thought is the exciting work that you are doing and that we hope to see more and more architects, and critical thinkers who are not architects, theorize.

LW-B: In your memory, do you remember the yard being a swept space?

bh: Oh, absolutely! I remember the specific broom for the yard.

LW-B: Yes, and cooking outside . . .

bh: And having to care for that space. This is something that was really exciting for me to think about—theorizing the yard as a public space, the yard as a place of display—because this is something valuable that I continue to draw from Alice Walker's essay "In Search of Our Mothers' Gardens," because those gardens were also about transforming one's space, one's shack, house, yard.

LW-B: The whole idea of domestic domain included more than the house itself. We need to think more about reclaiming the value of those places. We need to think more about spatiality, about the house and the yard and the interaction between the two. We need to think about the porch as a transitional space. And should that space of opportunity be called an African American architectural aesthetic? A transformation which recognizes our architectural intervention in New World environments?

bh: Overall, we have to think deeply about the cultural legacies that can sustain us, that can protect us against the cultural genocide that is daily destroying our past. We need to document the existence of living traditions, both past and present, that can heal our wounds and offer us a space of opportunity where our lives can be transformed.

Aesthetic Interventions

Always engaged with the issue of representation as a means by which the self is constructed and made visible, in her new work Emma Amos makes the canvas, the blank sheet of paper, a cultural site for critical exploration of art practices. Interrogating the way in which aesthetic sensibility is shaped by the particularity of artistic vision, as well as showing how that vision is informed by constraints imposed by a concrete politics of representation that maintains and perpetuates the status quo, Amos disrupts the essentialist assumption that a pure imagination shapes artistic work. Showing us that all art is situated in history, that the individual choice of subject matter reflects that situatedness, in her new work Amos articulates a vision of universality that coexists in a dialectical relationship to the particular.

Starting from the standpoint that the politics of racism and sexism create a cultural context wherein white male artists work within an art world that is predisposed to accord them recognition and visibility, Amos begins her new work by calling attention to the constraints that limit and confine all those "others" who are not in the privileged category. Within white-supremacist capitalist patriarchy, images of power and freedom are symbolically personified by the white male "subject," in relation to whom all other beings are constructed as unfree "objects." At the outer limits of otherness, then, one finds the image of Black femaleness, personifying within the existing culture of domination, powerlessness, a lack of agency, no capacity for transcendent vision. These traits remain the properties of the powerful. Any Black female who dares to claim them is out of place, transgressing boundaries, a menace to society.

Few African American women artists would understand this better than Amos. Making a commitment to art in the 1950s and moving from the sheltered comfort of privileged-class Southern Black life to the Central School of Art in London, and finally to New York City, where she hoped to come into her own as an artist, Amos knows firsthand the barriers that keep art a closed world only the chosen can enter. Like many Black artists, female and male, she can look back and identify the segregated world of Black culture as the location that first inspired her to choose to make art. In that world it was as natural for a Black female to claim art as a terrain for cultural exploration as for the sun to shine. Segregation meant that no one questioned Amos's right to claim art. Since she was raised in a home where art and Black intellectual work were valued, writers and artists were familiars in her world. The barriers and checks on creativity began when she left that protected space on the margin to try and make it as an artist in the mainstream art world.

Being the only woman member of Spiral, a group formed by Black artists in the 1960s that included Romare Bearden, Norman Lewis, and Hale Woodruff, Amos learned early to work around the sexism of men, Black and white, who did not take women artists seriously. Trying to show paintings that featured white figures, Amos came face to face with the racism of the art world, which felt it could best package her work, or that of any Black artist, by projecting it as always and only about the representation of Black images. Despite institutionalized systems of domination that discourage females from making a lifelong commitment to art, Amos continues to work. After years of being silent about the ways in which the politics of domination shape art practices, Amos began to speak out in the 1970s.

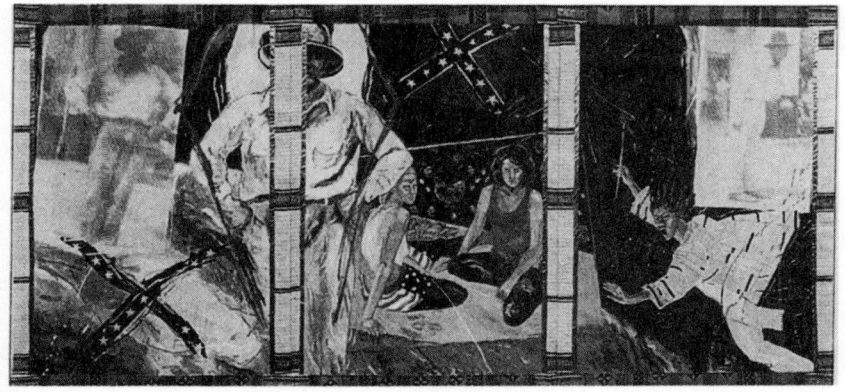

Emma Amos, The Overseer, *c. 1992.*
Acrylic on canvas with photo transfer, hand made weaving by the
artist and African fabric borders. 84" × 168".
© *[2024] Emma Amos / Licensed by VAGA at Artists Rights*
Society (ARS), NY. Courtesy of RYAN LEE Gallery, New York.

Her speaking was informed by feminist cultural politics, collaborative rebellion with other women artists, and engagement
with feminist publications.

While women artists are often encouraged to talk in interviews about the impact of racism and sexism on their lives and
work, it is common knowledge that an artist risks having her
work taken less seriously in the art world if the subject matter is
overtly political. Yet again and again artists from marginalized
groups, who continually struggle to create a cultural context
where their work can be recognized, find they must place artistic practice in a political context not only to identify the issues
but to overcome limitations, to create the space where boundaries can be transcended, where the work and the artist can grow.
Clarifying the reasons this resistance is necessary in *When the
Moon Waxes Red*, Trinh T. Minh-ha explains: "To challenge the
regimes of representation that govern a society is to conceive of

how a politics can transform reality rather than merely ideologize it. As the struggle moves onward and assumes new, different forms, it is bound to recompose subjectivity and praxis while displacing the way diverse cultural strategies relate to one another in the constitution of social and political life." Charting in her early work the social construction of the artist's identity in relation to the private world of kin and family, of loved ones chosen outside the realm of the familiar, in her new work Amos interrogates from the space of the unknown, the unfamiliar, the dangerous. Placing her own image in paintings and prints that depict a world where she could never "belong," Amos resists objectification and subordination. Subversively announcing her subjectivity via the imaginative appropriation of the space of power occupied by white males, she emerges from the shadows to call attention to subjugated knowledge. In the painting *The Overseer* she links repressive white supremacy to attempts to control and define images of whiteness and Blackness.

Exposing in her work the way racism depicts Black folks as objects rather than subjects of representation, Amos problematizes whiteness. Both in *Lucas's Dream* and in *Mrs. Gauguin's Shirt* she calls attention to the racialized sexism of white male painters like Gauguin, Samaras, and many others, who were never troubled by their rendering of the dark body in ways that reinforced white cultural imperialism. Of course, both historically and in contemporary times, when white artists choose to use Black subject matter in their work it is seen by the art world as a sign of their progressive inclusive vision. Critiques that question the nature of that representation tend to be viewed as bringing to bear unnecessary political criteria to the transcendent practice of making art. While Amos interrogates the sexism and racism that has shaped the artistic vision of many white artists, determining the ways they represent images of difference, her intent is not to censure but to illuminate through exposure. Presenting

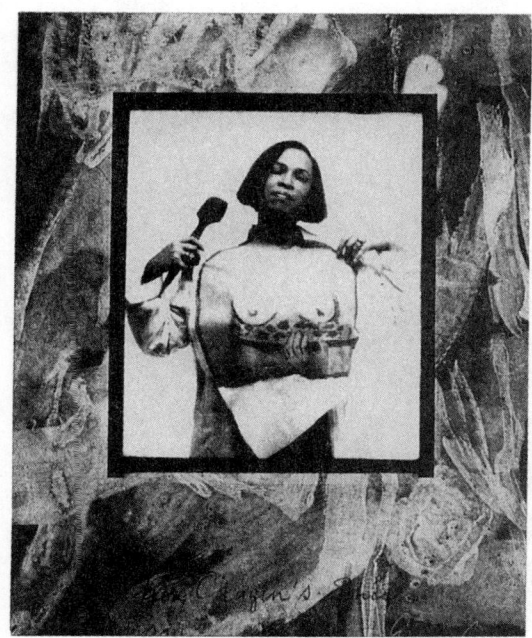

us with representations of white supremacy via her many images of the Ku Klux Klan in works such as *Ghosts* and *Captured*, she articulates the link between that whiteness which seeks to eliminate and erase all memory of darkness and that whiteness which claims the Black body in representation only to hold it captive. To resist that claiming, Amos challenges the use of Blackness as the space where whiteness can be redefined. To make that challenge she must lay artistic hands on the white body.

By laying claim to the white body through a process of objectification, visually represented in the painting *Work Suit*, and the print *Work Suit Try On*, Amos imaginatively appropriates the naked white male figure to gain artistic visibility. Subverting the paradigm to seize power, rather than deifying white male power, she pokes fun at it. Her white male body suit is not impressive. It looks ridiculous. A satiric comment on

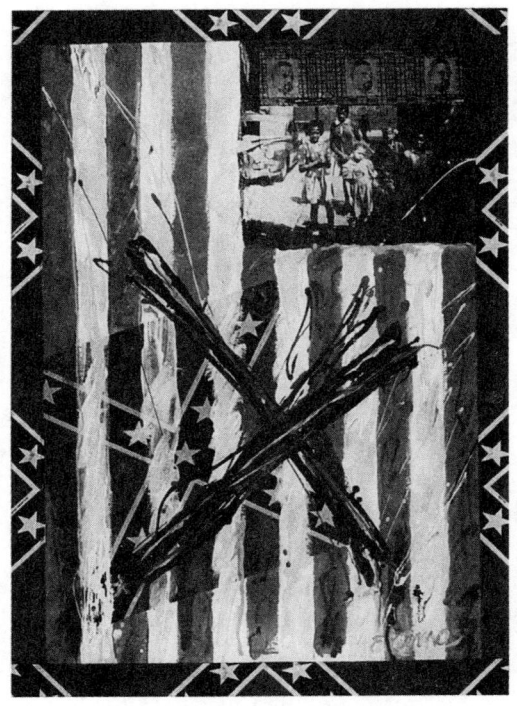

Emma Amos, X-Flag, *1992.*
Acrylic on canvas with photo transfer, handmade weaving by the artist and
African fabric borders. 58" × 40".
© *[2025] Emma Amos / Licensed by VAGA at Artists Rights Society*
(ARS), NY. Collection of Meredith Harper, New York;
Courtesy of RYAN LEE Gallery, New York.

the stupidity of categories, this playful mockery illustrates the reality of domination. In *Way to Go, Carl Baby* and *A. R. Pink Discovers Black* we are asked to reexamine race and gender in relation to control over the image. By reclaiming a site of image making inclusive of her subjectivity, and using it to critique and signify, Amos imaginatively dismantles the structures of race and gender privilege. This is the art of insurrection.

Linking her artistic practice with militant resistance to white supremacy traditionally personified by the revolutionary leader Malcolm X, in *X-Flag* and *Malcolm X, Morley, Matisse and Me*, Amos interrogates a politics of the visual wherein white male artists are frequently acclaimed when they use Black figures in their work while African American artists receive a message from the established art world that their use of white images will not be embraced, that even in the world of imaginative artistic practice no one will accept and condone Black artists toying with, controlling, shaping images of whiteness.

Amos asserts her right to work with the white image. Rather than regarding that image as "other," she urges recognition of the cultural mixing that calls into question an emphasis on racial purity. Critical of this type of narrow nationalism, Amos highlights what the Black British cultural critic Paul Gilroy in *The Black Atlantic World* identifies as "the theorisation of creolisation, metissage, mestizaje, and hybridity," terms that allow us to name "the processes of cultural mutation and restless (dis) continuity that exceed racial discourse and avoid capture by its agents." Against the backdrop of white supremacy, represented in painting and print by images of the Confederate flag and the Ku Klux Klan, Amos places images of that cultural mixing that occurs despite racism. She juxtaposes the reality of this cultural miscegenation with the fantasy of purity. Her work is in sharp contrast to that of artists who have used Black and white figures in ways that romanticize otherness, present it always and only as that which cannot be assimilated. Against those historical and current acts of appropriation where whiteness is figured as the sign of power and Blackness as a sign of powerlessness, Amos constructs an artistic landscape where there is parity. Her intent is not just to break the silence surrounding issues of race and gender as they affect subject; she intervenes and disrupts to lay the groundwork for a new vision of artistic freedom. That vision cannot be realized unless all the forms of censorship, both internal and external, are removed.

No doubt like many African American artists, once Amos understood that the art world was not as interested in the work she did that had white figures, she suppressed her own fascination with the interplay of different images. That self-censorship was ultimately more frightening than the narrow notions of Black art imposed by limited aesthetic understanding. Her new work repudiates this earlier censorship. More broadly, it challenges a traditional understanding of censorship as it affects artistic practice. Censorship is most popularly understood as a tactic used by the conservative right to control representation. Amos identifies those unspoken and unacknowledged forms of censorship that may emerge from an established art world that sees itself as always on the side of artistic freedom. Interrogating that world within the realm of the visual, she shifts the discussion away from a private behind-the-scenes talk about race and gender difference to a public "visual" discourse.

In her new work Emma Amos articulates a pedagogy of resistance wherein she calls for the linking of memory with power. Margaret Randall reminds us in *Gathering Rage* that "Authentic power comes from a fully developed sense of self, possible only when both individual and collective memory is retrieved." Linking her art practices to those of her peers in the works *X-Ray Showing Norman Lewis, Never for Vivian*, and *Fragments for Mel*, Amos lays claim to a legacy of participation in avant-garde art practices where Black presence is most often denied and erased. Again the issue is visibility—recognition.

Reworking the narrative of democracy and freedom, Amos evokes the flag, which appears again and again in her new work. However, it is represented as only a curtain, a veil that must be lifted if we are to see clearly the politics of our cultural reality. These acts of recognition, of both Black images and racial and cultural realities, come via acts of transgression and resistance, border crossings, and by participation in the cultural revolution, which Amos evokes through her use of the *X* symbol. In this work, *X* appears as the chosen space of marginality where the oppressed and exploited exit from a history that denies them subjectivity, refusing to be object, rejecting association with this dynamic. This refusal is highlighted in the print *Standing Out*, where the Black male thinker is set apart, watching the silhouetted white male and female appropriate space. It is this chosen position of "outsider" that liberates the Black male figure. Free of the established dominating order, a freedom gained by dislocation and disassociation, by the dynamics of struggle, Black artists are empowered to be self-defining, critically reflective, able to challenge, revise, and rework history. Art is revolutionized in the process. Freedom of expression is made more inclusive.

The rejection of domination as the only point of contact between those who are different that takes place in these prints and paintings does not lead to a reversal wherein Black power substitutes itself for white power. Instead, it allows for radically different liberatory visions of freedom to emerge. In this free world, identities are not static but always changing. Crisscrossing and crossbreeding become mutual practices, and the power to explore and journey is extended to all. Writing about the need for an insurrection that does not simply mirror the dominant culture in *When the Moon Waxes Red*, Trinh T. Minh-ha reminds us that "To disrupt the existing systems of dominant values and to challenge the very foundation of a social and cultural order is not merely to destroy a few prejudices or to reverse power relations within the terms of an economy of the same . . . Aware that oppression can be located both in the story told and in the telling of the story, an art critical of social reality neither relies on mere consensus nor does it ask permission from ideology." Defiantly, Amos places her image among the repressive fascist forces of white supremacy in *Blindfolds* and *The Overseer* to counter a cultural politics of exclusion and denial that would separate the practice of artistic freedom from concrete struggles for liberation. One struggle makes the other possible, not just for African American artists but for any artist. The convergence of possibility that is hinted at in the painting *Malcolm X, Morley, Matisse and Me* is an example of how Amos's work rejects a binary approach to the politics of difference that would have everyone's identity be fixed, static, and always separate. She replaces this paradigm with one where mixing is celebrated, where the cultural interchanges that disrupt patterns of domination are dismantled so that an ethic of reciprocity and mutual engagement forms the aesthetic grounds where the subject can be constantly changing.

Straighten Up and Fly Right: Talking Art with Emma Amos

bell hooks: It's the afternoon of May 12, 1993. This is bell hooks in conversation with Emma Amos. Emma, from where you are right now, has being an artist been a source of fulfillment for you?

Emma Amos: I can't imagine being anything but an artist. Yes, I think definitely a source of fulfillment. When I was a little girl, that was the only thing I ever wanted to be.

bh: Girlfriend, but how did you know there even was such a thing as an artist, as a little girl?

EA: I think I knew. All I did was draw, and I got responses to it when people said, "You're an artist," you know, "a little girl artist."

bh: That's wonderful.

EA: When I was in elementary school, I won poster contests and things like that. And when I was about nine years old, my mother tried to get Hale Woodruff to work with me a little. Hale was teaching at Atlanta University, making these gorgeous murals. And he must have laughed, and said, "A little girl! Are you kidding?"

bh: Well, I can tell you must be talking about a segregated Black environment, because people said you were a little girl artist, not that you were a little Black girl artist. Which reminds us that when we are in the context of segregated Black communities, gender differences are highlighted in a way that race is not highlighted. So you knew that there was something different about your desire to be an artist because you were a little girl?

EA: Yes. I don't think I knew I was a Black artist till many years later.

bh: Thinking of you beside Elizabeth Catlett in her late seventies, I think, here's this continuum of powerful Black women artists. Can you talk a bit about the evolution of coming to see yourself as somehow a Black artist? Using what the philosopher Cornel West calls a "race transcending vision," that little girl who was dreaming of being an artist wasn't thinking, "I'll grow up and be a Black woman artist" but "I'll grow up and be an artist." What's the point at which we move into seeing ourselves as both racially defined and defined more explicitly by gender?

EA: I became more aware of being identified by race when I attended college in Ohio. I learned that I was definitely different, because this was a mostly white college.

bh: You went to Antioch.

EA: Yes, after a completely segregated growing-up time, in Atlanta, with a segregated high school. And the colleges— Atlanta University, Spelman, Morehouse—had wonderful people. I mean, I didn't know that there was anything "wrong" with Black intellectuals, because I was completely surrounded by them.

bh: Absolutely. In retrospect, I see that when I was painting my little pictures in art class at my all-Black high school, it seemed perfectly natural that art should be a terrain of exploration essential to our intellectual development, and it's only when you move in different circles that you begin to question that.

EA: Well, even more after Antioch. Then in London, as an art student, I had that wonderful feeling of release. The English didn't dislike me because I was Black. They disliked me because I wasn't English. They also disliked Hungarians, and they didn't like French people, or any foreigners. It was a great revelation.

bh: I remember one of the earliest conversations I had with you. I was talking about my own pilgrimage to Europe, and how it was such a disappointment to me that I didn't find that special freedom there that Black expatriates had talked about. You said that the Europe you traveled to was that kind of moment, where you felt a greater sense of freedom and possibility. Talk about that some, because we hardly hear anything about Black women expatriates.

EA: There were and are a lot of them. A lot of women artists did go study, in Paris usually. It was a wonderful time for me, because I was in London with some other Black intellectuals. David Levering Lewis was there, and Preston King, a young man—he's one of *the* Kings—who left Alabama to go to Europe and never returned because, as a Black man, he refused to be drafted. I understand he's a professor in Lancaster, and a well-known lecturer. Anyway, I was in London when these people were there, in addition to picking up wonderful artist friends. Some of these people are still my friends. It was like a continuation of Antioch, really—that feeling that I belonged to a broader group. Young people going to school now segregate themselves.

Black students eat with each other and pressure each other to live in the same houses, doing all the things I wouldn't have imagined doing.

bh: That's because we grew up during the pain of segregation and were curious about what we could learn by moving into different circles, we felt we were being denied knowledge— experience. I don't see that longing to experience all kinds of difference in order to grow in many young people now.

EA: I think you're right. Did you feel especially that any institution was going to be *the* place?

bh: I thought that everything was going to be an adventure. Coming up in the segregated South, my notion of an artist, of the bohemian world, came from novels and books, and it wasn't realistic. Emma, what was it like to have that experience of journeying to Europe and then coming back here? How old were you?

EA: The first time I went to London, I think I was nineteen. I stayed there for a year and a half, went back to graduate from Antioch, and then returned to London to work and graduate from the Central School of Art. I think I was through with that whole thing when I was about twenty-two. And I went back to Atlanta and took part in what now seems like the galvanizing of energy and people that would lead to the civil rights movement. I spent this wonderful year meeting a whole bunch of bright, excited young Black folks, eager to make their mark in the world—people like myself.

bh: Unlike many young Black women, you did grow up in a milieu where Black intellectuality was celebrated and embraced.

Can you recall what this was like?

EA: I didn't know how special it was to grow up in that milieu until I went to college, went away to England, spent time in New York, and discovered that most people assumed that Blacks from the South are from some sort of plantation area. They don't have a true picture of the metropolitan areas in the South, or at least they didn't then. The assumption that you are unlearned, and that nobody in your family ever went anywhere or knew anything, was very painful. One of the reasons I did the piece *A Reading at Bessie Smith's Grave*, was to publicly thank my father for being a catalyst for the people that are in that piece.

bh: Describe those figures.

EA: The narrative of the piece is imaginary. It's about race and class, which is difficult for anybody to discuss in this country because there's not supposed to be any class system, and of course there is. I used my father as the centerpiece. My mother and father are first cousins, and my father had been apprenticed to his uncle, my mother's father, who had a beautiful drugstore which stood on a corner of "sweet" Auburn Avenue across from "Big Bethel" A.M.E. church. Daddy had gone to college in Ohio, and he's the one who told me to go to Antioch, because it was so liberal, it had Black students, even then! That was the only place I ever wanted to go.

Anyway, even though my father had this very respected uncle, his side of the family was poor, so he worked his way through college as a Pullman porter. He loved sports and all the things young Black men (with fresh images of slavery in their heads) admired in the 1920s and 1930s. Joe Louis was his hero then, and he read a lot.

In this picture there are references to W. E. B. DuBois, who

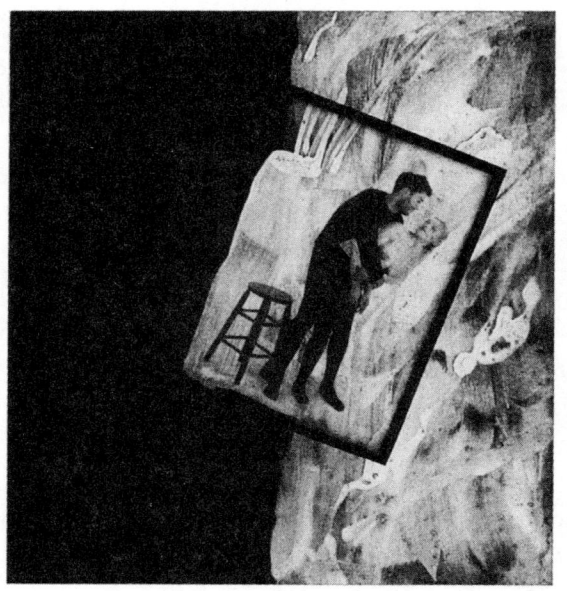

Emma Amos, Lucas's Dream, *1994*.
Photo transfer with silk collagraph. 22" x 19".
© *[2025] Emma Amos / Licensed by VAGA at Artists Rights Society*
(ARS), NY. Courtesy of RYAN LEE Gallery, New York.

came to our house when I was growing up, and to Langston
Hughes and Countee Cullen. Both my mother and father
bought us those writers' books, and we grew up reading them
and others. Zora Neale Hurston would come through Atlanta
on her trips to gather information for her anthropological work
(she was studying at Columbia with Franz Boas), and she would
come to my father's drugstore. He would get a whole bunch
of guys together, and after the drugstore closed they would sit
around drinking bourbon with Zora. And she would tell stories,
and they would tell stories (and she would write those stories
down). She came several times, and Daddy said she was wonderful. He said she could tell the raciest stories you ever heard. So I

wanted her to stand outside the reading, watching and listening, although in reality neither she nor Joe would have been invited by anyone but my father.

This story is really about class, because there never would have been a reading at Bessie Smith's grave if it weren't for me imagining my father bringing everyone together. W. E. B. DuBois wouldn't have thought that Bessie was one of the "talented tenth," right? She was just a blues singer. I think Paul Robeson would have come to a reading at Bessie Smith's grave, so I show him holding a songbook that belonged to her.

Then there was the problem of where Langston Hughes and Countee Cullen stood in this connection. I've read as many things as I could, and I'm not too clear on anything other than that Langston had this problem with Zora. They seemed to be after the same white woman's money. I did this piece as a response to David Lewis's book *When Harlem Was in Vogue*, where he gave Zora maybe a couple of lines, maybe a page. I asked him why he didn't give her more space, when he gave so much space to Langston Hughes. And he said it was because she had her hand out to that white woman. And I said, "Langston Hughes had his hand out, too!" They were both deep in the pockets of this white woman, whose name was Charlotte Mason. Anyway, I thought if a famous historian can use or not use something because he has an attitude toward it, then I as an artist can do that, too. And that's exactly when I painted a history I'd never read.

bh: Since the very beginning, you have been combining dream and reality in your work, surreal elements with concrete information about Black history. It's great to look in the face of that Joe Louis character in your painting, because it's very different from seeing photographs of Joe Louis. What strikes me most in your image is the color brown, the shadows in his face. The image has an intensity that suggests both his passion for his sport and also the turmoil of being a Black man in sports during his day.

EA: He was vulnerable in the same way that Zora and Bessie were vulnerable to fame, to misreadings and to high expectations. People used to cringe when they heard Joe Louis speak, because he didn't use proper English. But when he spoke he said wonderful things. He always thanked his mother after a fight, and when you think about our current jailed prizefighter, did he even have a mother, and would it ever occur to him to thank anyone?

bh: Clearly, Mike Tyson's early state of orphanhood has affected his ability to respond positively to his own self-image or to representations of women and the concrete reality of women.

Talk about your movement from the Black intelligentsia of the South to the big city of New York, and what that meant for you.

EA: Well, coming to New York with my portfolio of prints and all the painting I'd done, I thought I was a grown-up at twenty-three. I ran around trying to get a job teaching at the Art Students League, and Cooper Union, and I'm sure they were all laughing at me, but I didn't get the joke. They just said, "Oh well, we're not hiring right now," and I was sort of crazy to think that I could actually teach in one of those places then.

bh: What is most impressive about that period of your life is your certainty that you were an artist. Tell me more about what it felt like trying to establish yourself here in New York. One thing that distinguishes people of your upbringing from the South is that there are also all these other artists here. It's a much more competitive world.

EA: First of all, the community of artists is really big and intimidating. I think there were periods when I didn't know where to find other artists. I just lucked into meeting a group who were supportive of me when I was assistant teaching at the Dalton School for that first year. I was making peanuts, but I made valued friends. When I decided to leave Dalton, having studied textiles in England, I took a job as a weaver/designer with Dorothy Liebes, the famous textile designer, who respected my work as an artist more than my design experience.

I decided I'd better go back to school, and I chose New York University because it was convenient and I could work as a designer and go to school at the same time. It was kind of a mistake, because it wasn't Yale, you know, which would have been the validation supreme. But I met Hale Woodruff at New York University, though I never had a class with him.

bh: Did he remember you?

EA: Oh, he certainly did. And he apologized to me for having been reluctant to teach me years before. Hale was really mentoring me. I would go by his office and show him my work. He very much liked the prints that I had done in England, where I was a printmaking major in art school, and he started telling me about this group called Spiral. He said if I would lend him the prints, he would take them to Spiral and show them.

bh: What did he tell you about the group?

EA: He didn't tell me anything, except that Romare Bearden and Norman Lewis and some other men were members of this group. And it was up to me to find out who in the world they were.

bh: Were you the only woman in the group?

EA: I was the only woman and I was the youngest member, when they did invite me. I'm not sure they invited other people by looking at their work, but they were very nervous about having a woman in their group, and they wanted to make sure I was a real artist and not a dilettante or something. I think that they asked me to join the club (which met once a week for discussion) instead of women they knew, because those women represented some sort of threat, and I was only "a little girl."

bh: So that's where sexism entered in. It wasn't that they wanted to protect their male group. You have said that the group "talked about what it meant to be Black, and whether we must use our jazz and African influences, and do the same sort of work."

EA: I've tried to remember many times what it was like to be a member of Spiral. Mainly it was me listening to Norman. I know I spoke, but I can't imagine what I said. Norman talked about being a member of the Willard Gallery, and he talked about the problems of painting abstractly and being confused with being a Black artist and painting Black subject matter. He had been a figurative painter during the Works Progress Administration era. Those are some of his most beautiful works. But he had also been a member of the group of white artists that met at the Cedar Bar, including de Kooning and Ad Reinhardt, who was his friend, and Jackson Pollock, and that whole gang. In all the writing about that group of abstract expressionists, they had eliminated Norman, and I think some of his anger was because of that.

bh: When you see the film clips of that group, it's interesting how the camera practically erases him. He just comes across as this dark blob. His features are not visible, and the only thing that alerts us to his presence is his kind of shadowy, dark outline. *EA:* Right. So that's one of the things we discussed. The other was that Romy wanted to discuss negritude. Negritude was the big thing right then, and I hadn't read Senghor. I didn't really know what they were talking about. Some of them had taken part in that festival in Dakar, and so they were really up on it.

bh: What was your relationship to other Black women artists at this time?

EA: I didn't really know them. I knew of Faith Ringgold, because they mentioned having met her at some forum. I knew of Vivian Browne, but she didn't become a friend until several years later. And I knew of Betty Blayton Taylor because she had the children's art carnival at the Museum of Modern Art. I knew that there were Black women artists.

bh: I look at you now and I think of you as such a powerhouse in terms of bringing women artists together to have intellectual discussions about art. Where were you then? Were you caught in that traditional notion of the lone artist?

EA: I think so. That's a problem even now. Young people coming out of school are coming out of isolated campus environments or isolated art establishments. Coming to New York, they know there's a pantheon of names, but they think they're the only one of a given age. I like to reach out to those people.

bh: Let's talk about your encounter with Romare Bearden.

EA: Romy was very articulate and very smart and he knew his history, and he was not argumentative, as was Norman. Romy was not flashy. In personality, he was kind of like the glue for that group. His work he kept pretty much to himself except for one episode I remember, where he had been cutting out these magazine pieces and he brought them to a meeting and he wanted everybody to work on them together. This was a form of dealing with negritude, and he wanted to know if we could do something together and if something unique would come out of it. He wanted everybody to make clippings, and, somehow or other, nobody wanted to do it. I don't remember Norman's words, but I remember his attitude was "I don't want to do what you want to do. If you want to do that, go off and do it." And Bearden went off and did it by himself.

I didn't really know that he was famous. I knew that he was an exhibiting artist. It was kind of a shock to me to discover that just because you had regular exhibitions, you were a star to the Black community, and probably to the small white community that bothered to find out that there was a Black artist named Bearden.

bh: Bearden wrote about the negative response from early Black viewers of his work, especially that work that began to focus on what a lot of people saw as the low life, or the underclass.

EA: He definitely changed what he was doing, because he had been an abstract expressionist, as had I.

bh: Why abstract expressionism? When I began to develop my own idea of myself as a young artist, abstract expressionism, and the work of de Kooning particularly, was work I truly identified with. Is there some reason that we as African Americans have been drawn to abstract expressionism, more than to other movements?

EA: It's my theory that artists are extremely influenced by whatever is going on at the time they're coming into their powerful vision, whatever it is. And so even though I had been a figure painter as a teenager and I had taught myself watercolor as a child, as soon as I got to London and saw my first abstract expressionism—and it was the American abstract expressionists that I saw there—I became one. I just claimed that I'd always been one. Bearden, who was very important in the WPA period, painting many of the types of figures he would return to later, probably became an abstract expressionist with the first wave.

bh: It wasn't the central movement when I was trying to develop as a young artist. It was the freedom it suggested, that we could do all these things, the very kinds of things we see in your work now. You could have some realistic image at the same time that you could do something that would totally undermine it. I saw it as a place of possibility in painting. What abstract expressionism had that your art has so much of, Emma, is a quality of motion, a sense that there was truly an engagement with paint.

EA: Well, those are the things I wanted to deal with. Romy dealt with it in a different way. And Norman was not so much the paint-flying abstract expressionist as he was the quiet, solidly grounded, Ad Reinhardt sort.

bh: Would you say that about Charles Alston as well?

EA: I didn't know Spinky's work. And Spinky was rarely at the meetings after I joined. When he came, he didn't speak very much. It's only now that I've seen his work that I've come to appreciate it, but he was a star to Bearden and to Norman Lewis, because he'd become well known before they had.

bh: When did you begin to think critically about yourself as a woman artist and as a Black woman artist?

EA: I don't think I really began to think critically about myself until the late 1980s. Teaching drawing and painting at Rutgers, I realized that I had to know more. I had to be able to stand back and critically assess my own work if I was going to teach all these people who painted and drew very differently. Mini-malist art was beginning to wane, and I was meeting figurative artists again. Leon Golub, another Rutgers professor and a fig-ure painter, was having this great explosion of interest. I had to learn how to put what I do in some kind of perspective.

Earlier, I think the civil rights movement made me more critical about what I was doing. I could not in good conscience paint just lovely colored pictures with brushy strokes without having some of the pain and angst of the things that I wanted to say about women, Black women in particular, in the 1960s. I did that, but without anybody telling me what to do, or any-body looking at the work, or any of the men responding to it in any way. The work was never shown.

bh: I know you respect Elizabeth Catlett deeply. Where was your consciousness? Did you know about her work?

EA: I knew about her only through what the men said, and all the men said about her was that she'd been married to Charles White. She was just an appendage as far as they were concerned.

bh: So here was this incredible sculptor and they could not acknowledge that.

EA: Right. They were not in the teaching mode. They couldn't tell me where to look.

bh: It has always been your contention that when a Black woman artist walks into the studio, it is a political act. When did you begin to say that? How did the feminist movement impact on you?

EA: I think I began to know that nobody cared about what I was doing in the 1960s. I learned that by listening to the trials and tribulations of the guys, and also because I was not making little concentric circles as I made a splash in New York—I was just sinking to the bottom of the pond, with not one little bit of notice that I was there.

I had my first child in the late sixties, and then I had another one, and there was just a little window of time in 1970 when a very well-known dealer was brought to my studio. She said she liked the figure paintings of the late sixties, but she could only show my work in 1970 if I painted her a whole new show. And that was impossible. Here I was, pregnant with my second child. Now, young women have assistants, have babies, and continue to work. They want it all. At that time, I didn't think that was possible. I had no female role models.

bh: But through it all—through this lack of role models, through this late-blooming feminist consciousness—you remained extraordinarily dedicated to the vision of yourself as an artist. I think that's really important.

EA: I had a lot of help. Bob Blackburn, at the Printmaking Workshop, was one of those people who insisted that I keep working while the children were growing up. But the real awareness came in the late 1970s, after I'd done my television series and had this big star turn that didn't have a thing to do with painting.

bh: Let's talk a little bit about that television series.

EA: During the seventies, when the children were little, I bought all these looms and was teaching weaving in the Village. I hadn't woven since I was a textile designer, but it seemed to be a way to make a few bucks. (I tell students that you have to have a hustle. People are not necessarily going to buy your pictures. They don't, even now, buy my pictures enough to pay the rent.) There was an enormous crafts boom in the seventies. Everybody was knitting, crocheting, and weaving, and I had full classes.

bh: The feminist movement brought a reinterpretation of these particular arts, and one of the things that disturbs me in reading some of the older material about you is the way people somehow saw weaving as not "real." There's a clear artistic continuum between the weaving that you were doing and your relationship to textiles and fabrics and how you interweave them into your art now. I think it would be very different for you to be starting out today as a weaver, because the way we see weaving has changed. Feminist art criticism has done a lot to challenge our perception of women artists working in fibers and with fabrics. Faith Ringgold's quilts are a great example.

EA: Well, I certainly knew not to admit that I was a weaver, because people held it against me. It was just a smart thing to keep your mouth shut and not to admit it.

bh: Another thing that I think distinguishes you from other women artists, as well as specifically Black women artists of your time, is that you have grown intellectually and artistically into someone whose work is informed by feminist thinking and practice. Could you talk a little bit about that?

EA: Well, I think I taught myself. My television series was called *Show of Hands*, and I was cohostess with a white woman who was a wonderful writer and a quiltmaker. It had been my idea, but WGBH in Boston was very nervous that a Black woman would have a show all by herself. I was on this star trip for about a year and a half, running back and forth to Boston to tape the series, and the series was built on the theory that an artist could learn any kind of craft if he or she put their mind to it. So we did shows on woodworking, on stained glass, on weaving, quilt making, clay, jewelry—it was great. What I think that show taught me was to be secure, that I could learn how to do something, that I could take it through to an end. It taught me how to speak in groups without being nervous, and I loved it. But when it was over, it was really over, and I had been a media star in Boston and a nothing in New York. I had to figure out a way of bringing that craft element that I had been developing into the art work. I got a studio in SoHo and started to relearn being an artist.

bh: I think your work has a very postmodern quality. You work so much with notions of fragmentation. I think of the images of falling. One of the things you said early on about those images that fits with what cultural criticism is saying is that you were producing those images in those historical moments when the world was beginning to shift. There was this decentering of Western civilization that we now talk so much about, and in that decentering process there has also been alienation. Lots of Black people, lots of women of all races and ethnicities are asking, "Where are we?" It's as though the ground shifted and we are floating or falling, as so many of your pictures suggest. To me, that falling in your work is a statement about what was happening and what is happening.

EA: One of the most important elements in my work is movement, and it's wonderful to hear you talk about it because I get so little critical response to it. I feel that the static work that I was doing in the sixties had no place once I learned about the women's movement, once I learned about how I was being considered as a Black artist. And so when I make a painting, I am trying to use both the expressiveness of the paint flow and the movement of whatever it is I'm using, so that everything is in flux. Sometimes I even tear figures apart and have arms and legs going in different directions. The metaphor of falling helped me discover that I wanted to invent people in the air, because that was a way of having absolute movement. They are not standing on the ground, in doorways, or looking out of windows. There's nothing that is stationary. This is a thing about flux.

bh: The falling images give you this sense of disruption, and yet the work really doesn't make a value judgment about it. It doesn't say it's bad for life to be disrupted. Instead, it interrogates the meaning of stability. In many of the pieces, certain things remain intact even as others are drifting, falling. This raises questions about constancy in the middle of change. What things remain solid for us in flux? This is truly expressive postmodernism—it says that we're not in that period when everything is stable and clear, and there are possibilities of loss but there are also possibilities of being found. I also think about falling in relation to the notion of surrender. Other people who've written about your work have had a tendency to read the falling images solely as about descent into some negative possibility.

EA: Well, you're the first person who's noticed that this is not a horrible thing that's happening to people. I want people to look at the faces. I spend a lot of time trying to get the expressions right. I want these people not to look scared. And there have been only one or two canvases where there has been any fleeting suggestion of pain in the face of the person who's falling. I want to have connection between the eyes; I want the people to stare out sometimes. Sometimes I want the falling figures to interact with each other, to be looking into each other's eyes or to be looking away from each other. I want to bring a tension to the relationship.

bh: I think that sensation of falling in our lives is such a frightening sensation that perhaps part of why critics have a hard time interrogating those significations in the work is our own inability to deal with teetering on the brink. I'm surprised that no one has talked about that very energetic sense of possibility that comes in the falling work, that makes you feel the sense of movement. I was thinking of this as a sort of self-conscious artistic energy, a kind of strategy that always deconstructs or challenges the notion of concreteness, the specificity of gender, race, what have you. There's a way in which these paintings force us to think about the paint. No matter who is behind this work, the Black woman artist or any other static representation, ultimately it's really about the paint and about what's going on in those images.

EA: People don't notice the choices an artist makes. I have to make choices every time I make a figure. I have to decide what color that figure is going to be. I specifically like to use Black figures and white figures, and few people recognize my figures as white when they are white.

bh: Look at that group of artists in Spiral and think about which one of them has become the major figure, Romare Bearden. We don't see those white figures in Bearden's work. It's interesting that he was interested in negritude, because what many people most celebrate in Bearden are those pieces that could be seen through a lens of negritude. How would people respond had Bearden's work been packed with representations of whiteness?

EA: It's very interesting, because you had to be told that he was Black. Someone once asked me, "Why is it that Black painters always paint their figures darker than they themselves are?" I thought about that and it was absolutely true when I looked at my own work. I'd done self-portraits where I pictured myself as being much darker than I am. I've used that as a springboard, to try to include what we really see, which is one of the reasons I use so many different colors of skin tone in my paintings. I want to show the range of the people I see on the subway.

bh: It's precisely that choice that may lead your work not to get the kind of attention it deserves, because your work isn't announcing an explicit engagement with anything that can be linked to primitivism, to an exoticization of Black representation. Part of what your work compels acknowledgment of is the diversity not only of skin colors and our engagement cross-race, but also our own positionality. While I love the Romare Bearden work that focuses on representations of the underclass or the working class, the fact is that Black people inhabit many locations. What about us being able to make aesthetic choices highlighting other worlds, that history you came out of, for example? Those images aren't about primitivism. They aren't about a particular way of framing Black experience. They are a challenge to our very notion of Black experience, and part of Black visual experience is our engagement with whiteness.

EA: We know all about it. There is no part of whiteness that we don't know.

bh: Much more than many Black artists, you choose to use

those images. I think that is a challenge for a lot of the looking audience.

EA: I hope my work offers some clues to our problems and articulates a different perspective. I try to stand outside myself and exercise control over what I see.

bh: I know that you've read the theories of postcoloniality and that you've made those political interrogations. Your work poses a kind of postcolonial challenge because it's saying that, in order for Black folks to visually assert the range of our subjectivity, we must assert our right as well to paint those white figures that are so much a part of our reality. You're using a lot of the new work to comment on the white painter as colonizing subject. People like Ernst Ludwig Kirchner and Karl Schmidt-Rotluff use these African and Oceanic sculptures as inspiration. White painters like Modigliani worked with Black images, but somehow that became an expression of a certain kind of power, of being a subject. As a full subject, you have the sense that there is no area of representation that's closed to you. And partially what you've wanted to assert, Emma, is that you, as a Black woman artist, are a full subject and there is no area that's closed to you. You don't get positive feedback for that in the looking world. The gaze that looks at your work is, as you just said, unable to see these white images.

EA: They're not able to see them. I don't know whether anybody else understands what I'm dealing with in this newest work. It's about just what you said—the way white painters have the freedom to use dark figures and to use the dark other. And, somehow or other, when I do the opposite it's not given the same leeway. We're not in the same game!

bh: I was struck and moved and saddened by a comment William Majors made about Spiral. He said that one of the problems with Spiral is that you couldn't criticize each other's work, and what I hear you saying is that there are ways that people haven't yet talked critically about your work. This is one of the major dilemmas all artists in marginal groups, and specifically African American artists, face. My concern with regard to the Basquiat show at the Whitney was that so many critics overwhelmingly focused on autobiography, as opposed to talking about the work. Speak some about how you think critical work in art also illuminates the possibility of what one can imagine, paint, what have you. Is there a positive relationship between the development of one's art and there being a body of critical work that addresses that art in its complexity and fullness?

EA: The average critic will write, "Isn't it interesting that there's a Black artist doing . . ." whatever it is. Since the first year that I came to New York, only Arlene Raven, Lucy Lippard, and a few others have written about my work in the same way that they write about white artists. There are very few chances for Blacks, other nonwhite artists, and women to get their work critiqued. This is for many reasons—among them, that there is so little good criticism written, that writing about "the other" is a low priority, and that the white critic feels safe focusing on the Blackness and otherness of the artist instead of learning to look at the art.

bh: When we look at work like your *Water* series, we can't just see it through the lens of race or Blackness, because those figures are suggesting so many other things. They're suggestive of one's relationship, again, to space, to what spaces we occupy. There's the whole sense of rebirth. And I wanted to talk about the way your work tries to frame memory. In the introduction to *The*

Evidence of Things Not Seen, James Baldwin has this incredible passage about memory, where he says:

> . . . what the memory repudiates controls the human being. What one does not remember dictates who one loves or fails to love. What one does not remember dictates, actually, whether one plays poker, pool, or chess. What one does not remember contains the key to one's tantrums or one's poise. What one does not remember is the serpent in the garden of one's dreams. What one does not remember is the key to one's performance in the toilet or in bed. What one does not remember contains the only hope, danger, trap, inexorability, of love—only love can help you recognize what you do not remember.

Why has memory—both historical memory and personal memory—been so crucial to you in the development of your work? I think about the psychohistory of African Americans, and how our sense of ourselves as a people was radically transformed by the movement from the agrarian South to the industrialized North. In some ways, your own individual autobiography also attests to how we are transformed by that: You are that Southern Black girl raised in a certain kind of protected environment, where your value and worth were acknowledged, coming into the North. And I see in your recent work the construction of a genealogy, what Derrida talks about in his work on the palimpsest. I see you tracing yourself, going back. I think about the work you're now doing with photographs that your "Uncle George" took at a totally different historical moment, but you're linking those things.

EA: I'm glad you brought up photographs, because I've always loved them. My family's photographs were just stunning, and then I inherited George Shivery's photographs from Mississippi and Tennessee, taken in the 1930s. And I've now started taking my own photographs. Photography is interesting because it seems not to lie, when of course we know that it does lie, because it's very selective about what it shows. Painting is assumed to always lie, because we have so many options when we set paint on canvas. We can change a Black model to a white model, which is what the French painters did, I guess, a hundred years ago, because Black models were cheaper. There were lots of Africans in Paris to pose for them. You can detect, in some of the figure paintings, the figures of Black Africans with white skin. That's lying. The camera does that, too, but in a different way, and now I'm playing with that theme.

But back to the question that you asked me about memory. A photograph can tell you that you were standing on the beach with your mother and your brother in 1947. Painting gives the artist a chance to manipulate the background, charge up the colors, add texture. Combining photographs with painting is making me use a sense that I don't even quite know how to articulate. It's manipulating memory that's real, because it's painted, it's photographed. I don't know how to say it better, yet. It's tricky.

bh: I think that's an eloquent way of putting it. There's always this will on your part to explore different media and different ways of expressing, and I think that's really exciting. You're not, as some people who have not looked at the range of your work might presume, stuck in the work you were doing years ago. There has been constant change and development.

You've been doing new work with Malcolm X images and with notions of the Ku Klux Klan. That links your work to, say, the kind of work that someone like Carrie Mae Weems is doing

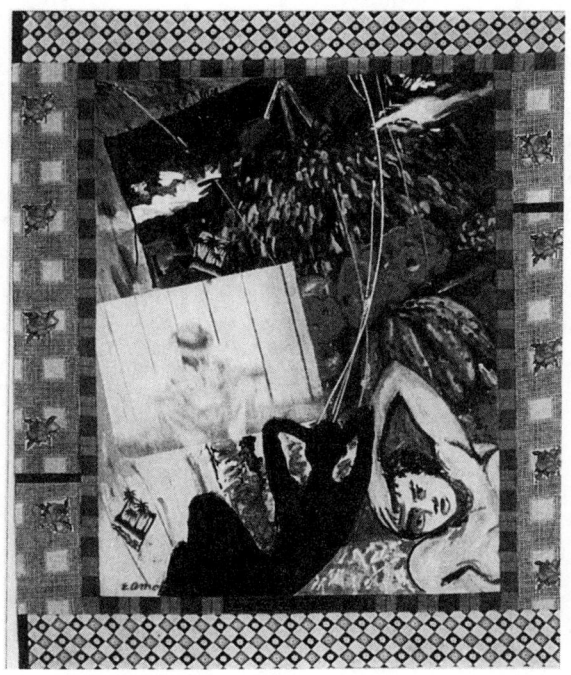

Emma Amos, Malcolm X, Morley, Matisse and Me, *1993.*
Acrylic on canvas with photo transfer, handmade weaving by
the artist and African fabric borders. 74" × 61".
© *[2025] Emmas Amos / Licensed by VAGA at Artists Rights*
Society (ARS), NY. Private Collection, DE; Courtesy of RYAN
LEE Gallery, New York and Art Finance Partners, New York.

in photography, or Andres Serrano. But you're not just working with a specific photographic image, you're mixing—you're
working with paint, you're working with paste-up, you're working with different things. Talk about what you want to convey
with those mixings.

EA: The Malcolm X image I've used lately has been printed

on African fabric I found on 125th Street, and I border all my pieces with African fabric or fabric I've woven.

bh: Even this bordering is about your using art to construct that historical diasporic continuum. You don't come out with that kind of overt image that says we are connected to Africa; you use that fabric that says there is this link. And I think that's one of the powerful movements in your own being, as someone who starts with weaving. It really invites you to an African past and carries you into this present where you can find Malcolm X on a piece of African fabric.

EA: They loved him in Africa. They saw him as a beacon. But I started using the *X* as a symbol of how hardly anybody gives a damn what I say. I don't want that to cut off other meanings of the *X* when I use it in my paintings to erase, to cross out, to show that I am silenced. The *X* symbolizes many thoughts.

bh: That's the kind of interrogation that was at the core of the Black Muslim use of the *X*: "Let's not only erase the slave master's name, let's reappropriate in that act our own capacity to name." That's part of what I see you doing in your painting, and it's interesting that you work in such abstract images and at the same time have been doing this whole series of very non-abstract portraits of women that you hope to leave as a legacy for your daughter. To some extent, that too becomes a critical intervention, because, like you, she has not been, and will not be, that young girl in her twenties thinking she was the only one. Because she'll be surrounded by not only the representation of community but the concrete power both in the images of those women and in the act of your honoring those images. I think that act is about establishing a different relationship both to yourself as a woman artist and to the entire community of women artists, and the strength of this work demands that other people do this also.

EA: They can't X the work out. *The Gift* is not possible to negate. That's what I'm calling this group of paintings of my women artist friends. Those women are too powerful to ignore. These friends sat for me as my support, as my mother's friends had supported her. I give them to my daughter India as her support, and I hope anybody who sees them will realize that there's something powerful and strong about women artists, about womanhood.

bh: Earlier in your career, when you talked about the falling images, you talked about "things out of control." You said. "Children try to save families. Families reach out for each other and books, art, memories, and ancestors rush past." And you say, "Reacting too late, regretting lost things, praying for future while falling past home." We see a kind of shift in your own work. Falling is no longer that central metaphor, because there is a kind of grounding that you are offering. It says, indeed, that this is the ground we stand on. This is you moving into history, becoming, at each stage of your life, artist, subject, more and more a woman of power, decolonized in that no group of people determines and contains your will to paint, to represent. That's why there's such a sense of history being made visible in your work.

In closing, Emma, what would you like to see happen in relation to an audience response to your work? Do you feel your work is seen enough? I remember, when I first came to see you, my astonishment that so much of this incredible, marvelous work of yours was not on other people's walls. And I know that's been changing. What could change that even more?

EA: That sounds like it might have to do with the marketplace, which has never really been interested in me. So I have no idea.

bh: That's exactly what I'm asking. If Black women artists—and all marginal artists, to some extent, who have not been chosen as the latest one—are always dealing with a marketplace that does not respond to them in the same way, then one does have to reconceptualize oneself as an artist. Clearly, you have not painted and do not paint for monetary reward, for a certain kind of fame and glory. You document so well both in art and interviews that there is this whole apparatus of domination, of racism, sexism, all of those things, that ensures a certain kind of silencing or negating of work that does not centralize whatever white people want to see Black artists doing at a given moment. But you have to have some kind of oppositional framework. I would think that many young Black women might think, "Well, how could I dedicate myself to being a painter?" I talked at the Cooper Union recently, and when you go on that floor where people are being painters, you don't see people of color. There is this sense that the area where we have least to gain is in the area of painting. So could you talk about that oppositional framework of affirmation that enables you to keep painting?

EA: I think that I've had to learn that success is not going to come to me the way it came to the blue-chip artists, and that only a small number of artists are really successful in the marketplace, anyway. And it's not going to be me, or, if so, it's going to be a late splurge on the order of what happened to Alice Neel, Elizabeth Catlett, or Faith Ringgold. Faith didn't get really well known until she had been out there for at least thirty years. Hustling that job, that painting—working hard and doing it without a lot of responses. I'm doing exactly what I always wanted to do, and that's what keeps me going. As an eight-year-old, that's what I wanted. Now I've got what I wanted!

Intervening Printmakers: Talking Art with Margo Humphrey

bell hooks: There's no doubt in anyone's mind that you are an exciting printmaker, Margo. There are not many African Americans, in general—and women, in particular—who have chosen to give to printmaking the kind of devotion and commitment that you have. Because we know that in the art world painting gets the most attention, artists who work mainly with printmaking rarely receive major attention. Yet you remain dedicated to the work.

Margo Humphrey: There is a challenge in printmaking. It is physical. Understanding the chemistry of an element that you're working on, whether it be a lithographic stone or a lithographic plate, is like a science. As an artist seeking out the best medium, initially I did not choose printmaking. I wanted to do sculpture. When I was in school, if you wanted to work in sculpture it was very difficult. At the time it was dominated by males—very macho. I found that working in printmaking gave me space. I no longer had to worry about work being damaged or broken, I could put things down and clean up in my own territory. Psychologically, this drew me to printmaking. Artistically, I like drawing. I like the physical process of making a mark, the image created; I like tonal levels. And you can't really do that as much in painting. However, in a sense, printmaking allows me to paint in that I use a liquid. It also allows me to be graphic. Making a print is challenging—you need a certain expertise.

Printmaking is based on multiples, not on a singular image. There is a challenge when you are working with the etch and the arch of whatever element you're working on. These factors determine the impressions you can get.

bh: Many people look at your prints, see the bright colors, the playful imagery, and don't see the deeper foundation of the work, don't understand the technical skill and creativity that go into making beautiful, compelling prints. This can only change as the work of printmakers is given greater attention and no longer devalued. The art world and our culture in general devalues printmaking.

MH: I have been an artist my entire adult life, and I see colleagues who started when I started—back in the sixties, right out of high school—who work in a different medium, either painting or sculpture, and their work is definitely more appreciated. I really like printmaking and have always wanted to represent my culture in this area. I have felt a need to do this work. It requires such a high level of expertise and skill. You cannot stumble. You just can't be a good printmaker without disciplined work, without the necessary training and without continual practice. It's learned and acquired over the years. I've worked almost thirty years to perfect my printmaking—particularly to make lithographs, working on stones and plates. I started this process the first year after I finished high school, honing my technical skills. Historically, most African Americans have worked with their hands. The history of slavery, the fact that Black folks were forced to do manual labor—the dirty work—makes some of us devalue any work that is messy labor. That's one of the reasons painting and sculpture are seen as more intellectual. They rarely require as much manual labor as printmaking.

bh: Your prints conjure up a mythopoetic universe. Your themes are metaphysical. They express artistically the ideas in the fiction of Borges, Lorca, Toni Morrison. Like these writers, in your work you bring familiar everyday images together with deep layers of meaning, evoking a feeling much like the experience one has watching a film such as *Like Water for Chocolate.* You are concerned with the metaphysical realm, the life of the spirit, and you focus that concern by drawing on diasporic Black culture—the experiences of the Black Atlantic world, connecting that focus with universal issues such as spirituality, unity with the earth, concern for the planet.

MH. I've always wanted my work to be universal. When I was a young artist, the role of the Black artist was hotly debated. Some folks wanted our work to be mere political propaganda. So I really searched for a deeper meaning, to be in touch with my artistic vision as a way to understand why I was doing this work in the first place. I did feel that the art had to have a message. And I sought that message in the things closest to me. Much of the work I do is autobiographical. It may examine the deeper philosophical meaning of our emotional states—for instance, a broken heart or anger. I work to convey the intensity of these states in my work. I also want the work to convey technical expertise, even as it draws one into a narrative. I am fascinated by symbols. I want the work to be multilayered. To not be superficial I use color to provoke, to startle, to engage the viewer in a particular narrative process. My engagement with color was intensified by travel. Visiting Fiji, South Africa, East Africa, Uganda, and teaching in those places, looking at the cloth, the color of the earth, I was just amazed by the impact color can have. In Fiji, I was very impressed by the way greens and blues worked together. I was impressed by the people within that environment, their use of color. When I went to Nigeria, everything was very brown and dusty, yet still very colorful. The color in my work tells the story of the use of color in Blacks' environment in both Africa and the diaspora.

When I was at Stanford University, a white professor—William Schockley—was insisting on the biological inferiority of Black people, arguing that we were not as intelligent, and actually claiming that this lack of intelligence was evident in the art we made. He devalued these very textile arts I am inspired by: quiltmaking, weaving, etc. Yet I know it requires intelligence, as well as artistic vision, to take a thousand threads and weave a work, discover a pattern. The skill and artistry is never simply "intuitive." I never wanted that word to be used to describe my work. The art that I make is intentional. The stories are personal, and I draw on African American experience—that to me is the foundation—but the values in my work transcend the specific and address the universal as well.

bh: Absolutely. I use the word *metaphysical* to describe your work, because you highlight human longing for spirituality, for self-realization. You use color to evoke the ontological. I think of all the works on "color healing"—on the power of color to transform the psyche, to change our state of mind. For the most part, this metaphysical understanding of the power of color is not common knowledge in our culture.

MH: Yet color can change everything.

bh: Absolutely. In your art work you bring together knowledge gleaned from diverse wisdom traditions—from Asia, Africa, the Caribbean, and, of course, from the West. The philosopher Cornel West constantly tells us that even though the West is decentered, the intent is not to repudiate the West but to highlight that which is most interesting to us as African American people about the West, to fuse the best of contemporary white Western cultures with non-Western ancient traditions that are close to our heart. That's here in your work.

MH: The color is a challenge. When people enter a gallery and see my work, it really engages them. To me color is a tool of power I use to engage audiences, to share my thoughts: it's the impetus behind the work. I combine colors in ways that you cannot ignore. You can enter the work the way you dive into a pool. You splash in, and then you get into this pool of information and begin to experience the work. It's just like a diver surfacing. You can shake your thoughts, then go back into the work and enjoy it. You can splash around and begin to experience each section on its own terms, discovering what it means to you, examining your reaction.

bh: It's this critically self-conscious element in your work that leads me to see critics as misguided when they use terms like *neo-naive* to describe the work. You clearly draw so much on different intellectual traditions, the new discoveries about ancient Egypt, the writings of people such as Ivan Sertima in his *They Came Before Columbus*, the texts of postcoloniality, etc. Really, we are no longer seeing ourselves and Blackness through the eyes of the colonizing culture. This cultural resistance to domination, to colonization, revisionist history, this is there in all your work. In your reworking of *The Last Supper* you draw again from the West, from the work of Leonardo, but you extend your focus to include Blackness.

MH: One aspect of *this* print is that there's a male who is a savior. I transplant the white male, putting the Black male in his place, so that we can look to ourselves for our own salvation. Salvation is within. I have a piece of sculpture that I'm working on called *Jesus*, and then it's hyphenated, *Jes-Us*, so that we can see that it comes from us, the rebuilding of our culture, of our attitudes toward the women in our culture, the attitudes toward children and whoever's going to partake in this new vision. The work is also about empowerment, about thinking of Black women and men as powerful and already with power from the start—not going someplace to get it, but being power in itself.

bh: Well, of all the contemporary artists I can think of, particularly among African American artists who highlight heterosexuality and conflicts between power and desire, you display in your work the most consistent vision of reunion between Black males and females. The vision encompasses both the realm of eros, the erotic, and spiritual reunion. That is made evident in pieces such as *Making Magic* and *The Getaway*. We see this reunion.

MH: Making Magic is an extension of the experiences that my husband and I had when we were young married people coming into a deeper knowledge of the spirituality of being together. That knowledge comes not just when you're physically intimate; it comes when you are engaged in everyday ordinary activity. In *Making Magic* there's a couple who have their hands in a container. The idea for this piece came to me when we were cleaning out a closet. Doing this, we were so close, deciding what was to stay in the house and what was not going to be part of the house. The things that we talked about had nothing to do with the work we were doing. We were communicating on such a high level. There needs to be more communication on a spiritual plane. It needs to be woven more into our relationships.

bh: Margo, your work really fuses those physical and spiritual levels. Like in the new piece *The Kiss*, where you see a combination of the notion of an eros that lifts us beyond the realm of the physical, even as you give us those powerful images of the physical, the tongue, the lips. What inspired *The Kiss?*

MH: I've always wanted to do erotic images. I'd done too many shows of work by African American artists and had not seen images of couples making love. And I wondered about this when we have so many erotic songs—the music of the Coasters and the Drifters comes to mind. These are classical, beautiful ballads that are still being played today and are so erotic. When you hear these songs, and almost anybody who lived through the sixties in this country knows which songs I'm talking about, these incredible ballads, there is such eroticism. Yet I go to shows of Black artists' works and I see so few depictions of intimacy in relationships despite these passionate, passionate love songs. And I thought, "Well, let me just step into this territory, let me talk about the intimacy and the passion. Let me put some of that out there." I really wanted to do an erotic series. Some of the pieces I'm doing represent this experimentation with new subject matter. I want the work to be enjoyed. I don't want anybody to be repulsed. Our culture's in a real sexual revolution with the impact of AIDS. Intimacy is part of the human experience. It needs to be expressed in visual work by African American artists.

bh: One element I see in your work that is not often visible in visual art is imagery depicting sexual ecstasy. *Midnight Lovers* reminds me of images in tantric art, especially the position that the male and female are in: you depict a union of souls, of body, mind, and spirit.

MH: Midnight Lovers is really about intimacy, lovers who engage in mutual consent and a mutual level of communication. It is about equality, shared desire. When you look, you notice the male and female are always on the same level. Here they are on earth—in intimacy, close together—and then here they are in paradise, the heavens.

bh: That union in the heavens is there, the lovers facing each other, and in *The Getaway* they're in the clouds together.

MH: And in *Midnight Rendezvous* the lovers are in this wonderful garden, this mystical garden of love with the flora and fauna, so I depict intimacy in diverse ways. In *The Getaway* this man and woman are truly in love, and all he's doing is just touching—his hand is on her heart—and so he is just pulling her through the sky and they are together. The allegory depicted on the bottom part of the image is the feeling of the woman, in that he is taking her away and she is on this wonderful, wonderful ride. The tiger that appears represents the sexual energy and all that's contained in that. The sky has chili peppers floating down, which is a sign, in the ethnic culture I come from, that their love is hot, intense. My grandmother used to cook with lots of chili in New Orleans. It's all very sensual.

bh: Sensual is precisely the word. It's the deep sensuality of the color in your work that often leads people to ignore the incredible depth of political and intellectual imagination that informs this use of color. Here I am thinking of your new work, *The Haitian Compassion Suite*, which compels audiences to think deeply about politics. Your work has that marvelous quality of not being in-your-face political propaganda in any way, always being true to the imaginative realm, the artistic vision, while having a political vision as well. In this work, that vision is the redemptive sense of Africa, a sense that Black people in the diaspora need to connect to restore our integrity of being. These themes are present in all your work, from its very beginning to now, whereas in *The Haitian Compassion Suite* you focus on immigration, identity, and nationality.

MH: This work has autobiographical roots—I have relatives from Port of Spain. This connection generated my concern with Haiti; it was about my family. I had such a hurtful feeling when the news showed refugees fleeing on a boat while the United States government was turning away Haitians at our shores. People were jumping overboard and drowning. I looked at this and had visions in my head of Africans in slave ships jumping overboard. It was as though history were repeating itself. I needed to talk about that. It was such a deep sorrow that I felt. I wanted to talk about the beauty of these Black people, to show that their lives are valuable, that their culture is valuable. Making art highlighting their predicament was a way for me to let people see what is actually happening. Then I decided that I couldn't just talk about the people in this one boat. I had to talk about their whole culture. I used the work to convey information about a beautiful naming ceremony in Haitian culture, how they have a cleansing ceremony. I also went back to emphasize the injustice and the inhumanity of imperialism and racism directed toward these people, who turned to their gods and their inner thoughts for solace and substance. They seemed to be deserted by everyone. And I wanted to call attention to that situation with art. It is really deep. As an artist, I felt I needed to be politically engaged. This is a sociopolitical war. It needs to be talked about. I haven't gone to Haiti and drawn the bodies in the street. That is not where my artistic temperament lies, to talk about the atrocity firsthand. With art and imagination I can bring to people's mind the beauty of a culture. As they think about this beauty, the culture, they can also think about what's happening to it.

bh: That complex vision comes through in pieces like *A Monument to Faith* and *The Ceremonial Baptism.* In these pieces you seem to strive to create images that do not encourage the viewer to feel sorry for the Black people in the boat. You depict the magnificent cultural retentions, especially those spiritual beliefs that sustain Haitians and all of us Black people in our moments of extreme crisis. In so many ways, your work is a kind of archeology of belonging, a search for home. It's amazing to me how many times structures of home appear in the work, both on the individual, personal level and on the global level. We often forget that Black people are an exilic people, that we live in exile, that there's a way in which we long for home, for homecoming. It seems to me that these yearnings are celebrated in your work. It is so prophetical. You take representations of Black love and romance that we see also in the work of people such as Jacob Lawrence and Romare Bearden. Yet you expand these images, taking them to a deeper level. In your work there is a vision of gender unity and interdependency between male and female that we don't see in the work of these male artists. There's also that prophetic vision of Black liberation that celebrates gender equality. Often when people evoke Africa and ancient spiritual traditions, they highlight the male figure exclusively. You give us a prophetic vision that highlights the Black female wisdom tradition. We see that in a piece like *Lady Luck Says Come Take a Chance,* that element of mystery and prophecy that's there in Voudou, that's there in Santeria, and that's in Christian evocations of grace. There's this fusion of mysticism and a prophetic tradition in your work.

MH: I was raised in a home with many different religions, from Lutheranism to Jehovah's Witness. My mother was a Sunday school teacher. I was always involved in different religions. Living in the midst of such religious intensity, I didn't like institutionalized, brand-name religion. I was into spirituality and want mystical spirituality to just be there throughout my work. In *Lady Luck* specifically, I talk about life here and in the hereafter. There are birds in this print, ghost birds, to guard you in the afterlife. There are two birds on the right and left that guard you through your life here on earth. The mysticism is there in nature, and everywhere. The work celebrates this.

Representing the
Black Male Body

A revolution happened in feminist discourse when race was included as a category of analysis informing the construction of gender identity. As a consequence, feminist visions of the body politic were expanded. Racist assumptions about African Americans that had always been accepted were challenged. An overall critique of sexist and racist standpoints in various disciplines created necessary interventions and change. As the feminist movement progressed, discussions of the body were highlighted, focus on the "politics of the body" was centralized. Yet, as Susan Bordo emphasizes in her introduction to *Unbearable Weight: Feminism, Western Culture, and the Body*, the groundbreaking role that feminism played "in developing a 'political' understanding of body practice is rarely acknowledged." Calling attention to ways in which contemporary scholars engage a historical understanding of body politics, Bordo stresses that there is a tendency to move from Marx to Foucault in a manner that erases "the intellectual role played by the social movements of the sixties (both Black power and women's liberation) in awakening consciousness of the body as 'an instrument of power.'" Inspired by the critical thinking of Black females engaged in the feminist movement, the revolutionary interventions created in feminist theory begin with the call to reassess the body in relation to the question of race.

The Black body had always received attention within the framework of white supremacy, as racist/sexist iconography had been deployed to perpetuate notions of innate biological inferiority. Against this cultural backdrop, every movement for Black liberation in this society, whether reformist or radical, has had to formulate a counterhegemonic discourse of the body to effectively resist white supremacy. In reformist agendas, that discourse invariably took the form of repression and erasure. If Black men were seen as beasts, as rapists, as bodies out of control, reformist movements for racial uplift countered these stereotypes by revering the refined, restrained, desexualized Black male body. If Black women were depicted as sexual savages, hot pussies on the lookout for ready prey, then these stereotypes were countered by images of virtuous, repressed Black ladyhood. Radical militant resistance to white supremacy, typified by the sixties' and seventies' Black power movements, called out of the shadows of repression the Black male body, claiming it as a site of hypermasculine power, agency, and sexual potency. That celebration was combined with a critique of white racist stereotypes. Black male writers and activists, from Eldridge Cleaver to Amiri Baraka, were talking through the body.

This focus on the Black body was extended and rendered more complex as Black female engagement in revolutionary feminist thinking led to an interrogation of sexism both in regard to ways in which white racist aesthetics subjugated and colonized the Black body and the ways in which the segregated spheres of Black life sanctioned Black male domination, subjugation, and exploitation of Black females. Importantly, the critical work of individual Black women writing feminist theory broke new ground by constructing an intellectual framework for critical discussions of the Black body from a standpoint that considered race, gender, and class. Much of this work emerged from critical thinkers who were both Black and gay (Audre Lorde, Pat Parker, Joseph Beam, Essex Hemphill, Hilton Als, Marlon Riggs, to name just a few). Feminist and queer theory established a broader context for discussions of Black body politics.

Ironically, psychoanalysis, as the established academic location that most engages a discourse of the body, was one of the few disciplines where white critical thinkers were unwilling to reassess their work in light of contemporary interrogations of racist biases in the development of specific epistemological frameworks. The rigid refusal to consider race as at all relevant on the part of feminist critics using psychoanalysis to reformulate critical thought in relation to gender served as a barrier, making it impossible for a substantive body of diverse work to emerge that would expand our understanding of the body politic, that would no longer erase the Black body. While many white women engaged with feminist thinking had found a necessary link between feminist politics of the body and psychoanalytical discussions, individual Black women doing feminist theory often found it difficult to constructively use psychoanalytical frameworks to discuss Blackness because we felt that work could not be done effectively without an initial interrogation and deconstruction of the ways in which racial and racist biases have informed both the academic field of psychoanalytical thinking and scholarship and the realm of clinical practice so as to devalue and exclude race. Despite these barriers, courageous individual critical thinkers are increasingly using psychoanalysis in discussions of race. It remains abundantly clear that it is useful for Black critical thinkers (and our allies in struggle) to engage feminist theory and psychoanalysis as ways of knowing that broaden and illuminate our understanding of Black subjectivity—of the Black body.

From my years of undergraduate study to the present day, sustaining my interest in psychoanalysis has required reimagining foundations and inventing strategies of inclusion that make a space for thinking about racial identity. As an undergraduate studying the work of Norman O. Brown, I was profoundly moved by his insistence in *Life Against Death: The Psychoana-*

lytic Meaning of History that the purpose of psychoanalysis is "to return our souls to our bodies, to return ourselves to ourselves, and thus to overcome the human state of self-alienation." Both then and now I think about the meaning of healing the split between mind and body in relation to Black identity, living in a culture where racist colonization has always deemed all Black folks more body than mind. Such thinking lies at the core of all the stereotypes of Blackness (many of which are embraced by Black people), which suggest that we are "naturally, inherently" more in touch with our bodies, less alienated than other groups in this society. The absence of critical frameworks that look at the convergence of racism and sexism in systems of domination that privilege the Black body rather than deny its carnality, only to exploit that embodiment in ways that create a modality of dehumanization and estrangement different from the one Brown refers to, creates serious theoretical gaps in any understanding of our collective body politic in this society. Brown did not have Black bodies in mind when he asserted that "the dehumanization of man is his alienation of his own body." For Black bodies, the fear has not been losing touch with our carnality and physicality but how to be in touch with our bodies in a way that is liberatory, that does not confine us to racist/sexist paradigms of subjugated embodiment.

Acknowledging the primacy of race in relation to feminist and psychoanalytical thinking about the body politic is a critical standpoint that has consistently led me to focus on the Black male body. When I first began to study feminist theory, I was puzzled by feminist scholarship that would talk in universalizing generalizations about how patriarchy equates the female being with the body and the male with the mind, because I was so acutely conscious of the way in which Black males have always been seen as more body than mind. Full recognition of this difference would have disrupted the neat binary gender polarities much feminist and psychoanalytical theory embraced. For the Black male body to receive substantive critical attention within psychoanalytic discussions, distinctions must be made between conventional ways of seeing the male body and the way racism disrupts and alters that understanding—the way it informs notions of identification, desire, fantasy. Calling for such a disruption in the essay "Fear of a Black Penis," Kobena Mercer shares this crucial insight: "Psychoanalytic concepts now float freely in debates on cultural politics, but there is still a stubborn resistance to the recognition of unconscious phantasy as a structuring principle of our social, emotional, and political life . . . It is in the domain of race, whose violent and sexy phantasia haunts America daily, that our need for an understanding of the psychic reality of phantasy, and its effects in the body politic, is greatest." Any liberatory visual aesthetics of the Black male body must engage a body politic that critically addresses the way in which racist/sexist iconography refigured within the framework of contemporary fascination with the "other" continues to be the dominant backdrop framing the way images are created and talked about.

Within neocolonial white-supremacist capitalist patriarchy, the Black male body continues to be perceived as the embodiment of bestial, violent, penis-as-weapon hypermasculine assertion. Psychohistories of white racism have always called attention to the tension between the construction of Black male body as danger and the underlying eroticization of that threat that always then imagines that body as a location for transgressive pleasure. It has taken contemporary commodification of Blackness to teach the world that this perceived threat, whether real or symbolic, can be diffused by a process of fetishization that takes the Black masculine "menace" and renders it feminine through a process of patriarchal objectification. Current patriarchal "feminization" of the Black male body is a process that takes place primarily in an aesthetic realm where the image produced has altered ways of seeing. In *The Male Nude in Contemporary Photography*, Melody Davis explains the term *feminization* this way: "secularized, men will lose their potency and force . . . they will become subject as are women to conditions, like pregnancy, beyond their control . . . they will become the sign for exchange value, and, as is the custom for women, be mere object, voids for the gaze." The equation of Black men with body, nature, the feminine appears in the rhetoric of nineteenth-century white male abolitionists. In a celebrated 1863 speech before the American Anti-Slave Convention, the white abolitionist Theodore Tilton urged white males to let go fear of their Black counterparts: "In all those intellectual activities which take their strange quickening from the moral faculties—processes which we call instincts, or intuitions—the negro is the superior to the white man—equal to the white woman. The negro race is the feminine race of the world." After slavery ended, Black men were constructed as feminine by white-supremacist rhetoric that insisted on depicting the Black male as symbolically castrated, a female eunuch.

In resistance to this construction, Black males cultivated and embraced the hypermasculine image. Richard Mohr's contemporary analysis of white gay male fascination with projecting this same image can be easily applied to Black males (straight or gay) who feel the need to counter theories of emasculation and mutilation by projecting the hypermasculine physique. In *Gay Ideas* Mohr reminds us that "under the burden of inherited sexual typographies, liberation is found in a working through of past oppression, a working through in which the constituents of oppression become morally diffused by being incorporated into and transformed in the self-creation of an oppressed minority's development of a positive ideology of and for itself." Historically, visual representations of the hypermasculine Black male were seen mostly in the photographs of sports figures. Two individuals who personified the use of the hypermasculine image as a means of resisting racism are Jack Johnson and Joe Louis. Fiercely handsome, these two Black males symbolized for Black people of their generation, and Black men in particular, via their rebellious masculinity, an assertion of militant resistance to racial apartheid. The contemporary African American painter Emma Amos works with the image of Joe Louis to chart a cultural genealogy of Black resistance in a five-part piece titled *A Reading at Bessie Smith's Grave*. In this huge painted plate Joe Louis stands between Zora Neale Hurston and Miles Amos, the artist's father. Louis is one of the mighty forces uplifting the race. Amos uses the full frontal solitary image of Louis in a silk collograph piece titled *Joe Louis*, which is painted with one color, a dark shade of brown. Dressed in boxing shorts, wearing his robe, hat on his head, hands in pocket, Louis is the ultimate image of Black male "cool." His cool pose conveys the feeling that resistance comes "natural" to him. For Black males of his generation Joe Louis was the embodiment of colonized Black masculinity asserting radical subjectivity. Though sexualized and eroticized by women and men of all races, Johnson, Louis, and the many Black sports figures who followed in their wake made their bodies political symbols. That legacy extended into the 1960s, when Black male athletes in all sports defiantly opposed white supremacy.

Conservative change in this politicized visual representation of the Black male body began to occur in the late 1970s with the commodification of Blackness, particularly the use of the Black male body, mainly that of sports figures, in television commercials to sell products. When that use of the Black male body converged with an overall change in cultural ways of seeing maleness that condoned the "feminization" of male bodies to sell products, the images that appeared were no longer directly challenging or subversive. Ironically, this cultural change was generated in part by feminist critique, the men's movement, and gay liberation. Appropriated by market forces, the subversive potential of the displayed male body was countered. This is especially the case for Black males, whose radical political agency is often diffused by a process of commodification that strips their bodies of dignity. Although the bodies of Johnson and Louis were commodified, the process was one that exploited and sensationalized political issues such as racial separatism, economic inequality. Rather than opposing those forms of commodification that reinvent the Black male body in ways that subordinate and subjugate, today's Black male athlete "submits" to any objectified use of his person that brings huge monetary reward. Black male capitulation to a neocolonial white-supremacist patriarchal commodification signals the loss of political agency, the absence of radical politics.

The quintessential symbol of the fetishized eroticized Black male body as an object of spectacle is the image of Michael Jordan. Repudiating identification with a politicized notion of Blackness, Jordan, though quite wealthy from his sports career, lends his image to the moneymaking schemes of the mainstream culture no matter how much his image is made to appear silly, ridiculous, even monstrous. In the commercials where he speaks to the cartoon figure of Bugs Bunny as though they are equals—peers—his elegance and grace of presence is ridiculed and mocked by a visual aesthetic that suggests his body makes him larger than life, a fantasy character. This visual image, presented as playful and comic, dehumanizes. Even though I agree with the cultural critic Michael Dyson's insistence in his essay "Be Like Mike" that Jordan's image has subversive potential in that "his big Black body—graceful and powerful, elegant and dark—symbolizes the possibilities of other Black bodies to remain safe long enough to survive within the limited but significant sphere

of sport," outside that realm Jordan lends his image in the service of a visual aesthetic that reaffirms the repressive racialized
body politics of the dominant society.

As a ruling-class person in this society, Jordan stands in total
contrast to the historical Black sports figures who were fighting
for equal pay for equal work. Even though many of those Black
male bodies were easily seduced by monetary reward, they did
not have the luxury of presenting an image of political neutrality, which Jordan tries to do. However, Jordan is not politically
neutral. His politics are rooted in both imperialist and capitalist
notions of power and conquest. The place where he articulates
that location is not in the realm of sports but in the picture books
that lay out his Black male body for public display. In *Rare Air:
Michael on Michael* Jordan boasts, "I've never been a vocal kind of
guy. My leadership in practice or games has always come from
the way I approach the game, and the way I play once I step on
the court . . . If you don't bring your level up to compete with
me then I am going to completely dominate you and I'm going
to talk trash to you, and about you while I am dominating."
Couched between sexualized images of his Black male body,
these statements act to eroticize both the world of homosocial
male bonding sex-segregated sports and to affirm the realm of
conquest. These "action" statements work to counter the passive
objectification of Jordan's Black male body in the accompanying images. In the introduction to *The Male Nude* Melody Davis
talks about the way in which the female body, especially the
nude, is usually portrayed as passive, reminding us that Freud
talked about the terror of passivity in men, the fear that passivity signified castration. Davis suggests that "the exposed male
body provides a field for sadomasochistic action so that the male
body, if not directly active, is the 'embodiment' of the action of
other men, of God, a superhuman male." In *Rare Air* (the very
title suggesting that he is like rare meat, raw, a freak of nature)

Jordan submits to a process of visual objectification that renders his Black male body passive in ways that feminize it. He must counter that violation with the hypermasculine in words that convey and assert action and domination, with the insistence that on the court he dominates using verbal humiliation as well as physical prowess. Symbolically, then, in the language of Black masculinist vernacular, he is the dick fucking the other dude over, turning him into a pussy. Central in this metaphor are both the trope of female domination and homophobia.

To counter the "soft" image created by subjugation via commodification, the Black male body must refigure its hardness. For a hypermasculine Black athlete such as Mike Tyson, that refiguring must be played out both in the boxing arena and via the assertion of sexual dominance over the female, even if that means one must rape. To many sexist Black male supporters of Tyson, the champion boxer was merely being "fucked" by the dominant white male. Supporters defended Tyson to counter this rape even if it meant they had to disregard the reality of his aggression and devaluation of a Black female body. The insistence on an assertion of "a dick thing" masculinity, both in real life and in the image, creates a structure of denial that allows Black male bodies to deny the loss of agency via the process of patriarchal capitalist domination, and to see the arena of sexist domination of females and homophobic subjugation of gay males as the place where those losses can be recouped. Rather than critique and challenge patriarchy and heterosexism, these Black males play the game, reproduce the subjugated image.

The commodification and fetishization of the Black male body in popular culture, particularly in advertising, is mirrored in the art world. That mirroring was made most public by the controversy surrounding the photographs in Robert Mapplethorpe's series *Black Book*. Just as it is possible to find sites of opposition in the visual aesthetics of Michael Jordan's image, in some instances Mapplethorpe's images disrupt and challenge conventional ways of seeing. Subversive elements within any image or series of images, however, do not necessarily counter the myriad ways those same images may reinscribe and perpetuate existing structures of racial or sexual domination. It is so obvious as to almost be unworthy of note, and certainly not of prolonged debate, that racist/sexist iconography of the Black male body is reaffirmed and celebrated in much of Mapplethorpe's work and in that of his predecessor and colleague George Dureau. The danger embedded in the images these two artists have popularized lies not so much in the perpetuation of obvious racist stereotypes that they exploit and reify, but in the manner in which public response privileges this work and thereby subordinates all other image making of the Black male body both by insisting that it reference or mirror this work and by continually foregrounding these images in ways that erase and exclude more compelling oppositional representations. Melody Davis's book *The Male Nude in Contemporary Photography*, cited several times in this essay, is a perfect example of this problem. Even though Davis critically trashes Mapplethorpe, aggressively calling attention to the way in which his images are racist, noting that he "seldom fetishized whites in the purely objectifying manner he had toward Blacks," her work also does not counter this tendency. By publishing and talking only about images of the Black male body photographed by white males, Davis does not subvert the racist agenda of inclusion/exclusion, of domination and control. She frames her critique by juxtaposing Mapplethorpe's images of the Black male body with the photographs of George Dureau, and in doing so maintains a colonizing schema wherein racially unaware whites determine who holds the more politically correct "right" to the Black male image. Although Davis chooses to insist in the critical text accompanying these images that there is a major difference in standpoint reflected in the work of these two artists, that difference is simply not visible in the images. As Mapplethorpe's work and similar work by other artists is enshrined, receives ongoing attention and reward, this success, and the way it is hierarchically privileged (particularly in critical writing), pressures photographers working with images of the Black male body to react—to position their work in relation to this body of work. This becomes another colonizing process that recentralizes Mapplethorpe's work and reinforces its prominence/dominance.

Reaction can engender oppositional representations. Certainly the African American photographer Lyle Ashton Harris deploys images that critique and counter Mapplethorpe's, as does Glenn Ligon's installation *Notes on the Margin of the Black Book* which reappropriates Mapplethorpe's series in order to critique, expose, and challenge. Ultimately, however, the visual hegemony of these nonprogressive white male–owned and –operated images of the Black male body, along with the historical racist/sexist iconography they mirror, can only be countered by the production and curatorial dissemination of a substantive body of oppositional representations from diverse locations. To break with the ruling hegemony that has a hold on images of the Black male body, a revolutionary visual aesthetic must emerge that reappropriates, revises, and reinvents, giving everyone something new to look at. That visual aesthetic is already visible in the work of artists such as Moneta Sleet, Emma Amos, Carrie Mae Weems, Lyle Ashton Harris, and a host of others.

In order for this oppositional aesthetic to emerge, attention may need to shift away from the Black male nude. The assumption that Black males are more "authentically" situated to create visual interventions has to be challenged, and more progressive critical work needs to be written that is theoretical and historical and that foregrounds a variety of work. From the archives of history we will find works such as Esther Bubley's photograph of two Black men in conversation, *Greyhound Bus Terminal, New*

York City, 1947, and we will hear anew what that work reveals about the male Black body. Fully clothed in suits and hats, the body parts that are most distinctive in this image are the faces and hands. While one man looks alluringly casual but questioning, his gaze fixed on the other man's face, his companion's body is tense and controlled. The hand on his hip is a gesture suggesting annoyance, that the man may be "reading" his subject. To know the journey of the Black male body that this image charts requires a critical engagement beyond that of passive consumption. Similarly, the image of the Black male in Carrie Mae Weems's photograph *What are the three things you can't give a Black person* cannot be understood or fully appreciated without some background knowledge of Black male subjectivity, the history of working-class men, the "fields" in which they labor. Another Weems photograph that challenges conventional ways of seeing Black male bodies is titled *Jim, If You Choose. . . .* Juxtaposed with text that reads, "Jim, if you choose to accept, the mission is to land on your own two feet," this image deconstructs homosocial bonding between white and Black men and the received messages about masculinity that come from the white-dominated mass media. It calls for accountability and an assertion of autonomous agency in the construction of self. Jim is positioned as contemplative—a thinker. Like the two Black men photographed in the Greyhound bus depot, more than forty years earlier, this man is not positioned to entertain, delight, or titillate us. We must dare to empathize and enter his world if we want to understand the nature of his subjectivity, his struggle.

In the artistic self-portrait of the photographer/cinematographer Arthur Jaffa we are offered another challenging image of Black male subjectivity: the whites of Jaffa's eyes positioned behind the camera, the photographer shooting himself working, catching himself charting new visual journeys, speaking to the Black male body that is himself. Still another image of the Black male body that challenges, that reframes and talks back to the Joe Louis collograph, is the photography of Marlon Riggs on the set of *Tongues Untied*. Intellectual, academic, filmmaker, gay diva—yet which of these identities, if any, does the image express? Like Louis, Riggs wears a hat, a mock tie. Unlike Louis, whose gaze is masked, whose eyes look down, Marlon has his eyes wide open. His is a direct gaze sharing vulnerability, but also challenging, urging, tenderly taunting us to embrace his image, to give it the long-denied recognition and love.

Oppositional representations of the Black male body that do not perpetuate white-supremacist capitalist patriarchy will not be highly visible unless we change the way we see and what we look for. More important than the race, gender, class, or sexual practice of the image-maker is the perspective, the location from which we look and the political choices that inform what we hope those images will be and do. Lyle Ashton Harris has set an aesthetic agenda: "I see myself involved in a project of resuscitation—giving life back to the Black male body." As that life is made more visible in images, as the diversity and multiplicity of perspectives emerge, the vision of radical Black male subjects claiming their bodies will stand forever in resistance, calling us to contestation and interrogation, calling us all to release the Black male body and let it live again.

The Radiance of Red:
Blood Works

Dead bodies do not bleed. As children, we marked the intensity of our bonds with outsiders by sharing blood, by cutting our flesh and pressing it against the cut flesh of another. Our blood mingled, we were now one, kin, no longer separated. In the novel *Maru* by the South African writer Bessie Head, to share blood is to know another person in a space beyond words: "They did not greet one another. Their bloodstreams were one."

Females in patriarchal society, far more than males, must engage the culture's conflicting and contradictory relationship with blood. Men envy women's capacity to bleed. As the feminist poet Judy Grahn chronicles in her book *Blood, Bread, and Roses: How Menstruation Created the World*, this male response grows out of fear: "It has been said that women's blood was held in awe and terror because men saw that 'she bled and did not die.'" Men usurped the power of blood and claimed it as masculine. Woman's blood became a sign of death and danger. She must be punished for bleeding, set apart, the sight of her blood made taboo.

Everyone raised in the Christian church learns to see the blood of Christ as redemptive. On communion days, we drink the symbolic blood to be one with God, to acknowledge the sacrifice of blood that makes growth and new life possible. I vividly recall my first communion, the solemn collective calm that descended as we all raised our glasses to drink together, the preacher's voice as it broke the silence to command us in the words of Christ, our Father, "Take and drink. This is my blood which was shed for the remission of your sins." We learned then that the blood of the Father is precious, sacred, a sign of compassion and forgiveness. In that same church, we learned that female blood is unclean. No female could walk across the altar for fear that her impure blood would contaminate the purest place of the holy.

Our culture trains the young menstruating girl to hide her blood, to make a secret of the fact that she has crossed the gender threshold that biologically separates her from male peers. Her blood, like that of Christ, is a sign of transition, an indication that an old self has died and a new self has been born. She becomes fully female through the act of bleeding. And it is this blood, not the absence of a penis, that most dramatically marks her difference from the male. Yet the blood that transforms her being is not sacred; it will not be cherished and blessed like the blood of the Father. It is, instead, the sign of her inferior status, her subordination. As Grahn testifies, "Taboos all over the world indicate that in childbirth rites the point of awe and fear was women's blood, not the birth of the baby." Girls learn to hide all signs of bleeding—"the curse," as it is euphemistically called in patriarchal culture. This bleeding, once the source of power, has become a sign of shame.

No wonder, then, that reclaiming the power of blood has become a central metaphor in the contemporary feminist movement's challenge to sexism and sexist oppression. Patriarchy can be undone only as the blood of the woman/mother regains status, is once again held in high esteem. To create a shift in cultural thinking about blood, taboos must be broken. Blood must be taken out of the shadows and made visible.

When he began to use blood imagery in his work, the photographer Andres Serrano shattered the cultural taboo that prohibits any public celebration of blood that is not an affirmation of patriarchy. By coincidence, he began this work at precisely the moment when the mass media had begun to warn us that our vital substances could be lethal. Serrano's fascination with bodily fluids also coincided with a more general revulsion at the sight of blood. Hence, the work was destined to be seen as provocative. But the truly radical aspect of Serrano's blood photographs transcends these specific elements of cultural tension; it resides in their fundamental disruption of conventional patriarchal understandings of the significance of blood in our lives. In these works blood is a subversive sign.

The critic Hal Foster's essay "Subversive Signs" begins with the declaration that "the most provocative American art of the present is situated at such a crossing—of institutions of art and political economy, of representations of sexual identity and social life." Foster contends, "The primary concern is not with the traditional or modernist properties of art—with refinement of style or innovation of form, aesthetic sublimity, or ontological reflection on art as such. In short, this work does not bracket art or formal or perceptual experiment but rather seeks out its affiliations with other practices (in the culture industry and elsewhere); it also tends to conceive of its subject differently." Serrano's blood photographs disrupt the neat, binary opposition that Foster constructs between art informed by "situational aesthetics" and art that uses more formalist traditional approaches. It is precisely Serrano's strategic merging of traditional aesthetic concerns with the social and political that gives his work its particular edge.

One of the first photographs in which Serrano used blood, *Heaven and Hell* (1984), depicts a cardinal turning away from a nude white woman whose hands are bound and whose head is flung back. Blood streams down her body. This photograph indicts the church as a primary site for the reproduction of patriarchy. Pornographic sadism, captured in this image by the look of satisfied desire on the cardinal's face, enables the patriarchal male to solve the dilemma of his own ambivalence via rituals of brutality. In the book *Pornography and Silence*, Susan Griffin reminds us that man must destroy the emotional part of himself to ease his terror in the face of what he desires:

> In one who is afraid of feeling, or of the memory of certain emotions, sexuality in itself constitutes a terrible threat. The body forces the mind back toward feeling. And even when the mind wills the body to be silent, the body rebels and plagues the mind with "urgency." And the body, seeking to be open, to be vulnerable, seeking emotional knowledge, is threatened, punished, and humiliated by the pornographic mind.

Serrano's symbolic representation of the split between heaven and hell mirrors the sadomasochistic severing of the connection between body and mind.

With this image, Serrano not only graphically calls out the agency of the patriarchal church in the perpetuation of sexualized violence against women and the destruction of the erotic, he also comments on the use of the female nude in Western art. For those in the know, the white male dressed as the cardinal is the artist Leon Golub, but the female nude remains unknown, unnamed. Here Serrano registers the link between the white-supremacist patriarchy of the church (note that the cardinal's robes are similar to those worn by Klan members later photographed by Serrano) and structures of hierarchy and domination in the mainstream art world. Golub, though celebrated in that world, is not representative of the conservative white mainstream. He is the white transgressive male figure caught in the logic of contradiction.

That art world, which continuously marginalizes women and nonwhite men producing art, makes a place for transgressive white males, reincorporating them into the body of the Father they have rebelled against. Woman's deradicalized nude image, on the other hand, is fixed, trapped in the static hold of the patriarchal noose. In *Old Mistresses: Women, Art, and Ideology*, the art historians Rozsika Parker and Griselda Pollock emphasize the myriad ways that patriarchal ideology is both made and transmitted by the manipulation of images:

> In art the female nude parallels the effects of the feminine stereotype in art historical discourse. Both confirm male dominance. As female nude, woman is body, is nature opposed to male culture, which, in turn, is represented by the very act of transforming nature, that is, the female model or motif, into the ordered forms and colour of a cultural artifact, a work of art.

Serrano reproduces this pattern in *Heaven and Hell*, yet he radicalizes it through his depiction of the dripping blood. He exposes the violation—the assault on both the woman's psyche and the psyche of those of us who consume the images, often with pornographic glee. By showing the blood, Serrano pierces the screen of patriarchal denial and demands that we acknowledge what we are really seeing when we look at the female nude in Western art. He forces us to bear witness, either to confront our complicity or to declare our resistance.

A similar demand for the deconstruction of visual allegiance to patriarchal church and state is called for in later images such as *Blood Pope III*. In this photograph the blood that covers the contented pope's face is not a marker of innocence. It is the exultation of the guilty, the demonic gloat of the sadomasochistic murderer who does not seek to deny the pleasure he derives from domination and death. Serrano uses religious imagery to expose the contradictions in organized or institutionalized religion, particularly the Catholic church. His work critically interrogates the structure of patriarchal Christianity even as it celebrates the seductive mystical dimensions of spirituality. The mystery and the majesty that shroud religious experience are extolled in the photographs of *St. Michael's Blood, Crucifixion, Precious*, and *Blood Cross*. Artistically, Serrano assumes the mantle of the religious mystic who has been initiated into certain secrets of the church. The ritual initiation he performs for his viewers involves both the deconstruction of traditional patriarchal Christianity and the return to a quest for an ontological spirituality.

While challenging the traditional church through a process of graphic desecration and dismantling, Serrano's work also explores and celebrates the individual's quest for spiritual ecstasy. In the introduction to *Thomas Merton on Mysticism*, Raymond Bailey emphasizes that mysticism has always been a threat to the organized church:

> The intensely personal nature of mysticism is inclined to arouse hostility within religious institutions, structures that see in it a threat to discipline and authority. The mystic strives for a direct experience of the absolute without intermediary, institutional or otherwise. Within Catholicism the rise of monasticism with its contemplative orientation occurred during the period of organization and hierarchical power in the Church . . . The pursuit of direct religious experience as manifested in Church history in the monastic, pietist, and charismatic movements has provided at various times an oasis for the spiritually thirsty who could draw only dust from the structures of organized religion.

Serrano juxtaposes the oppressive church hierarchy with the world of engaged spirituality, typified by the image of *St.*

Michael's Blood. Like the Christian mystic, Serrano artistically re-creates an iconography of sacrament where it is the individual expression of spirituality that is deemed most sacred. That sacredness is present in the ordinary dimensions of human life, in our bodily functions, the urine and blood that mark us. It is only through recognition of the commonness of human experience—in contrast to the elitism and separatism imposed by systems of domination that reinforce the powers of church and state—that individuals can live in harmony, without engendering violence against ourselves or others. Contrary to the teachings of the organized church, the individual must be able to accept him- or herself in order to live in peace with others.

This awareness, Merton claims, leads to the understanding that the individual is a "sacrament of God": "Christian personalism is, then, the sacramental sharing of the inner secret of personality in the mystery of love. This sharing demands full respect for the mystery of the person, whether it be our own person, or the person of our neighbor, or the infinite secret of God." Serrano transposes this notion of sacrament to a world of art practices where the individual artist must realize his or her expressive vision via a process of self-realization.

Just as Merton and other religious mystics turn Western metaphysical dualism on its head by insisting that salvation lies in human self-awareness, Serrano insists that artistic self-actualization can be found only in devotion to an aesthetics of transgression wherein all allegiances to fixed static understandings of creativity must be let go. Art practices, canons of art history, and all "great traditions" must be interrogated. Essentialist understandings of identity—gender, race, nationality—must be questioned. And hedonistic reveling in the transcendent powers of the imagination must be celebrated.

Critics ignore the ritualistic playfulness in Andres Serrano's work, yet that spirit of reverie is central to an aesthetic vision wherein one dares to bring together the sacred and profane, to defamiliarize by provocation. In the introduction to *Arresting Images: Impolitic Art and Uncivil Actions*, Steven Dubin describes his own visceral response to the Serrano photograph *Milk, Blood:*

> As the grandson of a kosher butcher, my immediate reaction was "You don't do this; you don't mix milk and meat. It just isn't done!" Once again this reaction startled me, for although I do not observe kosher laws, this image struck me as a violation of a very basic sort. Categories which I long ago rejected intellectually, I suddenly desired to uphold emotionally; they seemed natural and inviolable. But not only had they been juxtaposed, they seemed to bleed into one another down the middle of the photo. Unthinkable, and yet here was the record of this transgression.

In this photograph, Serrano flaunts symbolic transgression as a form of ritualistic disruptive play. His point is to remind us that the imagination is a powerful force, one that can lead to a revolution in vision, thought, and action. The blood photographs are as much a commentary on the place of art and aesthetics in ordinary life as they are interrogations of Western metaphysical dualism. Although his work has been seen as pretentious and arrogant, an in-your-face display of very obvious improprieties, Serrano very consciously chooses to work with the most familiar iconic images. His point is twofold: to deconstruct the notion that great art must emerge from "noble" subject matter and to challenge conventional understandings of beauty.

Indeed, one of the most disturbing aspects of Serrano's blood photographs to many viewers is the startling beauty of these images. The blood that we associate more and more with a world of impurity, violation, and death is spectacularly transformed in these photographs. Whether it is the beautiful displays of menstrual blood in the *Red River* series, the distilled images of *Piss and Blood*, or just the bold luxury of *Blood*, this work challenges the senses, demands that we see in bodily waste the possibility of a resurrection and renewal that empowers, that redeems.

To bring us back to blood as a life force, to counter the cultural images of dangerous blood (associated with the AIDS crisis), Serrano's work urges us to luxuriate in the ecstasy of red. This work is not solely an exploration of the cultural politics of blood, not solely an exploration of the cultural, it is also an artistic invitation to revel in the power of color. Celebrating the diverse meaning of the color red in *When the Moon Waxes Red*, the writer Trinh T. Minh-ha insists that it is the sign of contingency: "At once an unlimited and profoundly subjective color, red can physio- or psycho-logically close in as well as open up. It points to both a person's boundless, inner voyage, and the indeterminate out burning of the worlds of war. Through centuries, it remains the badge of revolution."

Serrano chooses to photograph blood only when it is bright, when it saturates the image with a sense of passion and warmth. Red makes the intensity in these images. Minh-ha contends that "the symbol of red lies not simply in the image, but in the radical plurality of meaning." Serrano's use of the color red is the indicator that we must not assume that the works address only what the images make superficially obvious. Each meaning of red is textured, layered, a palimpsest on which the photographer inscribes narratives of religion, culture, identity, art, and aesthetics.

Red is the color used to challenge our fixed visions of art and culture. Minh-ha says that red invites us to understand "that society cannot be experienced as objective and fully constituted in its order; rather only as incessantly recomposed diverging forces. These diverging forces, wherein the war of interpretation reigns," are ever-present in Serrano's work. He mixes them together in an elaborate gesture of border crossing and transgression; he announces that order is to be found by embracing the limitations of our capacity to know and control the universe. It is this vision that is evoked by the mandala image in the photograph *Circle of Blood.*

"An archetype released by the unconscious, the circle is a universal symbol of essence which is, which becomes, and which returns to itself; thus indicating how every form is in itself whole, self-consistent, a paradigm of a larger whole," Ajit Mookerjee explains in *Yoga Art.* "The mandala is wholeness. The never-ending circle transcends all opposition, imaging the ideal Self to itself." In *Circle of Blood,* the abstract image of wholeness converges with recognition that the circulating blood is central to continuity of being—that spirit of wholeness which the circle evokes. Even the thin band of yellow that encircles the red—suggesting sun and light—unites the very concepts of body and nature that Western metaphysical dualism tries to keep separate. Here nature's life-giving restorative symbol, epitomized by the sun, is reflected in the blood that circulates to renew life.

This same gesture of reunion is present in the photograph *Blood and Soil,* where again an aspect of the natural world (the earth) converges with bodily fluids to remind us of an organic framework of wholeness. These juxtapositions both interrogate and call for the restructuring of our priorities. While not as overtly transgressive as many of the Serrano photographs that use blood, these images are political and powerfully subversive. They challenge us to decenter those epistemologies in the West that deny a continuum of relationships among all living organisms, inviting us to replace this mode of thought with a vision of synthesis that extols a whole that is never static but always dynamic, evolutionary, creative. Though often overlooked, this is the counterhegemonic aesthetic vision that is the force undergirding Andres Serrano's work.

Acknowledgments

The publisher thanks the estate of Gloria Jean Watkins, and is grateful for permission to reprint the following copyrighted material:

"Subversive Beauty: New Modes of Contestation," from Felix Gonzalez-Torres exhibition catalog, 1994. Reprinted by permission of the Museum of Contemporary Art in Los Angeles.

"Diasporic Landscapes of Longing," from Fabric Workshop exhibition catalog, "Carrie Mae Weems," 1994. Reprinted by permission of The Fabric Workshop and Museum, Philadelphia.

"Representing the Black Male Body," from the Whitney Museum of American Art exhibition catalog *Black Male: Representations of Masculinity in Contemporary American Art* by Thelma Golden, 1994. Reprinted by permission of the Whitney Museum of American Art.

"Facing Difference: The Black Female Body," from "Lorna Simpson: Waterbearer," September 1993. Reprinted by permission of *Art Forum*.

"Altars of Sacrifice: Re-membering Basquiat," from *Art in America* (June 1993).